THE KINGDOMS OF CHRIST

'The kingdoms of this world are become
the kingdoms of our Lord and of his Christ'

The Revelation XI 15

THE KINGDOMS OF CHRIST

THE STORY OF THE EARLY CHURCH

Peter Bamm

365 illustrations, 18 colour plates

THAMES AND HUDSON · LONDON

Translated and adapted by Christopher Holme
Picture Research by S. Lang
Layout by Ian Mackenzie Kerr

© Droemersche Verlagsanstalt and Thames and Hudson London 1959
Printed by M. DuMont Schauberg Cologne · Western Germany
Bound by Van Rijmenam N.V. - The Hague · Holland

Contents

'But when the fulness of the time was come...'

WE IN THE WEST, who are the heirs of nearly two thousand years of Christian culture, find it difficult to form an exact idea of the Christian message as it was understood by those to whom it was first addressed.

For the disciples of Jesus, who were pious Jews, the fulfilment of the prophecies of their Holy Scriptures, handed down to them over two thousand years, and called by us today the Old Testament, was the proof that he was the Messiah whose coming had been foretold by the Hebrew prophets. Did they not see him with their own eyes? God, the Creator who transcended history, but who at different times and in various ways had manifested himself in history, had vouchsafed this final evidence of his divine purpose, which was to usher in the end of the world.

To readers familiar with the Hebrew scriptures, St Paul, in his epistle to the Galatians, was able to sum this all up in one half-sentence. 'The fulness of the time was come...' seldom has more been said in fewer words.

But supposing his readers had not been acquainted with the Hebrew scriptures, what would this pregnant saying have meant for them? For Paul was the apostle to the Gentiles, non-Jews who could not be assumed to possess knowledge either of the Old Testament or of Jewish religious thinking. Almost from the beginning Christianity was propagated as a universal religion, without discrimination in matters of race, sex, or social position. Why did this Christian message have such an instant appeal for all these different kinds of early believers? Here it is natural to look for some essential simplicity of statement. For instance, it has often been said of Islam, the youngest of the great world religions, that its rapid spread, no doubt primarily due to the Arab conquests, also owed a great deal to its simple, comprehensive formula – 'There is no god but God, and Mohammed is the prophet of God.'

In a like manner, we may feel, the message of Christianity can be reduced to a few essentials, as in the words of St Paul we have already quoted, words which would have carried at all times and in all places a universal appeal. But we cannot entirely rely on this intuition. It may be difficult for us to appreciate what the Christian teaching *meant* for those who first received it. On the other hand, we can readily appreciate what it *said* to those Jews who first heard and accepted it. For them it was not so much a simple new message as a complex one with which they were already familiar. It could be put in a succinct form only because no words were needed to explain, to those who had been brought up on them, the Hebrew prophecies, or the God they presupposed, or His previous revelations to the Jewish people. A bare allusion was enough.

In expounding the Gospel to the Gentiles, the apostles must necessarily have drawn on the Old Testament ideas and used its stories as an intro-duction to the story of Jesus. We meet with Adam and Eve, Daniel in the lion's den, Jonah and the whale, so widely in the early Christian relics that we can have little doubt of their having formed part of the basic in-struction given to all Gentile converts. But above all, these converts from a polytheistic world must first have been taught to believe in a unique tran-scendent God. We have in the New Testament an indication of the way in which this belief may have been introduced to them, for the account of the one God, 'in whom we live, and move, and have our being', takes up almost the whole of St Paul's address before the Areopagus at Athens as reported in the Acts of the Apostles. Only at the end, in this report, does Paul introduce Christ, and then not by name, but as 'that man' whom God 'hath ordained' and raised from the dead as 'an assurance unto all men'. 'And when they heard of the resurrection, some mocked: and others said, We will hear thee again of this matter.'

At this time neither the one God nor the resurrection from the dead can have been new, or even strange, ideas to the Athenians. In the works of Plato, written over four centuries earlier, God is frequently spoken of in the singular, without name, and the idea of a Creator, and also that of a world soul, are explicitly discussed. Later the Stoic system, which of all Greek philosophies gained the strongest hold on the Romans, had popularised the notion of an immanent God working in nature. The idea of life after death, again, was common to nearly all the religions with which the Greeks had contact, and a form of resurrection – a return from that life to this – whether as a universal principle in the transmigration of souls, or as a mythological and ritual event in the various fertility cults, was almost as widespread.

The spread of Christianity is not a matter of the conquest, by an uncom-promisingly new and strange religion, of a world given over to a totally different system of belief. As Kenneth Scott Latourette has argued in his history of that expansion, the problem is to determine, out of the confusion of religions and philosophies competing for the allegiance of the peoples under Roman rule, why this and no other faith prevailed. Christianity was not the first of the great religions to conquer, and become identified with, a whole civilisation and then to spread among many races of men. Nor was it quite the last. Though its success has been in many ways more

Time and the elements have failed to rob the delicate colours of the famous fresco of Piero della Francesca in Arezzo of their pristine beauty. This scene depicts the finding of the True Cross by St Helena.

striking than that of any of its rivals, it has one thing in common with most of them. Except as a result of military conquest, it has never achieved the conversion of a whole civilisation or highly organised culture other than that in which it first arose. It has never, indeed, secured more than a minority lodgment in any such culture. Christianity, it seems, was specially adapted to the Graeco-Roman environment: it could only flourish in other environments if it was able to take charge of them, as it were, and mould them to its own requirements from a more primitive cultural form. Once it had possessed itself, after a cultural struggle lasting four centuries, of the Graeco-Roman world and its State power, its further history became the history of that world and of the political systems that grew out of it – Byzantium, Europe, and Russia.

The character of this environment, then, in which Christianity arose, is of great importance for this story. Its political and geographical framework, first of all, was the Roman Empire, a world of Roman power and Roman law, but of a civilisation which was in all essentials Greek. After Caesar had brought to an end the terrible Roman civil wars of the first century B.C., Augustus gave the world the Pax Romana, the Roman Peace. It became a world of external security such as mankind was not to experience again until the end of the nineteenth century, and then only for a short while. One could journey from the Danube to the cataracts of the Nile, from the Euphrates to Spain, from Gaul to North Africa, without passport or visa. Nowhere was there a frontier to hold up the traveller. The storms of the Mediterranean – and those few bold practitioners of individualism, the sea pirates – were the only threats to universal security. Only within this framework is it possible to understand the astonishing distances which the apostles covered.

However detached a view we may take of the blessings of Roman security, the Pax Romana was a necessary condition for these missionary journeys of the apostles. At no other time in the whole history of the ancient world was there a state of political relations that could have made possible what the apostles achieved in their missionary activities towards the end of the first century. Later missions had much greater external dangers to contend with. The first missionaries of Christendom brought their message not to

Back in very early times the four Evangelists were allotted symbols, derived from a vision of St John. These symbols were recognized wherever Christianity was known. This picture occurs in the manuscript of a Persian diatessaron – that is a story of the life of Christ compiled from all four gospels.

savage and uninformed peoples but to a world in the highest degree civilized. Yet external security of living and travel, necessary though it was, was not the most important of the requirements for the spread of Christianity. More important still was the internal situation. The field in which the apostles sowed the seed of the new doctrine had been prepared for centuries by Greek civilisation. And this internal preparedness was due in the first instance to political events.

Three centuries before Christ, Alexander the Great had conquered the Persian Empire and advanced as far as India. The consequence of these tremendous feats of arms was that the Greek way of life spread over the whole of the newly conquered region. When the Romans some two hundred years later began to extend their power over the coastal lands of the eastern Mediterranean, the world they conquered was one which had become Greek. With all their diverse traditions, the peoples who now came under Roman rule had one thing in common – they admired Greek civilisation. Largely accepting it and fusing it with their own, they sent their sons, and sometimes also their daughters, to Greek universities to acquire a Greek education.

Gradually in this cauldron of cultures even the old deities of the East became fused with the corresponding Olympian deities. Greek temples were erected to the old Syrian weather god, Hadad. A full two hundred years after Christ's birth a large temple was built in Baalbek and dedicated to Jupiter Heliopolitanus, the old Phoenician god Baal. There was a Jupiter-Baal. There was an Egyptian Jupiter-Ammon. There was a Syrian Jupiter-Hadad. But one thing there never was – a Jupiter-Jehovah.

Yet at that time the rule of Olympus was a thing of the past. Perhaps it was only the resolute piety of the peoples of the East which had kept these old deities of the Greeks alive so long. The Greek philosophers recognised at a very early date that behind the wonder of creation there must stand a being of higher rank than the Olympian Zeus. The Olympian Pantheon, having the attributes of a State religion, survived the beginnings of Christianity by centuries. But in the world of those days, with its spiritual unrest and religious expectancy, there was a void which the old religion was no longer capable of filling.

It was a Hellenistic world – a complex of mixed populations and older cultures which had assumed a measure of uniformity under the successors of Alexander the Great. It had been conquered by the Romans and after all the upheavals and displacements of the preceding centuries it was beginning again to envisage the possibility of stable administration, prosperity,

This picture of the stoning of St Stephen is taken from the Topographia Christiana of Cosmas Indicopleustes. He was a Greek from Alexandria who travelled widely in the sixth century in order to get to know the Christian world at first hand, visiting Arabia and Ethiopia and roving as far afield as Ceylon.

St Jerome, one of the kindliest figures of Christian hagiology, was accompanied and protected by a lion while doing penance in a ravine in the Jordan valley.

and order. It was cosmopolitan in outlook and perhaps not on the whole disinclined, despite the violence and misery with which the coming of Roman rule was often associated, to accept Rome as the guarantee and symbol of a new political unity. The religious cult of Rome and its emperor, now associated with that of the Olympian gods, may well have seemed a natural expression of this political outlook. But there were deeper needs that it did not and could not satisfy. Safety of property and person and civil peace were not necessarily accompanied by peace of mind.

The Roman Empire was full of displaced persons – not only the multitudes of slaves who had been forcibly uprooted but also free men who had been impelled to migrate by the pressures of the times. Each one of these took with him to his new environment a fragment of another culture and the use of another religion, adding to the general confusion of cults and social values. Such people, too, in their rootlessness and personal insecurity, must have provided fertile ground for the spread of new religious practices and beliefs.

Among the more settled classes and in the higher intellectual levels religious scepticism was an attitude that had the redoubtable sanction of Athenian tradition, just as in our modern world it has the authority of eighteenth-century philosophy. Again as in our own day, its principal victim was the traditional, established religion. Towards other cults and philosophies the cultivated sceptic, then as now, might show a friendly curiosity and tolerant open-mindedness which in its own way could be as favourable to the spread of new doctrine as the spiritual hunger at the other end of the social scale. It was no doubt at these levels, too, that the Greek philosophical systems, combining moral principles and rules of conduct with theories of the universe, made their greatest appeal.

All these factors help us to understand how the apostles found such ready audiences in the Graeco-Roman world. This world, which had welcomed the mysteries coming from the East, was not unprepared to embrace the mystery of the birth and transformation of the Son of God on Earth, His human death, and His divine ascent to Heaven. But the apostles not only found audiences and won converts – this alone would not have distin-guished them from the preachers of all the other doctrines then current – they laid the foundations of a unique development which was to change the course of history. Why was it that precisely this doctrine, and not one of the others, maintained itself through all the centuries of bitter persecution by the upholders of the Roman State religion, and ultimately displaced it, becoming itself the religion of the Roman State?

There are two ways of meeting such a question. They may be called the answer from within, and the answer from without. The answer from within would find its reasons in Christian belief and Christian theology, appealing only to God's will working in history. The answer from without would approach the question historically, starting, as we have done in this book, from the Graeco-Roman environment and seeking to identify those features of Christian teaching by virtue of which it was so well adapted to make headway there.

What were these features? First among the advantages which Christianity had at the outset was its Jewish origin. That Christianity appeared as an offspring of Judaism is of vital importance. The Jews were the first people on earth whose God, as the Creator of Heaven and Earth, was completely transcendent. At the time of Christ's birth their tradition, enshrined in the Old Testament, was already one of great antiquity. The patriarch Abraham had received God's promise in the twentieth century before Christ, just as the empire of the Sumerians, in whose capital, Ur on the Euphrates, he was born, was about to collapse. For two millennia the Jews had preserved their faith in the one God and his law. The empires of the Sumerians, the Hittites, the Babylonians, the Assyrians had come and gone. We know today of whole civilisations which had disappeared so completely that the Greeks were unaware that they had even existed. Only the Jewish people had preserved its national identity through all these centuries of change.

Yet at the time of Christ's birth this people was already widely dispersed. There were Jewish colonies, as the historian Strabo expressly comfirms, not only throughout the whole Graeco-Roman world, but reaching into Asia. Indeed the Jewish *diaspora* had already begun in the eighth century B.C., at a time, that is, when the Greek city State of Miletus, on the coast of Anatolia, was just entering on its first great age. After his conquests of the Northern Kingdom of Israel in the middle of the eighth century B.C., King Tiglathpileser III of Assyria deported those he had defeated and settled them on the coast of the Caspian Sea. The victims of this deportation became known as the ten lost tribes of Israel. The dispersal was continued after the conquest of Jerusalem by King Nebuchadnezzar of Babylon in 587 B.C. Furthermore, we have evidence that Jewish colonies existed as far afield as in China before Alexander the Great.

From the very beginning these scattered Jewish communities played a decisive part in the speedy dissemination of the Gospel, and provided the apostles with points of support for their work in foreign countries. A very short time elapsed before the tidings of the life and death of Jesus, His crucifixion, resurrection, and ascent to Heaven, reached all the Jews wherever they might be. They were in contact with Jerusalem through the dues that every professing Jew paid yearly to the Temple treasury. It was these same Jewish communities, of course, which caused such difficulties for the apostles, when their leaders, taking the orthodox view that Christianity was a vexatious aberration from Judaism, complained about them and sought to embroil them with the authorities. But the violence of their opposition is also, no doubt, an indication of Christianity's early success.

There was one other way in which the Jewish communities probably facilitated the entry of Christianity into the ancient world. Judaism, particularly in its Hellenised form, was a widely known religion. Moreover, at this period, the Jews engaged in a deliberate missionary effort to make converts to traditional Judaism. Whatever success they may have had was likely to be of indirect help to Christianity. The apostles may well have found among their Gentile audiences many who were already acquainted with the God of the Hebrews and His law, the prophecies and the revelations.

The other strand in early Christianity was Hellenism itself. Greek culture, though resisted by the Pharisees, the Jewish sect who seem to have been Jesus' chief opponents, had made great inroads among the Jews. The Old Testament was translated into Greek as early as the third century B.C. The great Jewish philosopher Philo, who was living in Alexandria at the time of Christ's birth, attempted to bring the teaching of the Old Testament into agreement with Greek philosophy. The Apostle Paul was not only learned in the Scriptures, but also well-informed about Greek literature and philosophy. In his Athenian address already referred to he quotes from Cleanthes' 'Hymn to Zeus'. Greek was the language of dissemination of early Christianity, and the New Testament was written in Greek. Without going so far as to ascribe direct influences, we may safely contend that the Apostle's first audiences would have noticed many affinities between the moral teaching of the early Christians and things already known to them from the Greek philosophers. The love of one's neighbour – the most Christian of all the commandments – had already been taught and practised by Socrates.

It is significant in this context that among the early converts were many highly educated persons. For Christianity was not, as has sometimes been supposed, an affair merely of the humiliated and ill-treated, of poor people and slaves. It did make converts among these, and no doubt they outnumbered the rest, as they did in Roman society generally. But throughout its early history we are struck by the prominent part played in Christianity by intellectuals and also by people of means.

In its further development, the relations of Christianity with Greek philosophy were as important in their way as its relations with the Roman State. From the second to the fourth century Greek philosophy was, doctrinally, Christianity's greatest opponent. But just as the faith survived the State persecution and emerged ultimately all the stronger, so the fathers and councils of the Church wrestled for two centuries with their Greek adversary, and were eventually able, by superhuman efforts of thought, to come to terms with it and emerge victorious. The outcome of this struggle is the faith itself as it is known to us today. The system of dogmas elaborated by the early Church was forced upon it by Greek philosophy. As Adolph von Harnack, the German theologian and Church historian, has said: 'Christian dogmatics is a work of Greek philosophy grounded in the Gospel.'

And now, having sketched in the background, let us consider the impact the Christian message is likely to have had upon those first Gentile audiences of St Paul and his fellow apostles. Its elements of belief were in all essentials the one God and the Messiah, Jesus Christ. With these were associated a promise of eternal life. The Graeco-Roman world was, as we have seen, well prepared for monotheism. The Christian story of a birth, a death, and a resurrection had these ingredients in common with so many ancient fertility myths in so many of the cults known to people of that world that it must have struck familiar chords in the hearts of those who heard it. Only in this case the time-honoured ceremonial myth had taken concrete historical form. It had been enacted, not symbolically in a man-made rite, but in person by someone who had recently lived – by someone, moreover, whose character had been so exceptional and whose sayings and doings so extraordinary and persuasive that his disciples had gone out at his bidding into all the world to tell people of them and Him. In its central story Christianity was new but not strange.

When we turn from belief to practical matters, we find three aspects of the Christian way which from the very beginning seem to have distinguished it from every other way. These were its catholicity, its attitude towards the

This silver-gilt Byzantine reliquary of the eighth to ninth centuries is ornamented with cloisonné inlays. A crusader brought it back from the East for Pope Innocent IV. The precious little box was used to preserve a wooden fragment of the True Cross of Christ.

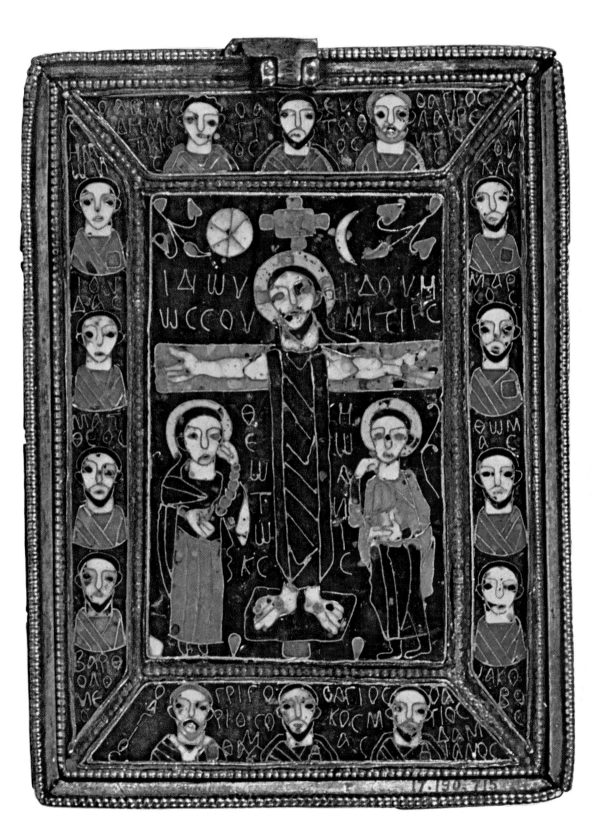

This eleventh-century Byzantine mosaic, representing the 'Anastasis' or resurrection at the Last Judgment, is in the church of the monastery of Nea Moni on the island of Chios. Christ stretches out his hand with the stigma, in order to awaken Adam and Eve from their graves to eternal life.

State, and its insistence on personal morality. First, then, Christianity was addressed to everyone of either sex, slave or free, to all races and all classes. To a world whose cosmopolitanism was seeking to express itself in closer association and closer fellowship Christianity offered the concept of human-ity. Doubtless among Christianity's rivals there were other systems which were nominally open to all and professed an indifference to social distinc-tions, but this teaching and practice of Christianity seems to have gone further than any. Christianity was not confined to members of one sex, as Mithraism, for instance, was confined to men, nor to those who could pass through the long and sometimes expensive processes of initiation demanded by other cults, nor to those versed in the philosophies. Roman rule was based on a stratified social organisation: there were Roman citizens, non-Roman free men, and slaves, with intermediate gradations. Christianity did not preach revolt against this system nor express opposition to it. But the practice of the Church implied a certain criticism of it.

This lack of social orthodoxy was balanced by an attitude of submission to the State which made early Christianity a more formidable movement, perhaps, than if it had been merely revolutionary. It was, by all accounts, a positive attitude, for which authority can be found in the Gospels. Just because Christianity was not indifferent to the State in the manner of the mystery cults nor hostile to it as was Judaism in its more uncompromising forms, but allowed the State a proper sphere in which obedience was its due, Christians were as deeply concerned with the State's morality as with that of individuals. It may be asked, then, why Christians were so bitterly persecuted by the emperors. But while they were upholders of order, there was a point beyond which they refused to go: they would not commit idolatry nor do anything unholy. This brought them into conflict with the State religion, and provided a standing pretext for official prosecution if one were wanted. Perhaps the authorities might not so often have taken ad-vantage of their status of permanent illegality if the Christians had not been at the same time so concerned with public order and morality. Because of this attitude Christianity was of all the competing cults and philosophies the only one capable of ousting the official religion and taking over its State functions. Long before Constantine's edict of toleration, there must have been moments when the emperors began to wonder whether Chris-tianity was to be regarded as just another religion within the Empire or as the alternative imperial religion.

At the same time, if public backing were needed for administrative meas-ures, there was always a ready source of popular indignation against the

Christians. For there was their insistence – and this brings us to our third point – on personal morality. This moral strictness must have involved the Christians in disapproval of many of the popular amusements of the day. Many of these, of course, were associated with festivals of a religious kind. The 'hatred of the human race' imputed to Christians in the time of Nero by Tacitus may have been a way of expressing a popular view that they were gloomy puritans hostile not only to established religion but to traditional amusements as well. The sacrificing of Christians in the Colosseum no doubt seemed an apt revenge for the pagan gods who presided over it, and the popular feeling which led, as much as any official policy, to the periodical orgies of slaughter there could claim to have a religious inspiration.

The Christians, on the other hand, were not alone in deploring the breakdown of moral standards in the early empire and the brutalisation of the masses. The preceding centuries of war and civil disorder had been disastrous in their effects. With the return of relative security there had been attempts at a moral revival, and many had sought a remedy in the Greek philosophies. Its moral system, which distinguished Christianity from the mystery cults, must have recommended it to large numbers of persons, to whom the Christians offered the spectacle of groups of people practising what they preached and strengthened to do so not so much by the light of reason as by a vivid system of belief.

Thus it may in truth be said that when the apostles set forth from the holy city of Jerusalem to bring the new tidings to this Roman Empire of Greek civilisation, they found a world which was awaiting them. For the central tenet of the new doctrine, that God had sent his Son to save the world, this political and cultural situation had no significance. But for the success of Christianity in its beginnings, the historical circumstances were of the greatest consequence. The historians teach us the course of history; its meaning is taught us only by history itself. 'But when the fulness of the time was come . . .' is an utterance in which St Paul tells us something vital about the meaning of history.

Taken from an icon probably of Abyssinian origin, this scene shows the prophet Elijah listening to his raven which sits above him in a palm tree. The writing above his head contains the name of Elijah. The Arabic inscription towards the bottom reads: Glory, glory to the Lord Sebaoth!

This picture of Isaiah praying, from a ninth-century Psalter, shows the great prophet offering up his soul to God. Recalling the antique manner, Night appears behind him with lowered torch, while Dawn as a cherub with upraised torch approaches him from the front.

THE BEGINNINGS of great historical movements have a fascination for the human mind. In seemingly trivial events there may be a significance that will come to light only centuries later when their full import for world history is revealed. Man is an enquiring creature. He wants to know. And what he wants to know of any great happening is how it began. But since beginnings are usually ill-documented and obscure, his natural curiosity leads him to fill up the gaps in the historical record with legends.

Legends are the despair of the historian. True, they can sometimes be shown to be false; but just as often a legend turns out to have a historical core. And in either case the historian has to recognise that the legendary elements in any great system of belief are not to be judged solely for their content of fact. They have other work to do, since they form part of the mythical framework in which a religion lives and from which it develops.

Christianity possesses in the Acts of the Apostles a very early historical source. It is by any standards a remarkable narrative, lively, topical, exhilarating to read and memorable in content. It often gives the reader the feeling that he is actually taking part in the events. There can be no doubt that it is based on documents that were written shortly after the happenings they describe.

There is in the whole of antiquity no single personality better known to us than the Apostle Paul. We know him through the documents transmitted to us, in all the variety of his life and character. And no doubt that is why his historical existence has never been seriously disputed by scholars and critics. This formidable man really lived; this is a fact that is universally recognised, and it has taken much of the force out of the arguments advanced against the historical existence of Jesus. For if we recognise the existence of the Apostle Paul and deny that of Jesus, we must conclude that the 'Jesus myth' was invented, out of nothing, in the course of a single generation. This supposition is too improbable to merit serious consideration.

The Acts of the Apostles gives us a good picture of the first generation of Christianity after Jesus' earthly journey. At many points this picture is filled out by legends. Much is still obscure. New discoveries will bring new insights, but we can expect that something will always remain unknown.

The story of the spread of Christianity into the world begins with the descent of the Holy Ghost on the day of Pentecost. As St Luke relates in the second chapter of the Acts of the Apostles, this event already had an international

character. The list of nationalities in the audience that had come together, every member of which heard his native tongue, mentions Parthians, Medes, Mesopotamians, Asiatics, Egyptians, Cretans, Libyans, Arabs, and 'strangers of Rome'. In his discourse immediately after, Peter addressed himself separately to the 'men of Judaea' and to those that 'dwell at Jerusalem' who were, we are told earlier, 'Jews, devout men, out of every nation under Heaven'. 'And the same day there were added unto them about three thousand souls.' These souls, gathered together from every corner of the world, must very quickly have spread the news of the 'wonder of the tongues' all over it.

Of the first Christians, the apostles and those they baptised, it is often said that they were no more than a small Jewish sect. It is hard to make sense of such an assertion. A sect, generally speaking, is strictly organised, intolerant; it has difficult rites for the admission of novices and prescribes severe rules for its members. All this, for instance, would be true of the community of the Essenes. They were a sect, as the decipherment of the Dead Sea scrolls and the excavations at Qumran have shown. The Nazarenes, as the community of early Christians was at first called, were anything but a sect in this sense. Organisation was just what they lacked. They admitted anyone who professed his faith in the Redeemer. Their baptism was a simple procedure. Only the rules prescribed by Christianity were strict. It is easy to understand why it took so long before the adherents of this new faith began to organise themselves. The early Christians were expecting the end of the world, with the second coming of Christ and the Last Judgment, in their own lifetime. In face of this tremendous prospect, earthly plans were purposeless. So it was that the new faith, though its long-term effect was to be the radical transformation of mankind, in its beginnings had no revolutionary character at all. The way of life of the early Christians is sometimes represented as Communist. Rather the opposite is the case. Communism regards property as so important that it devotes a whole philosophical system to its distribution. For the early Christians property was so unimportant that they renounced it entirely. Their principle was the love of one's neighbour. Far from being revolutionary, the new faith was more like a sapling that slowly grew into a tree – a tree in whose shade finally half the human race found room to shelter.

The small community of Christians in Jerusalem was regarded by the Jews with extreme distrust. This distrust was in no way diminished after they had procured the condemnation of Jesus by Pilate. There were some violent clashes. Then, as the result of an opinion given by the Pharisee Gamaliel, the Christians were left in peace. He declared, sensibly enough, that if the teaching of the Nazarenes were really inspired by God, it would be of little use to combat it. But if it were not, it would disappear of its own accord. With this judgment, Gamaliel at least showed that he put more trust in the wisdom and omnipotence of God than his colleagues of the Sanhedrin. So it was that the new faith, which was to develop into one of the most militant religions in the world's history, began by enjoying a long period of peace. During this phase the number of its adherents increased to a considerable extent.

The story goes that the apostles in Jerusalem were gathered in full muster about Mary, the mother of God, until she died and was taken up to Heaven. We can imagine what profound spiritual conflicts were experienced at this time by the founders of the young communion. They were all believing Jews, respecters of the Law of Moses, as their fathers and forefathers had been for more than a thousand years. They had been educated in strict monotheism. But now there was not only the one Almighty God, there was also his divine Son. The beginning of the Acts of the Apostles relates how Christ proclaimed to his apostles the baptism of the Holy Ghost. We know too little to be able to picture to ourselves exactly what the Holy Ghost meant for the apostles. It was without doubt something they actually experienced. For it was not till much later that the Holy Ghost became a theological problem, as the third person of the Trinity. The fact that God had a son was problem enough. These pious Jews, it must be remembered, were trained in theological argument. Since childhood, in their synagogues, they had been accustomed to sharpen their wits on the interpretation of Holy Scripture. They would have seen as quickly as their opponents the apparent conflict between the new mysteries and their monotheistic faith, and they must have been greatly disturbed by it. It was the main objection of orthodox Jews to the new faith that, if Jesus were the son of God, God was no longer the God of Holy Scripture. This profound problem was to exercise Christendom for centuries, and in fact it was not till the Council of Nicaea, held when the Roman Empire had already recognised Christianity, that it was finally resolved in dogmatic form. The apostles had not yet a New Testament to serve them as a help and support. Only the Old Testament, and they themselves, were the authorities of the new faith. The only source at their disposal, so far as Christ was concerned, was what they in person remembered of the Master and his sayings. How strong must their need have been to write down what was entrusted solely to their mortal memory!

During the period when the Jews left them alone, the apostles had time to accustom themselves to the fact that they, and no others, were the chosen witnesses of the Son of God's sojourn upon Earth. But the period came to an abrupt end. An action for blasphemy was brought before the Supreme Council against Stephen, one of the first seven deacons of the young communion. Stephen was stoned to death before the gates of Jerusalem. The first Christian persecution had begun.

The apostles set out to tread the path which Christ had commanded they should follow. The Gospel reached the Gentiles. And now the apostles were faced by the question which was to be decisive for the fate of Christianity. Was Christ only the Messiah of the Jews, or had he come to redeem all men?

There were thousands of Jews who recognised Jesus as the Messiah. They became Christian but remained obedient to the Law of Moses. Suppose the Jewish people as a whole had turned Christian. Christianity would then indeed have become a Jewish sect, and before a man could be converted to it he would have had to accept the Law of Moses. And so, apart from a few who had turned orthodox Jew for the sake of becoming Christian, the Jews would have remained the only Christians in the world. The historical success that Christianity has had would not have been possible. The Jews put the world in their debt for that obstinate attachment to their faith which safeguarded the revelation of God for close on two thousand years. It is a strange reflection that it was that same obstinacy which was responsible for the fact that Christianity did not remain Jewish, but became a world religion. 'God works in a mysterious way his wonders to perform!'

At the first Council of Christendom, the Council of Jerusalem, which was held probably in the year 49, this question, whether Christ had come to save only Jews or Gentiles too, was decided once and for all in favour of the doctrine that He was the redeemer of all mankind.

The Judaic-Christian community of Jerusalem had fled to eastern Jordania before the destruction of the city by Titus in the year A.D. 70. There it survived for five more centuries. For a long time, too, perhaps even up to the time of the prophet Mohammed, there were Judaic-Christian communities in Arabia. Later the Church proclaimed Judaic Christianity a heresy.

By its resolution less than half a century after Christ's birth the Council of Jerusalem promulgated the first condition for the new faith to become a world religion.

Barbed wire,
which was invented in the nineteenth century and has become a leading symbol of the twentieth, today divides Jerusalem into an Israeli and an Arab part. The wall from which the soldiers of the Arab Legion look across to their Israeli enemies was built by the Sultan Suleiman the Magnificent, who assured himself of a place in the memory of Europe by his siege of Vienna. But although barbed wire is an unfortunate fact of history, we look to Jerusalem for another, and more significant reason. Jerusalem is the only city in the world which is holy to three religions. Jews, Christians and Moslems in all parts of the world look upon this holy place with reverence. Jerusalem is also the only city on earth of which men believe that its counterpart is in Heaven. The old name of the city is Urusalim. In Ezekiel the Lord says of Jerusalem that her father was of the race of the Amorites and her mother of the Hittites. The name Urusalim occurs in Egyptian inscriptions as early as the twentieth century B.C. There is a later mention of the name in the Amarna letters to the Pharaoh Amenophis IV from one of his vassals.

The Descent of the Holy Ghost

on a fresco in Santa Maria Novella in Florence shows the Twelve
Apostles with the Virgin Mary in the room of the house in which the Holy
Ghost descended upon them, as described in the second chapter of the Acts
of the Apostles. Thronging the street are the people gathered from all parts
for the feast, which commemorated the giving of the Law by Moses on
Mount Sinai.

After Judas Iscariot had met his terrible end, only eleven apostles remained.
But the Twelve, of old a sacred number, had been determined by Jesus. So
Peter proposed that the twelfth apostle should be elected anew. Two candidates stood for election, both of whom had been together with the other
disciples since the day when Jesus had been baptised by John. They cast
lots, and the lot fell on Matthias. 'And he was numbered with the eleven
apostles.' This title of honour did not remain confined to the first twelve
apostles. It was conferred on St Paul and also on his companions Barnabas
and Silas. Moreover, right into the Middle Ages, messengers of the Gospel
who brought it to new peoples were called 'apostles'.

The presence of the mother of God at the descent of the Holy Ghost is not expressly mentioned in the Bible. Yet it is earlier stated that they 'all continued with one accord in prayer and supplication with the women, and Mary the mother of Jesus, and with his brethren'. After the feast of Pentecost, a profound and mysterious silence surrounds Mary, who is not mentioned in the New Testament again.

'The Heavens declare the Glory of God'

and the firmament sheweth his handiwork. Day unto day uttereth speech, and night unto night sheweth knowledge. There is no speech nor language, where their voice is not heard. Their line is gone out through all the earth, and their words to the end of the world.'

These words of the Nineteenth Psalm contain the prophecy that the Gospel will spread over all the world. So in this miniature, which comes from a Greek psalter of the year 1066, it is shown how each single one of the apostles preaches the Gospel to a different group of peoples.

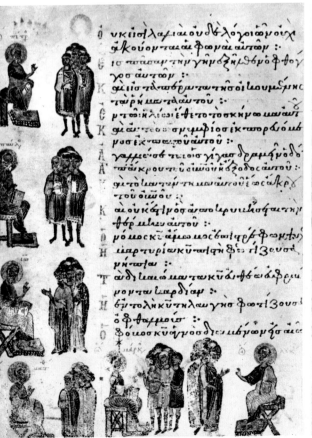

Among Christ's disciples

Peter is the dominant personality, as much for his weaknesses as for his strength. With the sword, Peter defended Jesus at the time of his arrest in the Garden of Gethsemane, only later to deny him thrice. When the Lord thereupon turned towards him and looked at him, he went out καὶ ἔκλαυσεν πικρῶς – and wept bitterly. The tears which Peter shed, out of remorse at his weakness under the starry sky of Jerusalem, were the bitterest ever shed by a human being. This austere Romanesque sculpture of the twelfth century gives an impression of the personality of this dynamic man, to whom Jesus promised the keys of Heaven.

The statue comes from France, from the time of the Crusades. The Middle Ages had an idea of Peter that corresponded much better to the personality of the New Testament accounts than does the Peter of the rather superficial legends in which a later age tried to make him into a kindly greybeard. Peter was the leading personality of the young community in Jerusalem. He directed it vigorously, cleverly, and successfully. His Pentecost sermon speaks with the voice of authority. It is he who, inspired by the Holy Ghost, baptised the first Gentile. Later he was for a time the first Bishop of Antioch, and after that became the first Bishop of Rome.

26

The Inscription of Theodotus,

written in Greek, was found some years ago in Jerusalem to the south of the site where the Temple had stood. On this stone Theodotus informs us that he, a priest, and son and grandson of a priest, has built a synagogue in which the Law is to be read and the Commandments taught, and a hostel with a water supply, for pilgrims from abroad. The stone of Theodotus belonged to a Hellenist synagogue in Jerusalem, in which Greek was spoken. In all probability it was also the synagogue in which Stephen preached, for he, to judge from his name, must have been a Hellenist Jew.

The Jews who came to Jerusalem from overseas for the most part no longer understood Aramaic, the language of the Jews of Palestine at that time. This was no doubt the reason why the inscription which Pilate caused to be put over Jesus' head was written in three languages – Aramaic for the native Jews, Latin for the Roman soldiers and officials, Greek for all those who had come from afar and understood only that language.

The fast-growing young communion

in Jerusalem was soon faced by practical tasks. Many of the newly converted sold their possessions and laid the money at the feet of the apostles. These sums were distributed to the poor, and to widows and orphans. The apostles seem to have proceeded in a rather high-handed fashion, for 'there was a murmuring of the Grecians against the Hebrews, saying that their

widows were neglected in the daily ministration.' We are all too apt to
assume that every single one of the first Christians was a great saint, and it
is rather a comfort to find that this was evidently not the case. Among these
men and women, too, there were individuals like ourselves, striving for the
highest and stumbling over the lowest. The fact that Luke has not omitted
this unchristian murmuring from his account shows what a reliable reporter
he is. Moreover, we can infer from this episode how quickly the new communion had taken on the international character of Jewry as a whole.
Seven deacons were elected to take the administrative work off the apostles'
hands. It is noteworthy that all seven had Greek names. One of these dea-

cons, Stephen, aroused the displeasure of the Supreme Council and of the High Priest by the many miracles that he performed. He was summoned before the Council. Instead of defending himself against the accusation that he was acting in contempt of the Law of Moses and the Temple, he made a violent attack on the whole Jewish people. At the end of his speech he had a vision, 'and saw the glory of God, and Jesus standing on the right hand of God.' And when he went on to tell the assembly what he was see-ing in his vision, the crowd took it as blasphemy and went wild with anger. He was dragged out of the city and stoned to death. Stephen was the first martyr of Christendom, the first witness of Christ. The Greek word means 'witness'.

The light of the divine apparition

has blinded the eyes of this powerful man, whom two armed companions have taken by the hand, while the groom leads his riderless horse by the bridle to the city gate. In the bowed attitude of St Paul the sixteenth-century Flemish master Heemskerk has managed to convey something of his torment of soul, after the vision of Christ which had been vouchsafed to him on the

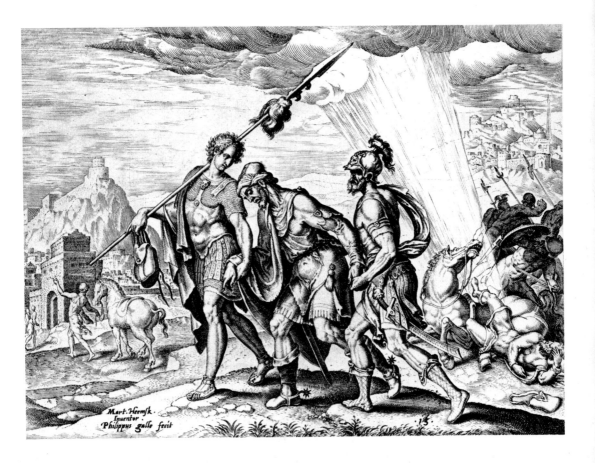

Mart. Heemsk.
Inventor
Philippus galle fecit
.15.

road to Damascus. The light has been perceived also by his companions but they have not heard the words spoken to him by Christ. Paul had set forth from Jerusalem for Damascus, in order to arrest the disciples of Christ there and bring them back to Jerusalem for trial. Only a few days later we find him preaching the new doctrine himself. The city gate of Damascus still incorporates a small portion of the Roman gate through which this group of people passed. These ancient stones were witnesses of one of the most important events in the history of early Christianity. Peter was the first disciple to baptise a Gentile, the centurion Cornelius. But Paul was the man who helped him convert the apostles to the doctrine that Jesus had come on Earth to redeem all men. Thereafter it was he who everywhere in the ancient world freed the new teaching from the tight shackles of the Mosaic Law and who made the conversion of the Gentiles his life's task. The greater part of the Acts of the Apostles is taken up with Paul's labours.

Damascus is an oasis
lying in the Syrian Desert between the spurs of the Antilebanon mountain range. Damascus was one of the more important great cities of antiquity and has survived the vicissitudes of history better than Ephesus or Antioch. The mountain in the background, Jebel Kasyun, is held sacred

by the Muslims because according to their tradition it was the place where Abraham received the illumination that there was only the one Almighty God. King David once conquered this city. And here it was that the harem and the treasures of the Persian King Darius, after his defeat at Issus, were handed over to Alexander the Great's general Parmenio. In the seventh century A.D. Damascus, under the Omayyad Dynasty, enjoyed a period of Islamic splendour as the first metropolis of the Arab invaders of the Byzantine Empire. The Caliph Khalid ibn al-Walid erected, in place of a church that had been built by the Emperor Theodosius I and restored by the Emperor Justinian, the famous mosque in which the head of John the Baptist is still a revered relic.

The Mosque of the Omayyads, though built to the orders of Arab princes, is an important memorial of Byzantine art. At the same time it can be counted, with the Dome of the Rock in Jerusalem, among the greatest works of Islamic art. The minaret in the centre of the picture is called Madinet Isa, the Minaret of Jesus. According to Muslim belief the spire of the Madinet Isa is the point at which Jesus at the end of time will again set foot on earth. Damascus is the city in which St Paul became a Christian.

'The street which was called straight' today still runs directly through Damascus from one city gate to the other. In Roman times it was adorned with columns on either side and some of these have been dug up. It was an elegant main street, full of the noisy life of an oriental shopping quarter. Here it was that Paul found accomodation in the house of a man named Judas. After three days of praying and fasting, the Lord sent to him Ananias, who laid hands on him and restored his sight. Paul had himself baptised and began to preach Christ in the synagogue.

The orthodox Jews in Damascus

were greatly incensed that the man who had hitherto been the most violent persecutor of the followers of Christ had now himself been baptised. They resolved to kill him, and Paul was forced to flee. As the Jews were lying in wait for him at the city gates his friends let him down by night over the city wall in a basket. The spot where this was done is still shown to tourists, and it is a fact that the lowest courses of the wall date from Roman times. Paul escaped this danger by a trick. He was to run into many more dangers, and did not always escape from them with so little hurt. The picture is from the Triumphal Column in the Cathedral at Hildesheim.

with the broken column and the marble figure, headless but still proudly enthroned in a deserted landscape, in the midst of gay spring flowers, is a part of the scanty remains of a whole city. In the time of Christ this city was a centre of public life. It was founded a few years before Christ's birth by Herod the Great. In honour of Augustus he called it Caesarea. Herod built for his city a harbour, which, on a coast so poor in natural inlets, met a great public need, and Caesarea later became the seat of the Roman governor. It was from here that Paul sailed for his native Tarsus when he had to leave Jerusalem soon after his conversion, fleeing from the Jews who were seeking his life, just as those in Damascus had done.

In Caesarea Peter baptised Cornelius, a Gentile and a Roman officer. An angel had commanded Cornelius to seek out Peter. The Holy Ghost commanded Peter to accept Cornelius's invitation. Peter entered the Gentile officer's house and baptised him together with his whole family and many other Gentiles who had come to see the holy man. By entering the Gentile's house and eating a meal with him, Peter, as an upright Jew, had broken the Mosaic Law. Because of this he was strongly attacked by the apostles and brethren in Jerusalem and called to account for it. His relation of what had happened, however, convinced the others that he had acted according to the commands of the Holy Ghost, and therefore rightly. The interdict had been broken. Christ was no longer the Messiah of the Jews alone.

'Then hath God also to the Gentiles granted repentance unto life.'

In Caesarea Paul was later to spend a long time in prison. Perhaps at one time or another it was up these steps, past this column, that he was taken to be examined by the Roman governor, first by Governor Felix, and then by his successor Festus. Here in Caesarea Paul had his famous interview with King Agrippa, whom he 'almost persuaded to be a Christian'.

In later history this site has other claims to fame, for it was here that Origen long lived and taught, and here that Eusebius, the first historian of Christianity, had his residence as Bishop of Caesarea.

The road from Damascus to Antioch

across the desert is an old Roman road. Everywhere about the Mediterranean remnants of such roads are yet to be seen, and some of them are still in use. The extensive road system of the Romans was a remarkable achievement. The most distant parts of the Empire were linked with the capital city by roads like these, and in the Roman Empire travel was generally convenient. The government courier service was astonishingly rapid. New ideas and new ways of thought moved quickly from one end to the other of this world empire. Over these ancient stones many of the apostles must have pressed forward through the sun's heat and the desert dust from the splendours of Damascus to the splendours of Antioch. The caravan camels loaded with expensive merchandise, officers and officials high on horseback, priests, beggars and scholars were their wayside companions. When a cohort of soldiers passed by, they would no doubt step prudently aside. The road system of the Roman Empire was an important element in the strategy of imperial defence. Later these same roads contributed to its downfall, for the conquering invaders could advance along them just as quickly as the defending troops.

Antioch on the Orontes

was famed in ancient times for its beauty, its riches and its immorality. In this treasure, found in Rome, the silver figurine representing Antioch is shown wearing a crown. On her arm she has a sheaf of corn. Her feet are planted on the prow of a ship. The figure at her feet is a personification of the river Orontes. Antioch today is a modest little Turkish country town, only the name of which, Antakya, recalls the past. Of its ancient glories very little now remains. From the height of Mount Silpius, at the foot of which Antioch lies, one can still make out from the traces discernible in the ploughed fields round the modern town, the city's former extent, along either side of the winding Orontes. Antioch was not one of the original Greek cities but was founded by Seleucus I Nicator, one of Alexander the Great's generals, as the capital of his new kingdom. Its first inhabitants were Macedonians, veterans of Alexander's campaigns. These splendid, fierce soldiers had many excellent qualities, but it is certain that they did not lead very moral lives. From the very beginning they impressed the stamp of their personalities on the life of the city. Antioch was reputed to be not only the most magnificent but also the most immoral

city of the East. The satirist Juvenal complained that 'vice flows from the Orontes into the Tiber.' Antioch prided itself on the fact that its marble-paved streets were illuminated at night, but perhaps this was necessary for security. It was in this Antioch that the 'Nazarenes', the adherents of the new doctrine, were first called Christians, and they were able to live fairly undisturbed here. A certain measure of toleration is usually associated with immorality.

For the beginning of Christianity the city of Antioch was of extraordinary importance. It was from here that Paul undertook his first two missionary journeys. From the city there were great caravan routes leading to Asia Minor, to Persia and India, and to Damascus, Jerusalem and Egypt. It was always a very lively city, a clearing-house for merchandise and ideas. It was from here that the Gospel spread into Syria and Persia. The first Bishop of Antioch was Peter. Later, towards the end of the fourth century, the famous John Chrysostom preached here. His surname in Greek means 'Golden-tongued'. His sermons, of which we possess thirteen volumes, are so lively that they would still be acceptable from many pulpits. As a preacher he was so beloved by his congregation that, when he was chosen Patriarch of Constantinople, he had to be smuggled secretly out of the city, because it was feared that the people would not let him go.

This beautifully worked silver chalice, a masterpiece of Byzantine Christian art, comes from Antioch, from about the time of John Chrysostom.

Tarsus was the birthplace of the Apostle Paul.
Here in his youth he visited the synagogue, and here he learned the craft of tent-making. Tarsus lies between the high mountain range of Taurus and the sea, in the fertile Cilician plain in southern Anatolia, only a few miles distant from the coast. In ancient times it had a harbour, which is today silted up. It was connected with Antioch by a trunk road, and through its harbour with the world. Tarsus, too, was a flourishing and wealthy city, whose inhabitants enjoyed Roman citizenship. The fact that Paul was a *civis Romanus* several times played an important part in his life story. Tarsus had a famous university, regarded as one of the chief centres of the Stoic school of Philosophy. Cicero had been governor here. Athenodoxus, the tutor of the Emperor Augustus, came from Tarsus. Antony and Cleopatra passed in Tarsus a rapturous spring, of which we may suppose that many anecdotes still circulated in Paul's boyhood. Even an Archbishop of Canterbury first saw the light in this city – Theodore of Tarsus, the organiser of the English Church in the seventh century.

But in Tarsus nothing of these ancient splendours has remained. Only the tentmakers still ply their craft there. Though now Muslim, they have chosen the Apostle Paul as their patron saint and take pride in the fact that he was one of them.

Before the Church of Panaya Chrysopolitissa in Paphos, Cyprus,
stand some ancient granite columns. They once belonged to the palace of
the governor Sergius Paulus. To this day they stand as witnesses of an
event which is related in Chapter XIII of the Acts of the Apostles. Paul
and Barnabas had come to Cyprus, and the governor Sergius Paulus sent
for them, desiring to hear the word of God from them. On the governor's
staff there was a Cypriot named Elymas who was a sorcerer, and who disputed
with the apostles. Paul struck him with a temporary blindness, and the governor
was so impressed by the supernatural powers of the apostle that he
became a convert. Once more, at this early period, it was a high Roman
official who went over to the new faith.

41

Of the miracles that Paul and Barnabas performed on their journeys,
one had an astonishing effect on the heathen. Raphael has depicted this
scene in one of his cartoons. When Paul had healed a cripple in Lystra, in
Asia Minor, the people took these two for gods. Barnabas they thought was
Zeus, and Paul his companion Hermes. The priest of the temple of Zeus
brought oxen and wreaths of flowers, to sacrifice to Apollo. Paul and Barnabas were of course horrified, and had great trouble in convincing the
priest and people that they were not gods.

Where St Paul first set foot

on the soil of Europe was the harbour of Kavalla. Before leaving the soil of Asia Minor, he passed through the ancient Troy. Not since Alexander the Great had made sacrifice at the grave of Achilles had the site of the Trojan War had been allowed to go unremembered. In St Paul's day a great temple of Athena stood on the presumed acropolis of Troy.

Even today the old Roman aqueduct still soars on its wide arches over the rooftops of Kavalla. Still in use, too, is the old road through Kavalla from Philippi to Thessalonica, shown in the picture below.

Philippi, as the excavations there have shown,

was not one of the great places of antiquity. Yet it had already been fortified by Philip II of Macedon, on account of the gold mines in the near-by Rhodope mountains. The city became famous through the battle of Phi-lippi in the year 42 B.C., in which Octavian and Antony overcame the murderers of Caesar, Brutus and Cassius. Philippi was a flourishing provin-cial city in the fertile Thracian plain. Sheltered by the mountains from the cold north wind, this smiling countryside looks out on the Aegean, across to the rocky islands of Thasos and Samothrace.

Philippi was the home of the first European woman to become a Christian. As a seller of purple, Lydia may well have been a fairly wealthy woman, and it was she who hospitably entertained Paul and his companion in her house. Lydia was not herself a native of Philippi, but of Thyateira, the township in which was one of the seven apocalyptic churches singled out by St John as typical recipients of open letters in the first chapter of The Revelation.

Lydia's whole household were baptised with the mistress of the house, and this suggests that her ideas of household management were of a sober, tradi-tional kind. Again and again we hear of this happening. It seems that, while laxity of behaviour began more and more to gain the upper hand in the great cities, the countryside still remained faithful to the old virtues.

In Philippi Paul and Silas suffered imprisonment,

and this as the consequence of an extraordinary episode. There was in the city a young woman with the gift of soothsaying. She ran behind the apostles, calling out: 'These men are the servants of the most high God, which shew unto us the way of salvation.' It was the plain truth. But Paul would not tolerate it. Even for an apostle it was too much to have a woman run behind him and ecstatically proclaim his mission to the people. Paul was 'grieved' by it, for even the truth may not be proclaimed by an unclean spirit. He drove out the evil spirit, and now the girl's master, who had earned a lot of money by her soothsaying, was angry with him. He dragged Paul and Silas before the magistrates. The people became incensed against them, and the apostles were beaten and thrown into gaol. That night there was an earthquake. The prison was shaken. The doors burst open. The prisoners were free. The gaoler at first wanted to kill himself, thinking that his prisoners had escaped. When he found that they had stayed there, he threw himself at their feet and had himself baptised. The further course of events is instructive in showing Paul's sense of pride. On the next day the magistrates sent court officials with instructions to free the two men. But Paul demurred. He was a Roman citizen, be said, and had been publicly beaten without trial. The Roman respect for law and justice, particularly when they had been violated, was shown by the manner in which the magistrates demeaned themselves to visit the apostles in person and politely request them to accept the freedom they had so miraculously gained. Paul acceded to their request and set forth for Thessalonica.

Thessalonica,

now known as Salonika, took its name from the sister of Alexander the Great. In the course of history the city has several times been destroyed, most recently in the first World War. Thessalonica lay on the Via Egnatia, the great Roman road that led to the Bosporus from Dyrrhachium, the present-day Durazzo. The Via Egnatia, the main street of the city, is still spanned by the triumphal arch of Galerius, which was put up at the turn of the third and fourth centuries. From earlier times, it is true, almost nothing has been preserved. Only one thing remains unchanged since the time of St Paul, and that is the wonderful view across the harbour to the snow-covered slopes of Mount Olympus. Here in Thessalonica, in full view of the old mountain home of the Greek gods, St Paul founded the first great Christian community on European soil. In St Luke's account of the Apostle Paul's stay in Thessalonica, two things should be noted. Here again the Jews contrived to stir up a public commotion against him. It seems that they always regarded this as a sure means of getting rid of this inconvenient man. What a Roman official desired above all was not to attract attention. So long as nothing was heard of him in Rome, he was always regarded as a good official. But in Thessalonica the Jews used this as a means of driving Paul out of the city. Among the accusations they laid before the magistrates Luke quotes the sentence, 'These that have turned the world upside down have come hither also.' They could scarcely have used such words if the Christians in these early times had been an un-important and unknown group. Another widespread preconception refuted by the account of their Thessalonican visit is the idea that originally Chris-tianity was an affair of poor people and slaves. Not only were many God-fearing Greeks baptised, but also some prominent society ladies.

The most dangerous pavements ever trodden by St Paul were those of Athens, although he did not in fact suffer the slightest harm there. And it was in Athens that he made his finest speech. The Agora of Athens has been excavated, largely by American archaeologists. One of the ancient buildings, the Stoa of Attalos, has been reconstructed exactly according to the ancient plans. When one wanders through the lovely cool colonnades of the Stoa, which houses a wonderful museum of the objects excavated here, one has a view of the Agora, the most famous market-place the world has known, and of the Temple of Theseus in the background. One can experience and appreciate the spatial harmony which is so characteristic of the great age of Greek architecture.

After it had lost its political importance, Athens was for centuries longer the cultural centre of the ancient world. Roman emperors decked out the city with magnificent buildings and accorded it high privileges. The university was famous, and only Alexandria ventured to compete with Athens in learning. To the Athenians the admiration accorded their city by educated people all over the world was as much a matter of course as

the admiration for Paris today is to the French. In Athens they knew everything and believed nothing. There could have been no more cynical audience than the assembly in the Agora addressed by St Paul. The 'mock-ing of Paul' taken from the Codex of St Gall depicts a scene one can well imagine as having occurred in Athens. Yet there were some among the audience who believed, notably the Councillor Dionysius, and a wo-man whom St Luke mentions, with special distinction, by name Damaris.

48

They had come, as always, to hear 'some new thing', not as seekers after truth, but to be entertained. Such a sophisticated audience would find it natural to make fun of this strange Hebrew prophet.

Bible critics have indeed questioned the whole episode of St Paul's address to the Agora, and sought to prove that it must have been inserted in the Acts at a later date. It is argued, moreover, that his Greek cannot have been good enough for him to make such a speech. But in the long run the compelling simplicity of the Bible narrative has carried more conviction than the critical conjectures. And as for St Paul's Greek, he wrote in the *Koiné*, the ordinary Greek of common use; using this language he was one of the most important contributors to one of the most successful books in world literature. He must also have spoken it with eloquence to make so many converts among the Gentiles of so many Hellenist cities.

1. Chateau d'Ephese ou d'Aiasalouc habité par les Turcs.
2. Ruines d'vn Chateau plus ancien ou est la porte aux basreliefs.
3. Eglise de S.t Iean convertie en Mosquée.
4. Le Village d'Aiasalouc habité par les Turcs.
5. Aqueduc ruiné.
6. Ruines du Temple de Diane.
7. Restes de la porte ou est l'inscription

8. La prison de S.t Pol.
9. Marais a la terte du quel étoit le Temple de Diane.
10. Ruines et quartiers de marbre.
11. Ruines et Colonnes vers l'Embouscheure du Caistre.
12. Lac.
13. Maison de pecheur.
14. Bac ou l'on passe la riviere pour aller de Scalanova a Smirne.
15. Pont et chemin d'Ephese a Smirne.
16. Chemin d'Ephese a Scalanova.

Ephesus, the city of Artemis,

was, like Antioch, one of the great cities of the ancient world. In the time of the apostles it had a quarter of a million inhabitants. It was a much older city than Antioch. While Antioch was founded at the end of the fourth century, Ephesus was probably a city of the Achaeans as early as the tenth century B.C. It was about the same age, therefore, as Peking. Yet, before the beginning of modern times, it had completely vanished from the earth. Not even a village stood on the site where it once had been. It took I. T. Wood, the British archaeologist, some years to find the Temple of Artemis. The clue was ultimately provided by a Roman inscription from the time of the Emperor Trajan.

Homer lived in Ephesus and the

Iliad mentions a meadow named Asia, which lay by the Caystros, the river
that runs into the sea at Ephesus. From this meadow the Roman province
of Asia, and ultimately a whole continent, took its name. The Temple of
Artemis at Ephesus, called the Artemisium, was for a thousand years, from
700 B.C. till its destruction by the Goths in A.D. 263, one of the greatest
sanctuaries of the Greeks. Herostratus, a man who wanted to win fame
quickly and easily (and had his wish, too) set fire to the temple, so tradition
has it, on the night in which Alexander the Great was born. Whereupon
the temple was rebuilt with all the more magnificence. The artist who in the
year 1608 made a picture of the then completely vanished temple has
succeeded in rendering fairly accurately what later reconstructions by
archaeologists have revealed. Today the place on which this famous building
stood is a water hole in which a few marble pillars lie scattered. Occasionally
a shepherd comes here with his flock to water his sheep.

Original columns from the Artemisium are to be found today in the Hagia
Sophia in Constantinople, and there are some magnificent marble slabs
from it in the apse of the church in the Monastery of St Catherine at the
foot of Mount Sinai.

Artemis, called Diana by the Romans, was the successor of Astarte, a very

ancient Asiatic fertility goddess. Artemis exhibits a head with the fine features of a Greek goddess and the numerous breasts that symbolise the Asiatic idea of fertility.

It was with worshippers of this Artemis that the Apostle Paul came into direct conflict. The silversmiths of Ephesus earned a great deal of money by making models of the temple. These they sold to the pilgrims who thronged to it from all over the world. Fearing for their sales, Demetrius, who seems to have been the master of the silversmiths' guild, stirred up a commotion against the apostle. The theatre in which the silversmiths held their noisy meeting has been excavated. The menaces of the mob compelled St Paul to leave the city. But he had already been three months in Ephesus, and the disturbance caused by Demetrius is a proof, if one was needed, that he must have had some success there. Paul was very attached to the community in Ephesus. One of his wonderful epistles is addressed to the Ephesians. On his last return to Jerusalem, when the presentiment of death was already casting its shadow, he stayed a short while in Miletus. He sent for the elders of the community of Ephesus to visit him, and there addressed them with those moving words of farewell that are recorded for us in the twentieth chapter of the Acts of the Apostles.

St Paul's voyage to Rome

was to be the last journey of this much-travelled man. On board ship Paul was the prisoner of the Roman centurion whose orders were to take him before the Emperor. They ran into a storm that lasted fourteen days. There appeared to Paul an angel who announced to him that all those on board with him would be saved. Paul informed the crew of the angel's message, saying that God had 'given him' all those that sailed with him. 'Where-fore, sirs, be of good cheer; for I believe God, that it shall be even as it was told me.' How different these words from those which in a similar situation a century earlier Caesar had addressed to his ship's crew: 'This ship will not go down. It bears Caesar and his luck.' The course of events when Paul's ship grounded is described by St Luke with seamanlike accuracy of detail. No old salt could have told the story better. The unknown island on

which they were all able eventually to reach safety was Malta. As the shipwrecked party, drenched and half frozen, were making a fire, a viper sprang out of the firewood and bit Paul in the hand. According to an old superstition the island people thought he must be a murderer, whom the vengeance of the Furies would not allow to live, although he had escaped the sea. But when nothing happened, they looked upon him, for the second time in his life, as a god. The centre scene on this leaf from an ivory diptych shows the incident.

The Acts of the Apostles ends with St Paul's arrival in Rome. We are told only that he lived in Rome for two years, more or less undisturbed in his own house, and preached the Kingdom of God. We do not learn anything from this source about his martyr's death.

St Paul is the author of a quarter of the New Testament. He wrote letters, the Epistles, to the members of seven Churches: the Romans, the Corinthians, the Galatians, the Ephesians, the Philippians, the Colossians, and the Thessa-lonians. In addition there is preserved for pos-terity a letter from him to Timothy, a good friend who accompanied him on his second missionary journey, a second letter, to Titus, who was also a friend of Paul's and later became the first Bishop of Crete, and finally the letter to Philemon. Paul infuses into his Epistle to Philemon so much affection and warmth of feeling that we may consider ourselves lucky to possess a document

that fills in the picture of this stern man with such kindly touches. The slave Onesimus had run away from his master Philemon. Probably, too, he had not left empty-handed. Both crimes, running away and theft from a master by a slave, were punishable by crucifixion. Onesimus had met Paul on his flight and had been converted to Christianity by him. And now, since Paul could not well cover up a crime punishable by Roman Law, he sends him back to Philemon with a letter. In it he even offers himself to make good to Philemon the loss he has suffered at Onesimus' hands. The disobedient slave has become an obedient Christian and does St Paul's bidding. This good deed had for St Paul one favourable consequence that he was never to know about. After the apostle's death, his letters were collected. It is surmised that it was Onesimus who performed this task from Ephesus and then published the collected epistles. One other fact is recorded of Onesimus. Eusebius says he was Bishop of Ephesus in about 110.

The writings of St Paul have perpetually affected the course of history, changing the world right up to our own day. St Augustine records in his *Confessions* that a passage in the Epistle to the Romans (XIII, 13–14) was the cause of his conversion, and Luther was decisively influenced in his religious development by this Epistle. St Paul's part in the foundation of Christianity are such that any matter of Christian doctrine is bound to involve questions about the theological views of St Paul and the nature of his personal contribution to Christian belief. These questions have often been the subject of controversy, and will continue to be so whenever Christianity is discussed. St Paul was one of the great writers of world literature and one of the truly great figures of world history.

THE REGION that extends from the slopes of the Caucasus and the south coast of the Black Sea to the deserts of North Arabia and the Indian Ocean is one of the great theatres of world history. Kings, statesmen, generals, religious leaders and philosophers, explorers and conquerors, heroes and saints, artists, scholars, martyrs and monks, all have played their parts on its stage. The crowds moving on and off, or waiting in the wings, were the peoples of the ancient world. Many a stretch of ground throughout this entire region has been drenched in blood, and the wars that have been waged over it can be counted in hundreds. Here, too, the German historian Ranke's bitter saying seems no more than the truth: 'Humanity's periods of happiness are the blank pages in the history books.' And yet this is the part of the earth in which three decisive elements of our own civilisation have their origin – its religion, its science and its art.

The alphabet was created by the Phoenicians. Science was born in the cities of Ionia on the west coast of Anatolia. From the islands off this coast come the medicine, mathematics and poetry of the West. Hippocrates taught on the island of Cos; Pythagoras was born on Samos; Homer was a native probably of Chios; Sappho, of Lesbos. From Palestine came the Gospel.

Some of the most ancient races of men have lived here since the Stone Age. The oldest city known to us anywhere on earth is Jericho in the Jordan Valley. It has a proved history of continuous settlement from the eighth millennium B.C. to the present day. Through all the changes of time the region has retained certain constant features. Again and again it has been invaded by warrior peoples, and there is no quarter of the compass from which such invasions have not come. Far back in prehistoric times it experienced those great east-west movements of peoples that originated in Asia and poured out over the isles of the Aegean as far as the mainland of present-day Greece.

It is conjectured that the Sumerians, the earliest people of whom we have written records, originally advanced into Mesopotamia by way of the Euphrates delta from one of the mountain ranges of the Iranian plateau or of Central Asia. Again and again, during three millennia, waves of Bedouin kept breaking in from the deserts of Arabia. Among them were the forefathers of the Hebrew people that later conquered Canaan. The last of these waves was the eruption of Islam, which reached southern France in the west and the foothills of the Hindu Kush in the east. The legendary

kings of Crete, as the excavations in Knossos have shown, extended their command of the seas to the coast of Asia Minor. And coming from the southwest the Pharaohs repeatedly conquered Syria as far as the Euphrates. Nothing is yet exactly known about the origin of the Hittites, a people speaking an Indo-European language whose empire in the centre of Anatolia lasted a thousand years, but had already been forgotten by Roman times. The records tell us, too, about the invasions of 'sea peoples', who were able to shake the power of Egypt and perhaps even conquered it. It is not known who these peoples were, but some think the Philistines of the Bible should be numbered among them.

The Empires of Assur and Babylon in Mesopotamia were a perpetual menace to all their neighbours. Again and again Syria was the scene of battles between these two great powers and Egypt. The Empire of Israel was destroyed by the Assyrians.

The Babylonians were followed by other peoples coming from the east, the Medes, and after them the Persians, whose expansion was stopped by the Greeks in the famous battles of Salamis and Marathon.

The Greeks, when we first meet them in history, in the first half of the first millennium B.C., were already established on the mainland of Hellas and all round the Aegean. They were descended from peoples who had come down into the mainland of Greece from the north in a movement lasting many centuries, the beginnings and exact details of which can only be conjectured, and from there spread out eastward over the Aegean. From the Aegean the Greeks sent out their colonising expeditions all over the Mediterranean, and by the time of the prophet Jeremiah the colonies of Miletus reached from the estuary of the Don in the Sea of Azov to the coast of Provence and Spain.

A rival movement of colonisation was that of the Phoenicians, who, starting out from the coasts of Syria, settled in North Africa, Sicily, and also Spain, and whose most famous centre was Carthage.

Later, Alexander the Great, in one great rush of conquest, swept over Anatolia, Syria, Mesopotamia, and Iran as far as India. There was also for a time, before the Romans came, a great Armenian empire, extending over wide areas of Anatolia. The Roman conquest was from the west, and for a few hundred years it brought peace to the lands between the Black and the Red Seas. The Romans, on the other hand, never succeeded in extending their dominion permanently across the Euphrates to the east, for the empire of the Parthians withstood Rome, just as that of the Sassanid Persians was later to withstand Byzantium.

At times northern Europeans – the Galatians of St Paul – and Goths from the Danube, invaded Anatolia. It was the Goths who destroyed the Artemisium of Ephesus, one of the greatest sanctuaries of the pagan world, even before the Christians had the chance to do so. Among their Christian prisoners were the parents of Wulfila, who later converted the Goths and translated the Bible into Gothic.

Byzantium for years had to pay tribute to Attila, the King of the Huns, who was established in Hungary, and who for his part had to fight numerous campaigns against the attacking Bulgars. Byzantium, during its last centuries the Christian bulwark of the West, was as often embroiled with the western Christians as with the enemies of Christianity. The Crusaders from northern and western Europe, who passed through the Byzantine dominions to wage war against the infidels and for two centuries maintained their Latin outposts in Palestine and Syria, often found it difficult to remember whose allies they were. And in the Fourth Crusade Constantinople was taken and looted of its treasures by the Franks, two and a half centuries before it finally fell to the Ottoman conqueror.

For the Turks were next on the scene. They came from the steppes by the Aral Sea; first the Seljuks, then the Ottomans – the only warrior people to succeed in subduing the Arab lands. The Egyptians got possession only of the Sinai Peninsula. Alexander the Great died of malaria just as he had completed the preparations for his campaign against the Arabs. The Romans, and more recently the British, failed in their attempt. The Most Christian Kings of Axum, in Ethiopia, did once, in alliance with the Emperor Justinian of Byzantium, subdue and rule over Arabia Felix, the modern Yemen, but only for half a century.

The Mongols penetrated a thousand miles further than the Turks. They came from the steppes of Inner Asia on their stocky horses, stayed a short time, and disappeared with enormous booty.

Later conquerors from the west were the Venetians, the Genoese, and the European great powers of the last century. The North was represented, when the first Russian fleet appeared off Constantinople in the ninth century A.D. Later, in their long wars with the Turks, the Russian pushed deep into Armenia from over the Caucasus. At that time they contented themselves with the sources of the Euphrates. Today they look to its mouth.

Here in this world of violence and slaughter, one splendid civilisation after another was created and brought to fruition, only to sink again into ashes. Again and again man raised his temples out of rubble and his cities out of smoking ruins. Again and again he wrested new crops from fields laid waste. In the extremity of desolation he never gave up hope, never despaired. And it was in this great theatre that the stage was set for an event whose very simplicity was to conquer the world.

A handful of men, with no assets but their own honesty of purpose, without power or arms, with hardly more than a crust of bread in their pockets, set out to give mankind a piece of news, a message, a new faith. The gospel, the good tidings they brought, consisted of an announcement, the most astonishing ever made, that God had sent his Son upon earth to redeem mankind from its sins and sufferings. Yet after little more than three hundred years Christianity had become the State religion of the Roman Empire.

At the geographical core of the new faith were the provinces of Syria and Anatolia. In the two hundred years between the reigns of Constantine and Justinian they became Christian lands, splendidly adorned with churches, illuminated by a new humanity, stirred by deep theological problems. Today there are hardly any Christians left in Anatolia, and within the boundaries of the ancient Syria there are only scattered communities like the Maronites of the Lebanon, or the Greek Orthodox Arabs of Palestine.

From this flourishing centre the new Christian culture spread to the neighbouring lands – to Georgia and Armenia from Anatolia, into Persia from Syria. In Persia, it is true, the Christians were in conflict with the teaching of Zoroaster, the State religion, and were never able to achieve any better standing than that of a minority, at best tolerated, and often persecuted.

The period of nearly two hundred years between the end of the Acts of the Apostles and the elevation of Christianity to a State religion is characterised by the scarcity of reliable information about its progress. They are the silent centuries. Silent, but not inactive, for as soon as the records recommence, we learn of great Christian communities, numerous bishops, and even more numerous martyrs.

If we consider it, a hundred and fifty years are not a very long time. We should have quite a good picture today of the battle of Waterloo or the figure of Napoleon even if none of us knew any more than what our grand parents had told us, just as they had heard it from theirs.

Bishop Polycarp of Smyrna, who suffered martyrdom at an advanced age under the Emperor Antonius Pius (reigned A. D. 138–161), had been a pupil of the Apostle John, and thus had personally known an eye-witness of Jesus' earthly journey.

We know very little of the written documents on which later Christian chroniclers depended. They are lost. But there is no reason to suppose that what we learn from them about the first and second centuries is incorrect. The legends that fill up these gaps allow us to make guesses about the rest. Some of these legends are quite fantastic, but others are plausible and convincing. And so we are not entirely without clues as to what was happening during the silent centuries, and there are one or two decisive facts which are universally recognised.

Let us now turn to the consideration of some of these.

The symbols of the four evangelists are encountered again and again in Christian art. Matthew's symbol was the angel, Mark's the lion, Luke's the bull, and John's the eagle.

The gospel manuscript that is kept in the Church of San Lorenzo at Chiavenna is encased in this twelfth-century binding of great richness and outstanding craftsmanship. On its cover the four symbols appear as part of an elaborate design incorporating gold filigree work set with jewels, mosaics, enamels and cameos.

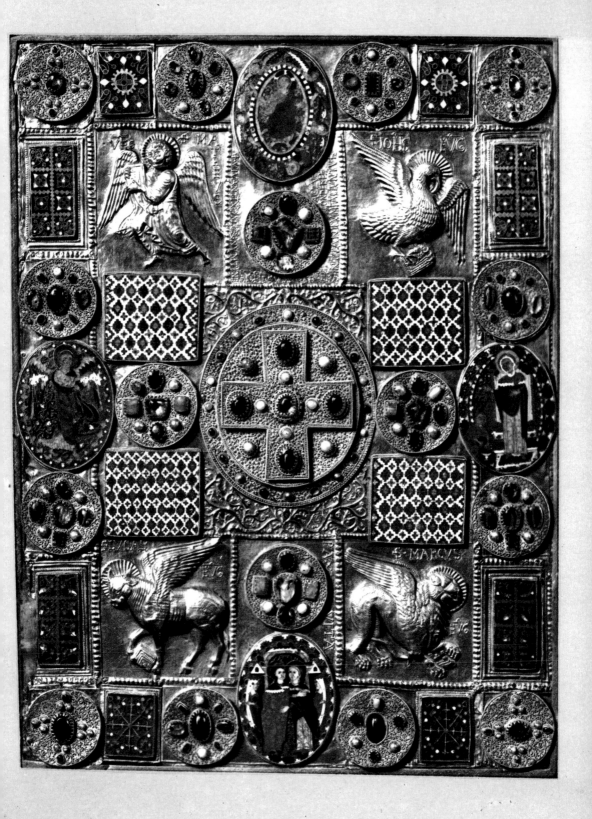

on both sides of an inconspicuous fragment of papyrus have furnished us with an isolated piece of information about the first of the two silent centuries in the history of early Christianity. The papyrus was acquired in Egypt in 1920 by the British explorer Grenfell. It found its way to the John Rylands Library in Manchester, where it has the catalogue reference 'Papyrus Rylands Greek 457'. In 1935 it was discovered that the textual fragments belonged to St John's Gospel. The passage is John XVIII, 31–33 and 37–38:

εἶπον αὐτῷ οἱ Ἰουδαῖοι Ἡμῖν οὐκ ἔξεστιν
ἀποκτεῖναι οὐδένα· ἵνα ὁ λόγος τοῦ Ἰησοῦ
πληρωθῇ ὃν εἶπεν σημαίνων ποίῳ θανάτῳ
ἤμελλεν ἀποθνήσκειν· Εἰσῆλθεν οὖν πάλιν
εἰς τὸ πραιτώριον ὁ Πειλᾶτος καὶ ἐφώνησ-
εν τὸν Ἰησοῦν καὶ εἶπεν αὐτῷ Σὺ εἶ ὁ βα-
σιλεὺς τῶν Ἰουδαίων;

'The Jews therefore said unto him, it is not lawful for us to put any man to death: that the saying of Jesus might be fulfilled, which he spake, signifying what death he should die. Then Pilate entered into the judgment hall again, and called Jesus and said unto him, Art thou the King of the Jews?'*

ἐγὼ εἰς τοῦτο γεγέννημαι καὶ ἐλήλυθα
εἰς τὸν κόσμον ἵνα μαρτυρήσω τῇ ἀλη-
θείᾳ· πᾶς ὁ ὢν ἐκ τῆς ἀληθείας ἀκούει
μου τῆς φωνῆς· λέγει αὐτῷ ὁ Πειλᾶτος Τί
ἐστιν ἀλήθεια; Καὶ τοῦτο εἰπὼν πάλιν
ἐξῆλθεν πρὸς τοὺς Ἰουδαίους, καὶ λέγει
αὐτοῖς Ἐγὼ οὐδεμίαν εὑρίσκω ἐν αὐτῷ αἰτίαν·

'To this end was I born, and for this cause came I into the world that I should bear witness unto the truth. Everyone that is of the truth heareth my voice. Pilate saith unto him, What is truth? And when he had said this, he went out again unto the Jews, and saith unto them, I find in him no fault at all.'*

Of this text the papyrus contains only a few words, but the context, as the drawing shows, can be identified without difficulty. From the quality of the papyrus and from the character of the script it can be determined that the document is from the first half of the second century. St John's Gospel is the latest of the Gospels. The period of its composition is assigned on textual evidence to the years between A.D. 60 and 90. So the fragment must have belonged to a codex which was written not later than fifty years after the composition of the original. The Rylands Library papyrus is the earliest New Testament document so far known. We learn from this find that only a generation after John had written down his account, the Gospel had already been read and transcribed. It is also clear that the text of St John's Gospel as we know it today is in substantial agreement with this fragment of the second century.

An unknown Gospel

is contained in the Egerton papyrus, which is now in the British Museum. This fragment, too, dates from the first half of the second century. There were originally more gospels than the four admitted to the New Testament in its present canonical form. Several of these apocryphal, non-canonical gospels have been preserved. We know, from the tradition, of others that have been lost. At Oxyrhynchus in Egypt a papyrus of the third century has been found with sayings of Jesus, some few of which occur in the New Testament, while others are unknown to us. St John, at the end of his Gospel, makes this significant comment: 'And there are also many other things which Jesus did, the which, if they should be written every one, I suppose that even the world itself could not contain the books that should be written.'

The fact that, finally and definitively, only four Gospels were admitted to the New Testament has its reasons in that love of mystical number-symbolism which was common to the whole ancient world. Number-symbolism was an important constituent of the teaching of the Pythagoreans. The importance of the number four in Christian symbolism has its origin in

Ezekiel and The Revelation. In the vision of the glory of the Lord with which the book of the prophet Ezekiel begins, there is the first mention of the four symbols that were later assigned to the evangelists. In The Revelation, St John returns to this picture. 'And the first beast was like a lion, and the second beast like a calf, and the third beast had a face as a man, and the fourth beast was like a flying eagle.'

The number four is also the number of the revelations to Noah, Abraham, Moses, and the revelation through Jesus Christ. So it was that the four Gospels became ultimately the four pillars of the Church. It is not known when the four symbols were assigned to the four Evangelists for the first time. Yet as early as the second century, St Irenaeus of Lyons laid down the fourfold nature of the Gospels as a canonical principle and established the correspondence between the four symbolic creatures of the Apocalypse and the four Evangelists. One of the earliest and finest representations of this symbolism has been preserved on the mosaics of Ravenna. This detail shows St Mark and his symbol.

Picturesquely situated

in surroundings of great beauty on the west coast of Asia Minor, Smyrna is today a great Turkish merchant city. Not only is it one of the seven cities which lay claim to being the birthplace of Homer, but also one of the seven apocalyptic communities, which were probably founded by the Apostle John. The second chapter of The Revelation contains a missionary letter of St John to Smyrna, in which this wonderful passage occurs: 'Be thou faithful unto death, and I will give thee a crown of life.'

Of Smyrna the noteworthy fact is reported that certain Jews in this city, not particularly firm in their orthodoxy, worshipped Jehovah under the name of 'Zeus Hypsistos'. This idea is not so outlandish as it may at first seem. There was in Greek mythology a father of gods and men, standing high above the Olympian Zeus who with his amorous affairs was the butt of the comic poets. This 'AllHighest' Zeus – Zeus Hypsistos – was worshipped without an image. It may have made an impression on the Jews. True transcendence cannot be ascribed to this Zeus Hypsistos. Yet his appearance is at least further evidence of the readiness of the Greek world to advance to a higher rank in the worship of the divine.

66

S. Polÿcarpi Capel.

The most famous Christian personality of the city was Bishop Polycarp. He had been a pupil of St John. His martyrdom under the Emperor Antoninus Pius in A. D. 155 is historically attested. He was sentenced, at the advanced age of eighty-six, to death by burning. Polycarp was such a famous man even among the pagans that the authorities must have had many earlier opportunities of proceeding against him if they had wanted. Why they waited so long is not known. As the flames were unable to make any impression on this holy man, a gladiator was ordered to kill him. He thrust his short sword right into the saint's heart. On the western slope of the mountain citadel near the stadium in which Polycarp was executed, his grave was long held in honour. The picture shows a chapel of St Polcyarp from a later period.

67

The Diatessaron of Tatian

was pieced together out of parts of all four Gospels. The author's literary intention was to write a connected story of the life of Jesus. 'Diatessaron' is a musical term meaning a harmony of four parts. Tatian was an Assyrian who lived in the second century and went over to Christianity in Rome. The Diatessaron, however, was probably not written until after his return home. The work was widely disseminated and was in general use in Syria till the fifth century. It was condemned by the Church, so that, apart from this fragment of papyrus, it is only preserved for us in late and incomplete translations into Latin, Arabic and Old High German. The papyrus here illustrated was excavated in Dura Europus.

Burnt in gold on glass,

the portrait of Christ on this fine fragment from the British Museum dates from the third century. The significance of the four smaller heads is unknown. The portrait of the handsome, beardless youth is completely different from all the later portrayals of Christ in ecclesiastical art.

68

A pagan testimony of great importance

is preserved in a letter of Pliny the Younger, in which he asks the Emperor Trajan for instructions as to how he should act towards the Christians. The letter was written about A.D. 110 when Pliny was governor of Bithynia.

Caius Plinius Secundus Minor led an eventful life as an administrative official of high rank. He was only nineteen years old when he held his first public office. In A.D. 100 he was consul, and after that governor of the province of Bithynia. He was the nephew and adopted son of Pliny the Elder, the admiral and natural historian who lost his life in the eruption of Vesuvius. He was a high-minded, perhaps rather vain, man, always ready to help any good cause, applauded as an orator and esteemed as a writer by his contemporaries. This highly educated man, who in his own writings denied the existence of gods, found himself faced with the unpleasant necessity of condemning to death, on grounds of State policy numerous Christians who refused to make sacrifice to the gods and the Emperors. One of the most significant things about Pliny's letter is what it leaves out. He does not explain to the Emperor what the Christians were. Evidently he had no need to. Barely twenty years after the death of the last disciple of Jesus, the Apostle John, this was general knowledge.

Pliny says he has released all accused persons who have made the required sacrifice and denied Christ. He gives a justification for this in which, again without meaning to, he pays tribute to the bravery of the early Christians. He had been told that no threats would induce a genuine Christian to deny Christ. Pliny gives an exact account of how the Christians really did nothing else but meet together on a definite day of the week. At this meeting, he reports, they sang a hymn to Christ and solemnly engaged themselves to commit no crime, to refrain from theft, robbery, and adultery and to keep their given word. They assembled for common meals, at which they consumed 'innocent foods', and they had given up even this custom after he had forbidden secret assemblies.

Thus the pagan governor describes the life of the early Christians exactly as we know it from Christian sources. But this man of so many intellectual interests is then seized by the desire to learn what is at the back of it all. The unlucky victims of this curiosity were two young slave girls who were deaconesses of the community. With a certain show of shame Pliny excuses himself for having tortured them, without finding anything but a 'distorted and boundless superstition'. Thereupon Pliny postpones any further trials in order to consult the Emperor, drawing his attention to the great number of people concerned, both in town and country. He mentions further (and this is very revealing) that the trials had already had a certain success. The deserted temples were filling up again, and sacred ceremonies which had long been interrupted were once more being held.

The Emperor's reply is a noteworthy example of classical humanitarianism.

He recommends the greatest clemency and expressly forbids the slightest notice being taken of anonymous denunciations, so as not to create an undesirable precedent. Anonymous denunciations, he says, are not worthy of modern civilisation. This modern civilisation existed two thousand years ago.

Clearly this authentic evidence from an objective source, at such an early period, has given valuable support to the more fragmentary testimonies of the same period from Christian sources.

The well-known account in Tacitus about the persecutions of the Christians under Nero in the year 64 also dates from the same time as Pliny's letter.

The pictures show a statue of Pliny in the Church of Como and a coin with the head of the Emperor Trajan.

This ancient olive tree

which stands near Bethlehem is no less deserving of our respect, as a living witness of ancient times, than the stone remains which the archaeologists dig out of the earth. As botanists are able to determine, this tree was already bearing fruit before Jesus Christ was born. Its dappled shade is a wonderful place in which to meditate on man's past.

The tree has seen the earth break into blossom more than two thousand times. Seventy generations of small boys have climbed about its branches. It has seen the burning of innumerable campfires, lit by shepherds, peasants, robbers and soldiers. The men have passed away, but the olive tree has remained.

The last cedars of Lebanon stand in a remote mountain valley, whose inaccessibility has saved them from being burnt as pillars in a temple fire or broken as ships' masts in a storm. Only as a symbol in the flag of the State of Lebanon is the cedar still crossed with the sea.

In stone, not much evidence of the first centuries of Christendom has been found in Syria. Buildings that were erected on sites traditionally associated with early Christian events have disappeared under later buildings of the Byzantine period. But the desert still keeps many secrets. What is still preserved there must far exceed in quantity those few remnants that have been dug up out of the sand.

Dura Europus

is the most important excavation of Christian archaeology in Syria. The city was founded in the fourth century B.C. by Seleucus I Nicator. The name, Dura Europus, is remarkable, and is of mixed Assyrian and Macedonian origin. The ruins lie on the banks of the Euphrates, here the border of the desert. Begun as a fortress, it was later a caravan city of the Parthians and ultimately a fortress on the eastern frontier of the Roman Empire. In the middle of the third century A.D. the city was destroyed. What was a terrible disaster to its inhabitants became a stroke of fortune for archaeology, for no other settlers came after them, so that nothing more was destroyed to make room for later building. In a few years the desert winds buried the ruins under the sand.

The rediscovery of the site was due to chance. In 1920, a British army captain, engaged in fighting the Arabs, had trenches dug on this spot; he discovered the wall paintings in the temple. In ten years' work a great part of the city was excavated by French and American archaeologists.

In Dura almost all the religions of those days were represented. Babylonian, Syrian, Phoenician and Arabian gods were worshipped. The Mithras cult had its place. A synagogue and a Christian church have been excavated. The synagogue dates from the end of the second century. The wall paintings from the synagogue are in the museum in Damascus.

The small building that served as a Christian place of worship was originally a private house. It was not taken into use as a church until A.D. 232, that is, just before the destruction of the city. One of the rooms of the house was a baptistery with wall paintings. These paintings today

are in America where a reconstruction of the baptistery has been built. It may be assumed that these frescoes were painted during a time of persecution. As a precaution the other rooms of the house were not adorned in a like manner. There is now not much to be seen of the frescoes, and what can be distinguished is comparatively primitive. All the same, the reconstruction allows us to believe that the room, though modest in scale, must have aroused feelings of awe in the worshipper. The wall paintings are of considerable importance for the history of art, since there are very few examples from such an early period still extant in the East. From these frescoes of Dura Europus we can learn something of the development of that Christian art which later was to adorn the whole of Europe with so many splendid masterpieces.

In the picture with the three Marys approaching the grave of Christ on Easter morning, the grave is not the cave hewn from a rock, of the New Testament account, but a sarcophagus. The angel at the grave, too, is missing. The picture was intended to remind the candidate, who would generally be an adult, that through baptism he was to be awakened to a new life, like Christ at Easter. The actual resurrection of Jesus is seldom depicted in early Christian art.

The two scenes, 'The Good Shepherd' and 'Adam and Eve under the Tree of Knowledge', which seem at first sight to have no connection with one another, are brought together in the same picture. The meaning is clear if we recall that Adam, the first man, brought sin into the world, while Christ by his coming brought the remission of sins. 'For as in Adam all die, even so in Christ shall all be made alive,' is how St Paul puts it (1 Corinthians XV, 22). The fresco is not only a fine example of the symbolism which animated the faith of the early Christians, but also shows that even at that date they were expected to be familiar with the Old Testament, or at least with those parts of it which were needed to make the New Testament intelligible. Such familiarity with the Old Testament, which would be expected of most Christian congregations today, can have been by no means a matter of course with the early converts unless they had been originally Jews.

The wall painting depicting Moses at the burning bush is one of the better-preserved frescoes in the synagogue of Dura Europus. Representations of living figures are extraordinarily rare in Hebrew art: the occurrence of so many religions in such a small place may have had a loosening effect on the strictness of traditional usage. The figure of Moses clearly shows Greek traits. It is without doubt a work of Jewish Hellenism. The shoe under the thorn-bush out of which God spoke to Moses refers to the passage Exodus III, 5: 'Draw not nigh hither: put off thy shoes from off thy feet, for the place whereon thou standest is holy ground.' In the chapel that pious monks have built on the site of the burning bush in the Monastery of St Catherine at the foot of Mount Horeb, every pilgrim to this day is made to take off his shoes before entering the chapel.

The silence of the desert

now broods over many places in which men once lived. Dr Nelson Glück, the President of the Hebrew Union College, who works as archaeologist on the project for the development of the Negev Desert in the south of Palestine, has excavated in this forsaken corner of the world a number of villages in which there was a settled population at the time of the Jewish kings. These settlements are thus two thousand five hundred to three thousand years old. Dr Glück estimates, from the sites already excavated, that there are in this once thickly populated territory another two hundred villages, churches and monasteries from the Byzantine period buried under the sand.

The ruins of Palmyra, the ancient Tadmor, in the midst of the Syrian

Desert, give us an impressive picture of the magnificence of these cities, in which Greek art, transplanted to the East and there transformed, blossomed out once more. Of Christian buildings no more than the traces have been found in Palmyra, although the city in the time of the Emperor Justinian was fortified as a point of frontier defence against the Arabs. The desert has always been a place of warfare, for the Bedouin tribes have been from time immemorial in conflict with the settled peasantry who tilled the soil.

Rusafa, too, lies in the Syrian Desert. It was built not far from the banks of the Euphrates, south of Dura Europus. In Rusafa the caravan route from Baghdad divides, one way leading to Palmyra, Emesa and Antioch, the other to Damascus. Modern desert buses still use the same track along which the camel caravans once plodded.

The reconstruction of the north gate of Rusafa shows the splendour and dignity achieved by the builders of this city so long ago in the middle of these endless wastes. Such places owed their wealth to commerce, their fertility to the presence of water, and their destruction to the covetousness of their enemies who wanted both. Rusafa, too, was a frontier fortress of the Roman Empire in the fourth century. Two martyrs, who were both to win great celebrity very soon after their deaths, met their end in Rusafa. They were soldiers of the imperial army, Sergius and Bacchus. After they had refused to deny their Christian faith they were first of all degraded. Then, as a mark of special humiliation, they were paraded round the city in women's clothes, and finally, after horrible tortures, they were beheaded. Their graves soon became places of pilgrimage and attracted many visitors.

Later the city was actually renamed Sergiopolis after one of the two martyrs. The first church to be erected in Rusafa in honour of Sergius and Bacchus dates probably from the time of Constantine the Great. Churches dedicated to them were soon to be found in many parts of the Empire. Rusafa today is completely abandoned. The recently excavated churches, one of which is prominent in the lower picture on pages 78–9, date from the sixth century.

Two solitary columns

towering above the site of the ancient city of Edessa, are reminders of a fragment of world history. They belong to a former temple, of which nothing remains, and which was probably dedicated to JupiterBaal. The city has had many names. Its Syrian and Armenian name was Urhai, and the Arabs still call it Ruha. The Greeks called it Edessa or Osrhoe, and its usual name today is Urfa. Christianity had already reached Edessa by the middle of the second century. Edessa was at that time the capital city of a little kingdom, under the dynasty of the Abgars. About the year 200, King Abgar IX became a Christian. He was the first ruling prince of whom this is recorded – one hundred and thirty years before Constantine the Great. Edessa became the spiritual centre of Syrian Christianity. It was here that the Bible was translated into Syriac.

The great saint and theologian of the Syrian Church is Ephraim the Syrian. He was born of Christian parents in Nisibis in A.D. 306, and lived there until it was conquered by the Persians, when he moved to Edessa where he founded his famous school. He was a great scholar, and his works were soon translated from Syriac into Greek. At the end of his life he withdrew from the world and became a monk. He died in 372.

King Abgar IX had an ancestor, King Abgar V, who was the hero of a famous legend. Abgar V reigned in Edessa from 4 B.C. to A.D. 50. The legend relates that he sent a letter to Jesus Christ with the request that he would visit him and heal him, and that Jesus wrote back to him in reply that after His resurrection He would send him one of His disciples. And so it was, according to this legend, that the Apostle Thaddaeus later came to Edessa, baptised the king and healed him. The Spanish nun, Etheria, who at the end of the fourth century went on a great pilgrimage to the holy places of the East, tells us in her account of it, which has been preserved, that she was shown in Edessa many copies of the letters of Jesus and Abgar. They were written, she said, in the Syriac language on parchment, and had great miracleworking power. The legend was later expanded to include the story that Jesus sent King Abgar a portrait of Himself.

Edessa is an important point in both ancient and modern history. Within the radius of a day's journey from the city the following events occurred:

Abraham left Haran, after the death of his father Terah, to move into the promised land of Canaan.

At the 'Fountain of Rebecca' Eliezer made suit, on behalf of Isaac, the son of his master, for the hand in marriage of Bethuel's daughter.

In the battle of Carchemish Nebuchadnezzar II of Babylon, in the year 605 B.C., defeated the Pharaoh Necho of Egypt. From Hierapolis, in 53 B.C., Crassus launched his ill-fated campaign against the Parthians, in which he lost his own life. From Hierapolis, in A.D. 363, Julian the Apostate, the last pagan Emperor to occupy the Byzantine throne, launched his ill-fated campaign against the Persians, in which he lost his own life.

In the time of the Crusaders, Baldwin, later King of Jerusalem, made himself Prince of Edessa. Then came the devastations by the Mongols, the Egyptians, and the hordes of Timur Khan.

In 1516 the city itself came under Turkish domination.

In 1896 in Edessa about a thousand Armenians who had taken sanctuary in the Cathedral of St George from a threatened pogrom by the Turks and Kurds were suffocated by the smoke from carpets soaked in paraffin, set on fire and thrown in.

81

The first 'pillar saint' in the history of Christendom was Simeon Stylites

He was born in Cilicia in A.D. 190, and entered a monastery when still a young man. But he found monastery life not ascetic enough, and withdrew into the Syrian desert, into a region which was about one day's journey distant from Aleppo. Aleppo, today a purely Arab city, has a mosque dedicated to Abraham and another to St Zacharias, the father of John the Baptist.

The Eastern Church was always dominated by the belief that the greater the sanctity of a monk or hermit, the more efficacious were his prayers and his intercession with Heaven. So St Simeon had attracted many of the pious or merely curious from the surrounding country, both near and far, and it was this which after a time induced him to mount a pillar, so as to pass his days on it in a yet more rigorous withdrawal from the world. But that of course made him still more popular. So he heightened the pillar several times, till he was finally at a distance of sixty feet from the sinful earth. By this time he had become reconciled to his popularity, and often preached from this altitude to the admiring crowds. He also wrote numerous letters to Emperor and bishops, giving them advice in worldly and ecclesiastical affairs.

In the illustration on the right the saint, sitting on the column, is deaf to the solicitations of the snake, the ancient symbol of evil and temptation.

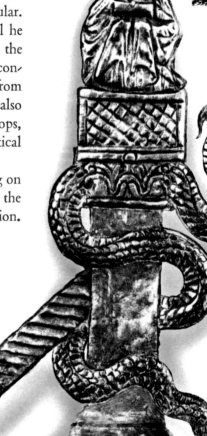

A very great sanctity here below carries always with it the danger for the soul of the sin of pride. It is therefore not quite certain that the height by which St Simeon was raised above his fellow human beings was also pleasing in the sight of Heaven. However that may be, Simeon stayed for forty years on his pillar, until at the biblical age of seventy he was released from his ascetic labours.

The church that was erected in his honour is still astonishingly well preserved. It dates from the fifth century. Set in the middle of the desert mountains, it presents, in combination with the ruined monastery, a most impressive picture. The church is a building of great artistic merit, its centre being an octagon, in which a remnant of St Simeon's pillar still stands today. Whether this octagon had a roof or was left open to the sky is a question on which the experts are not yet agreed.

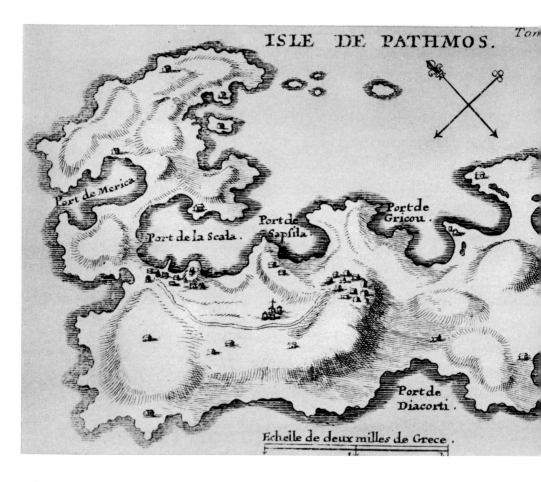

Port de Merica

Port de la Scala .

Port de Sapsila

Port de Gricou .

Port de Diacorti .

Echelle de deux milles de Grece .

In banishment on a lonely island of the Aegean

the Apostle St John in A.D. 95 had his great vision of the end of the world, and wrote it down in The Revelation. The Revelation of St John the Divine is the only prophetic book in the New Testament, and its mysteries have exercised theologians and commentators since very early times. In the first period of Christianity there were numerous prophets and numerous 'apocalypses' or revelations, which led to a deepening of the faith and a confusion of its doctrine. The Revelation of St John is the only one that was accepted as canonical and admitted to the New Testament, but it has many times been rejected by eastern theologians, and is not included in the early Syriac and Armenian editions of the New Testament.

Patmos is a small rocky island off the west coast of Anatolia, situated about fifty miles from the town of Ephesus. The cave in which St John lived lies beneath a mountain summit. When St John stepped out of his cave

into the open air, the beauty of this world lay spread out before his eyes: to the north, in the blue waters of the Aegean, gleamed Samos; opposite, the high mountains of the mainland of Asia Minor shone in the full light of the sun; to the south, the contours of the islands of Leros and Cos were traced with delicate lines on the horizon. The fearful vision of the end of the world, as St John saw it with his inner eye, was in moving contrast to the beauty of creation in which he lived. On the mountain summit above his cave there is today a monastery, built like a fortress, which was founded in the year 1088 by St Christodoulos. This monastery owns a valuable library. Scholars have for long argued, and are still not in agreement, whether the

John of the Fourth Gospel is the same as the author of The Revelation. At the end of the Gospel according to St John there occurs the remarkable passage in which Christ says to Peter of John: 'If I will that he tarry till I come, what is that to thee?' And 'then went this saying abroad among the disciples' that John 'should not die'. The evangelist's own comment on this interpretation is to reject it, and he leaves the reader to infer that what Jesus really meant was that he would come again before John should die. There is a very early tradition that St John is buried in Ephesus and in the fourth century a shrine was erected over his grave. Over this shrine at the beginning of the fifth century a basilica was built, and this was pulled down again when Justinian erected his great church in its place. The Church of St John at Ephesus was a place of pilgrimage until well into the Middle Ages. Then it fell into ruin until its impressive remains were excavated in our own time.

The throne of Satan

is the name given by St John, in his open letter to the congregation of Pergamon, to the citadel of this city. Situated between two rivers, it towers high above the plain. Adorned with a palace, splendid gardens, numerous temples, a theatre, and the famous altar of Zeus (which is today in Berlin), Pergamon was indeed a city of pagan magnificence. The Pergamene Kingdom was founded upon a treasure and ended as a bequest. In the third century B.C. King Lysimachus was the guardian in Pergamon of a treasure of nine thousand talents, the equivalent in modern terms of a sum of about twenty million dollars. After the king's death the regent Philetairos succeeded in appropriating the treasure to his own use. With this money he founded a new kingdom, as today one might found a firm. The Pergamene Kingdom, unlike most of the contemporary kingdoms, never distinguished itself in war. Attalus, its first king, who reigned from 241 to 197 B.C., was the first man of antiquity to make a collection of older works of art.
The royal library was famous, and contained 200,000 volumes. Antony later transferred it to Alexandria, making a noteworthy addition to what was already the greatest library of the ancient world. It was in Pergamon that parchment, that is, 'Pergament', was invented. A Pergamene scholar who had been sent as ambassador to Rome by King Attalus II was the author of the first Latin grammar. He had broken his leg, and in the boredom of convalescence he composed this work of meticulous pedantry, under the

consequences of which our schoolchildren still suffer today. Attalus III, instead of leaving Pergamon after his death to inevitable conquest and destruction by the Romans, took the better course of making it over to the Roman Empire in his Will. In the history of Christianity this city was of importance in only one rather unfortunate respect. It was in Pergamon that the first temple in honour of Augustus was erected. On the throne of Satan the divine worship of the Roman Emperor, which was to have such distressing consequences for the young religion, had its beginning.

We do not know how the Gospel reached Pergamon, but probably here, too, it was first preached in the synagogue, perhaps by St John. Very early, as we learn from St John's open letter, Pergamon experienced the two things that are so characteristic of early Christianity: the death by martyrdom of a believing Christian and the false doctrine of a heretic. Later, it became the

seat of a bishopric and many churches were built. One of these was sketched, in a state of comparative preservation, by Laborde, the French explorer, when he visited Asia Minor over a hundred years ago. The vignette (below) gives an attractive glimpse of Istanbul in the distance by the Golden Horn,

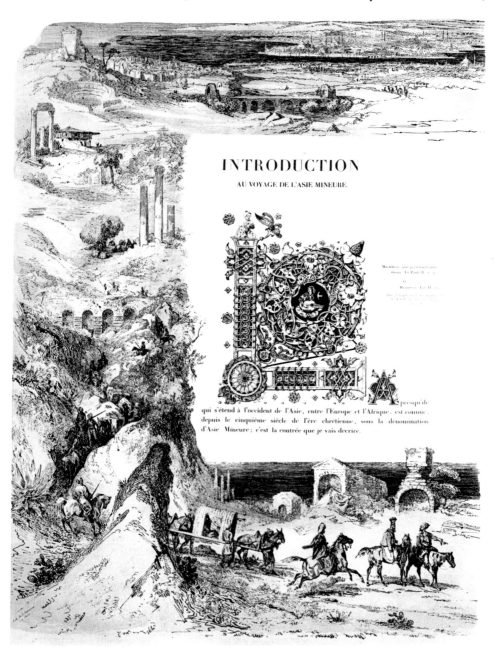

INTRODUCTION

AU VOYAGE DE L'ASIE MINEURE.

qui s'étend à l'occident de l'Asie, entre l'Europe et l'Afrique, est connue, presqu'ile depuis le cinquième siècle de l'ère chrétienne, sous la dénomination d'Asie Mineure; c'est la contrée que je vais décrire.

the old temple ruins, the aqueducts, and the wild and pathless Anatolian landscape. In Laodicea, too, the seventh of the apocalyptic congregations, there was a magnificent Byzantine church, as the ruins still show. Pergamon was destroyed by the Arabs in A.D. 761, and at the foot of the throne of Satan today, in the mosques of the little Turkish town of Bergama, only Allah is worshipped.

Bare, cold, treeless, poor in water, poor in stone, rich in salt –
such is the description given even by the ancient geographers to the country of Lycaonia, which lies in the interior of Asia Minor and extends from the Taurus Mountains in the south to the River Halys in the north. This land was one of the flourishing provinces of early Christianity, as is shown by the great number of its representatives sent to the Council of Nicaea. Nothing of its ancient life has been preserved. In this salt steppe, ruins have served from time immemorial as stone quarries. Nor were there in the early centuries either famous theologians or famous bishops in this ill-favoured land. It is the legend of a saint to which Lycaonia owes its fame.

Iconium, the capital city, had been visited by Paul and Barnabas. Thekla, a beautiful young girl, heard the Apostle Paul preach a sermon on chastity, and by resolving to remain a virgin all her life became the mother of all the nuns of Christendom. She went with St Paul to Antioch, where she was thrown to the wild beasts in the circus, but was there saved in miraculous fashion. An apocryphal story of Paul and Thekla was widely read in the second century. The picture shows St Thekla between two beasts, which seem well-disposed toward her. It is from the title page of a Greek menology of the twelfth century which tells the story of her martyrdom. A later Bishop of Iconium, Amphilochus, was one of those Cappadocian fathers who distinguished themselves in the fight against the Arian Heresy. Arius disputed the divinity of Christ, and his heresy was the subject of the Council of Nicaea, but continued to play an important historical part long after it was condemned there. There is a pleasant story told of Amphilochus. He had an audience with the Emperor Theodosius, and wanted to induce him to expel the Arian congregations from Constantinople. Amphilochus greeted the Emperor with all due respect, but paid no attention at all to his son Arcadius, on whom the title of Augustus had just been conferred. Theodosius became angry and gave him to understand that he considered any slight to his son as an offence against himself. Amphilochus answered, 'You do not allow a slight to your son. You must therefore believe also that God will not tolerate any blasphemies against His Son.' This simple logic convinced the Emperor, who thereupon forbade the Arians to hold divine service in the city.

The great city wall of Iconium, which is today called Konia, had a hundred and eight towers. It dated from the time of the Seljuk princes, who in the eleventh century had founded here a wide and flourishing and highly civilised empire that played an important part in the Crusades. This city wall has been torn down, and its stones have been used for road-building. Laborde has preserved its picture for us in the drawing he made while it was still standing.

This Isaurian silver shrine

was found in Cirga, to the west of Iconium, in a country so poor in Christian remains that it is a notable rarity. The shrine has been dated to about the year 500. In its manufacture 2300 grams of pure silver were used, which made it a piece of quite exceptional value, since in the ancient world the value of silver was much higher in terms of gold than it is today. The fineness of the craftsmanship is evidence of the high standard of the silversmith's art at that time. The medallion in the middle portrays two saints, probably Peter and Paul, with between them the Lamb of God and the Cross hung with jewels. It is not known whom the two female figures to the right and left represent. The lions on either side of these women are quite oriental. They recall the representations of Artemis that are found throughout the Aegean, such as this small relief, below, from Crete.

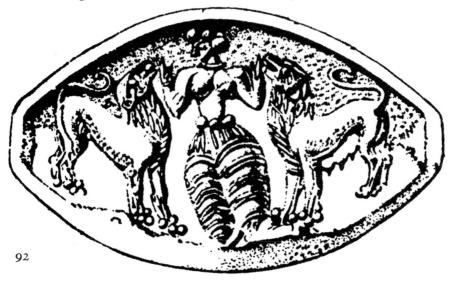

CHRISTIANITY originated in the eastern half of the Roman Empire, in an ancient culture that was predominantly Greek. Here it encountered scepticism and a spirit of curiosity but no moral system that made such uncompromising demands as its own. When it moved into the western half of the Empire, however, where the culture was Latin, Christianity found itself among the heirs of a morality which had once been in its own way just as definite as the Christian and no less stern. Where the Roman virtues had already fashioned a new world of power, the Christian virtues were to bring into being a new world of faith. After prolonged conflicts, a fusion of the two systems came about, and the product of this fusion has lasted till our own time.

The Roman Empire, when Christianity entered its history, was still young. Its growth had been extraordinarily rapid. Alexander the Great might perhaps never have heard the name of Rome, had not an embassy of proud farmers appeared before him one day in Babylon, seeking diplomatic relations with him. When Alexander thought of the West, it was the power of Carthage that came to his mind. He could not have suspected that the farmers of Latium would, in the course of the next hundred and fifty years, conquer Carthage, and that it would take them not much more than ten years after that to break the power of his successors and set up a protectorate over the eastern Mediterranean. The proud farmers were soon building a world empire which was to prove more durable than that of Alexander.

How old is Rome? As a settlement it is of great antiquity. Only three miles from the Vatican, on the Monte Mario, the remains of a Stone Age village have been excavated. Mythological tradition has it that the two sons of Mars, the twins Romulus and Remus, founded Rome in 753 B.C. Soon after their birth they were set adrift in a wooden trough on the Tiber. The trough grounded in the swamps that then covered the spot where Rome was later to be built, and the twins were reared by a she-wolf.

The oldest document known to us concerning the history of Rome is a treaty from 509 B.C., concluded between Rome and Carthage. This was the same year in which Tarquinius Superbus was driven out. The last King of Rome, he had no successor until Napoleon assumed that title some 2,300 years later. The Republic, the *Res publica*, was founded.

At this point of time not even the most far-seeing statesman in any of the great empires of the Mediterranean region could have predicted that Rome would become the mistress of the world. But this little Italian city was the home of the *Res publica*, a City State in which every free man was a *Civis Romanus* – a citizen as jealous in defending his liberties as he was courageous

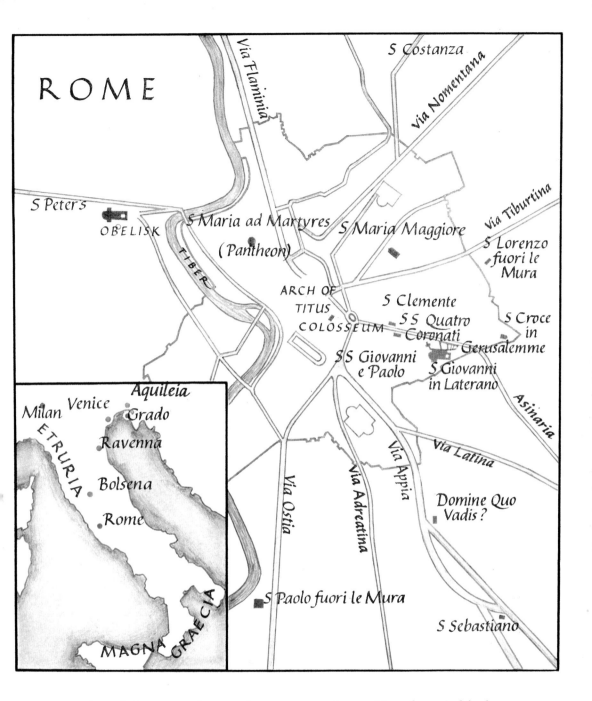

ROME

S Costanza

Via Flaminia

Via Nomentana

S Peter's

OBELISK

TIBER

S Maria ad Martyres

(Pantheon)

S Maria Maggiore

Via Tiburtina

S Lorenzo
fuori le
Mura

ARCH OF
TITUS

COLOSSEUM

S Clemente

SS Quatro
Coronati

S Croce
in
Gerusalemme

SS Giovanni
e Paolo

S Giovanni
in Laterano

Asinaria

Via Latina

Via Appia

Aquileia

Milan Venice

Grado

ETRURIA

Ravenna

Bolsena

Rome

Via Ostia

Via Adreatina

Domine Quo
Vadis?

MAGNA GRAECIA

S Paolo fuori le Mura

S Sebastiano

in resisting external aggression – a man who at this early period had some share in the ancient Roman virtues.

The religious fervour and the strict moral code of the early Roman began in the well-defined relationships of his patriarchal household, in which even the tutelary gods had their place, and rights and duties were assigned to all.

Outside the household, which was the nucleus of the State, the citizen took part in great religious festivals. At this early stage, reflecting the practical turn of the Roman mind, these festivals were all agricultural, associated with the procuring of results in field and orchard.

Later, as Roman power grew with conquest, this religion became gradually transformed into the religion of the Roman State, with its temples and priesthood. An important part of the process was the assimilation by the Romans of deities and religious elements from the peoples they conquered: the Etruscans and other Italic tribes, and above all the Greeks, first in Italy and then in Greece itself. This capacity for absorbing other cults is of the greatest importance for our story. Its causes can be looked for in two directions: in the character of the early Roman religion, which, seeing spirits everywhere, had no difficulty in adding to their number, and in the practical temper of the Romans which disposed them towards toleration. The process went so far that in the end it was the Greek gods of Olympus who to all appearances absorbed the Roman cults. But given the Roman religious temper, they would, for a time at least, have the same strict regard for the new as for the old. Thus, as the ancient cults were enriched and became the State religion, Roman piety became identified with Roman patriotism.

At the same time, the practical wisdom of the Romans developed into a statesmanship of world-wide vision. For their skill in waging war was matched, as it had not been in the case of the closely related Greek peoples, by political genius. It was this rare combination of qualities that created the *Imperium Romanum*. The Roman state expanded its dominion in a succession of wars, waged by the Romans in the two and a half centuries from the foundation of their Republic up to the beginning of their conflict with the world power of Carthage. It was not merely the lust for conquest that drove the Romans into these wars. It was more a strategy of defence, in which the Roman tactics were those of aggression.

They always saw clearly which of the enemies surrounding them and intending their destruction were the most dangerous, and by skilful diplomacy they would form a league of smaller allies against the greater enemy. Once they had gained the victory with the help of this coalition, the greater danger was out of their way and their weaker allies had become weaker still. The Romans then usually attempted to form an alliance with their defeated enemy. Such alliances were faithfully honoured from the Roman side, but the impatience of the new ally would presently play into the Romans' hands: the ally would revolt, and then the Romans would insist on 'unconditional surrender', destroy the rebel's military bases, and incorporate his territory in their own State. Such a State, consisting for the most part of former allies, conquered and deprived of their freedom, would naturally be somewhat unstable. But the Roman process of conquest did not end here. The most characteristic expression of the Roman genius was Roman law, and the conquerors trusted to the efficacy of their system of justice, together with good administration and the security and prosperity which they brought their subjects, to make the new territories in the course of one or two generations into reliable components of their State.

This procedure was repeated again and again. But, as the power of the new State extended its range, its opponents became more and more considerable. When central Italy, as far as the Adriatic, had become Roman, it was the Celts of northern Italy who had to be subjected. The Greek cities of the south sued for protective alliance with Rome, and so it came about finally in the year 265 B.C. that Rome was the undisputed mistress of Italy. The inevitable consequence of this power situation was that Carthage now became Rome's greatest opponent.

After its victories over Carthage in the two first Punic wars Rome found itself opposed, again almost automatically, by Macedonia. The States of the Greek mainland asked Rome for alliance and protection. After Philip V of Macedon had been defeated, and Rome had advanced to the coast of the western Aegean, the next enemy, soon to be defeated in his turn, was Antiochus III of Syria. There followed the Third Punic War and the destruction of Carthage, and so, after a further century, Rome had become mistress of the Mediterranean.

When Octavian, by his victory over Antony and Cleopatra at Actium in the year 31 B.C., had restored the unity of the Empire and its internal peace, he returned to Rome and became *Princeps*, the highest official in a constitution which remained republican. The State thus constituted, called by historians the Principate, lasted till the reign of the Emperor Diocletian at the end of the third century. It is of course true that it became more and more a matter of form, as the incumbents of the Principate turned more and more into absolute monarchs. This development of autocracy was one of the main reasons for the fall of the Roman Empire. Octavian was still the *Princeps*, holding his mandate from the Senate and people of Rome. Even the title 'Augustus' had been conferred on him by a resolution of the Senate. The *Imperium Romanum,* therefore, is historically only a little older than Christianity. Christ was born in Bethlehem, in the year 754 *ab urbe condita* (from the foundation of Rome), in the reign of the first Princeps, the first Augustus, and the fifth had probably only just succeeded to the imperial power when the Apostle Peter took up his residence in Rome, to become its first bishop. Through a long course of historical development these bishops of Rome were one day to become the spiritual successors of the secular rulers of the Roman Empire. To this day the Pope bears the title *Pontifex Maximus* (high priest), so long borne by the Roman Emperors. It was through Peter that the transient metropolis of a transient empire became *Roma aeterna*, that eternal Rome in which his successor still lives.

The fire of Rome in the year 64 and the persecution of Christians that the Emperor Nero thereupon instituted struck the young community like a bolt from heaven. The cruelties of this persecution were so excessive, according to Tacitus, that even the Romans, not noted for their compassion, turned turned away from Nero in disgust. Peter and Paul both suffered martyrdom. The persecutions of Christians in the Roman Empire lasted for three hundred years. They were of varying severity. The legal regulations in the different provinces were enforced with more or less strictness at different times. There were long periods of peace when the Church could grow undisturbed; but the threat of new persecutions was always present. Several bishops of Rome suffered death by martyrdom. There were historically attested martyrs in all the provinces of the Empire at almost all periods.

Despite the adverse conditions, the Church grew stronger and stronger. Anyone who professed Christianity therewith accepted the possibility of personal risk for his faith. Time and again the army of fellow travellers melted away in face of new persecutions, so the core of the Christian communi⁄ ties consisted of the real believers, those who genuinely meant what they pro⁄ fessed, who for the sake of their faith were ready to undergo any suffering. Their patient heroism had a power of conviction that won the Church new adherents, and always from among the finest individuals.

The legal ground of the persecutions was the statute regarding the payment of divine honours to the emperor and the sacrifices to the gods of the official State religion. A Christian was forbidden by his religion to do either. But his refusal was *lèse majesté* and therefore punishable by death.

Originally, then, the persecution of the Christians was in no way a persecu⁄ tion of their religion. Not until the last, most violent, and protracted persecu⁄ tions of Christians under Diocletian did Rome attempt to extinguish Christi⁄ anity as a religion and the Church as an organisation. The State suffered a complete defeat. When it came to the point, it could not exterminate the best element of its own population. The estimates of the number of Christians n the Roman Empire at the end of the third century are widely divergent. But even the lowest puts it at a twentieth of the population, that is, several million.

Rome had to abandon its campaign and the Christian persecutions ceased. Not much later, Christianity was recognised by Constantine the Great, and after a further generation, under Theodosius I, it became the State religion. The worship of the old gods was forbidden by law. The persecutions of the heathen began. The Church had become the ally of the State. Victory was complete.

The causes of this victory were to be found not only in Christianity itself and the steadfastness of its believers but also in the Roman religious environ-ment. This latter had much changed since the days of the Republic. The worship of the Roman State had found expression, logically enough and following eastern precedents, in emperor worship, and this, as a matter of State policy, was enforced by law. On the other hand, the hellenisation of the Roman gods had been accompanied by a decline in the old Roman piety. In an atmosphere of increasing scepticism and eclecticism the various Greek philosophical systems, some monotheistic, some atheistic in tendency, had great and confusing influence. Finally, with the conquests in the east the oriental mystery religions came flooding into Rome. Perhaps Christianity at first may have been regarded as just another of these. But for those who made its acquaintance the strictness of its moral code must have set it apart. For in Christianity some of the best of the old Roman virtues had found a new home. Unyielding strength of character, personal morality, piety, female chastity, submission to the State, love of justice – all the virtues of which Roman authors were lamenting the decline right up to the last years of the Empire had long since been revived in Christianity.

An important factor in the triumph of Christianity was the practical genius which showed itself in the secular organisation of the Christian Church. It was a great piece of good fortune for the Church's development that Rome was from the very beginning the centre of the new hierarchy. The Bishop of Rome founded his claim to be the first bishop of Christendom on the fact that he was the successor of St Peter, whom Christ had called the rock on which he would build his Church.

The Church built up its organisation on the pattern of the Roman State. The great city centres forming the key points of the Roman administration became the seats of the patriarchs and archbishops to whom the bishops of their regions were subordinated. The Christian Romans showed them-selves as much endowed with the Roman talent for administration as their pagan counterparts. The strict sense of the Romans for right and justice found its expression in the very early establishment of legal norms, out of which the canonical law evolved. The imperial claim of the Bishop of

Rome to have the final decision on all questions of faith gave this hierarchy an apex that commanded respectful obedience. The whole structure was so firmly knit that the Church lived on even after the State organisation of the Western Roman Empire had collapsed.

While Christianity was marching to victory, the decline of the Empire had begun. The statesmanlike principle of the Romans that tomorrow's possible enemy should be defeated today, had led, it is true, to an impressive expansion of the frontiers of Roman rule, but with the expansion of frontiers the number of enemies had correspondingly increased, till in the end they had become so numerous that the power of the State no longer sufficed to master them all. The strategy of defence was maintained, but its tactical instrument was attack, and there were no longer sufficient reserves to operate it. The statesmanship of the Romans had run its course, and their historical task was performed. The northern peoples, the Celts and the Germanic tribes (Lombards, Vandals, Goths) overran the western part of the Empire.

The Church was able to preserve the unity of Christendom until the schism of the year 1054, the year in which Byzantium separated from Rome. During this time the northern barbarians, to whom the future of Europe was entrusted long before they had any idea what Europe was, had been won over to Christianity. The same peoples who had brought about the collapse of the Western Roman Empire were destined in the later course of history to spread over the whole globe. This was only possible because the Church had proved itself capable of surviving the upheavals caused by migration.

The best of the old Roman virtues had seen a splendid revival in the Church. While the Hellenic East was fashioning a Christian theology that could hold its own with the intellectual disciplines of the Greeks, in the Latin West the traditions of the see of St Peter had their outcome in the Papacy, still the symbol of the world-wide unity of the Roman Catholic Church.

The grim legionaries keeping watch
at the sleeping Emperor's tent have no suspicion that a decision of world importance is being taken in his dream. An angel with the cross in his hand appears to the pagan ruler, and the angel's voice speaks to him, saying: ἐν τούτῳ νικᾶ – 'Under this sign be victorious!'

Catacombs, persecution and martyrdom

were long the dominant factors in the life of the early Christians in Rome
Considerable parts of the catacombs have been preserved to our own day.
We know from history about the persecutions of Christians. The martyrs
are known to us and reverenced as saints of the Church. But what has been
preserved and handed down to us was not the whole life of the Christian
community. Everyday life leaves few traces for posterity.

The early Christians did not for the most part live in the catacombs, as has been sometimes supposed. The catacombs were ordinary burial places of a kind usual in those days, and the burial of the dead inside the city walls was forbidden by law. In emergencies the catacombs served as refuges.

The building of burial catacombs ceased after the conquest of Rome by Alaric, the King of the Goths, in A.D. 410. They were gradually forgotten, and their rediscovery at the Renaissance was a sensation. The catacombs are

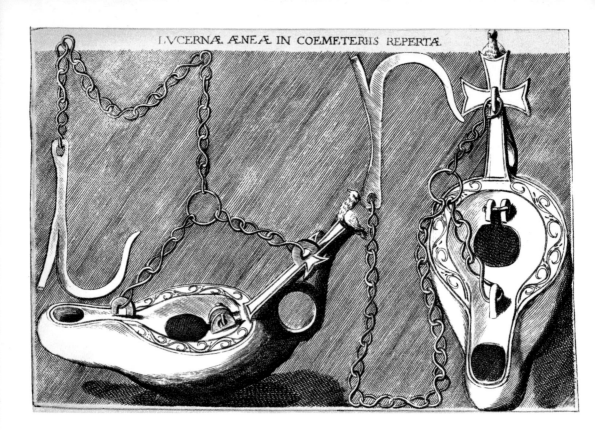

less mysterious than was at first believed. Still, we owe to them a great deal of information about early Christianity in Rome.

Rome, as the capital city of the Roman Empire, was a continual meeting place of Christians from the whole Mediterranean region. Thus from the very beginning the city was a clearing-house of ideas and experiences. And after the visitors had returned to their homes, contact was not broken off. St Paul was perhaps the first who had an extensive correspondence with the communities he had founded. The Bishops of Rome used to send news to the brethren in Greece and Asia Minor. The letter of Bishop Clement to the Corinthians, which has been preserved to us, can be dated as early as the first century. About the year 150 the 85-year-old Bishop Polycarp of Smyrna visited Bishop Anicetus of Rome. It must have been a stirring moment for the Christians in Rome to see and hear preach the man to whom the Apostle John had sent a written record of his revelation, and who had very probably been the first to read it aloud, to his congregation in Smyrna.

Very early there were Christian men, and especially Christian women, in the highest social circles with power to protect other Christians who were their clients: Flavia Domitilla, for instance, who was a granddaughter of the

Emperor Vespasian. Sometimes, also, there were broad-minded emperors, such as Alexander Severus, who had statues of Orpheus, Abraham, and Christ put up in his palace. Our own times have provided examples of the way in which a faith can keep itself alive despite all the menaces and pressures of a hostile State.

Just so, during the first three centuries A.D. in Rome, there was an everyday Christian life in which neighbourly love, prayer, and uprightness were cherished. Of this nothing remains, apart from a few pious wishes chiselled on the sarcophagi of the deceased, a few lamps and other objects of daily use adorned with Christian emblems. At the same time these were centuries full of violent conflict over theological problems, or about practical questions, or even about the powers of the hierarchy which was growing up inside the Church. The study of the numerous heresies during the time in which Christian dogma was first worked out is a science in itself. We are well informed about these struggles from the polemical writings, for and against, in which they have been recorded. Hundreds of the best minds of the age were needed to keep the true faith safe through the errors and confusions.

A stone witness

of the onset of the sufferings that were so long to tax the endurance of the early Christians was the obelisk which now stands in the precincts of the Vatican. It had known fully a thousand years of weathering under the rays of the Egyptian sun at the time when Nero had it put up in his circus. This

115

ancient relic comes from Heliopolis, near the modern Cairo. It was in the sixteenth century that the obelisk was set up in the square before St Peter's. In the Middle Ages the belief was widespread that the gilt sphere on its apex contained the ashes of Julius Caesar.

The monument would never have been preserved to our own day but for the experience of a San Remo seaman. With eight hundred workmen, a hundred and forty horses and forty rollers, the architect Domenico Fontana undertook the difficult operation of re-erecting it on its new site. During this work all the spectators were ordered under penalty of death to keep the strictest silence. But Fontana had not reckoned with the heat that would be generated in the ropes by the friction due to the enormous weight of the obelisk. The main cable began to smoke. An old seaman who understood how to handle tow ropes saw the disaster which threatened and shouted, '*Acqua alle corde!*' – 'Water for the ropes!' This courageous man, who had risked his life by shouting, was richly rewarded.

According to all the information we have, Nero's Circus, itself no longer extant, was the place where St Peter was crucified. So this event, one of the most important in the history of Christianity, must have been enacted in view of the mute stones of the obelisk.

The cameo, left, cut in rock crystal, shows a chariot race in a circus around a '*spina*', or barrier, adorned with an obelisk and two altars. Behind the altars stand the umpires. The figure on the high column to the right is a goddess of victory. In the foreground to the left stands the starter.

The Colosseum in Rome is, with the Amphitheatre of Miletus and the Temple of Jupiter at Baalbek in the Lebanon, one of the three largest ruins left to us by antiquity. It took fifteen hundred years for this imposing edifice of imperial ostentation to crumble into ruin. The Colosseum was princi-pally used for gladiatorial shows. In times of persecution its arena was one

of the places also where Christians were thrown to the wild beasts. The cross in honour of the martyrs previously stood in the middle of the area, but has since been moved to one side to make way for the excavations.

'Domine, quo vadis?'

When the Emperor Nero on the occasion of the fire of Rome suddenly ordered a pogrom of Christians, the anxious community begged the Apostle Peter, its revered head, to seek refuge in a place of safety. St Peter bowed to the wishes of his flock and left the city. But on the Via Appia he was met by Jesus. St Peter addressed to Him the famous question, 'Domine, quo vadis?'–'Lord, where goest Thou?' Christ answered that he was come to be crucified a second time. St Peter turned on his heel and went back to Rome, to end his life as a witness of Christ.

The earliest account we have of this episode comes from a manuscript of the second century, the *Acta Petri*. The story has often been dismissed as legendary, despite this early authority. Yet in the context of Christian belief there is nothing improbable about St Peter's vision. Christ, after His resurrection, appeared several times to the disciples. He appeared to St Paul outside Damascus. Why should he not have appeared once more to St Peter outside the gates of Rome?

The Roman citizen Paul,

as the Acts of the Apostles tells us, was brought to Rome as an imperial prisoner. Paul was then allowed to live for a long time relatively undisturbed in Rome. That is the last thing we learn about him from this document. It appears that he was once more set free. There are a number of indications which make it probable that he undertook one more missionary journey, his fourth, to Spain.

The relief, above, which depicts the beheading of the apostle, comes from the Tabernacle of Pope Sixtus IV in the crypt of St Peter's.

A surprising piece of evidence

for Christian archaeologists was a discovery made in 1894 in the crypt of the catacomb of St Sebastian in the Via Appia. There is an old tradition that during the persecution of Christians under the Emperor Valerian in A.D. 258 the mortal remains of the Apostles Peter and Paul, in order to protect them from desecration, were secretly brought into this crypt under the Via Appia. Later, St Peter was buried in the Vatican, and St Paul in the Via Ostia. In the year 1894 there was found under a small altar in the crypt an empty

PROIECTIO CORPORVM SS APOSTOLOR IN CATACVMBAS EX PORTICV VETERIS VATICANÆ BASILICÆ

grave divided into two parts. Undoubtedly this must have been the grave which had always been known to tradition.

Later, a small cemetery was established on this spot, in memory of the two Apostles. In this cemetery St Sebastian too was buried. He was a high officer of the Pretorian Guard, who suffered martyrdom under the Emperor Diocletian.

Over the crypt, in the fourth century, Pope Damasus erected a basilica, which was at first dedicated to the Twelve Apostles, and later to St Sebastian. This basilica became a place of pilgrimage at a very early date. It is one of the seven churches of Rome which the pilgrim is required to visit. In a room under the church, illustrated above, some two hundred inscriptions have been found in which Peter and Paul are invoked by name. There is something touching about the rough and ready manner in which the letters are scratched on the walls.

Immediately adjoining the catacomb of St Sebastian there is a Jewish catacomb of the third century. It is instructive to find that, at a time when the final expulsion of the Jews from Palestine was already a century old, most of the inscriptions are in Greek. Forty are in Latin, and only six still in Hebrew or Aramaic.

A last memorial to a great tradition

is the marble representation of the seven-branched candlestick on the Triumphal Arch of Titus in the Roman Forum. Forty years after Christ's death, twenty years after the first Council of Christendom, the meeting of the apostles in Jerusalem, 'high-built Zion' was conquered and destroyed by

Titus in consequence of a revolt of the Jews. No other people in world history fought for its freedom through so many centuries with so much courage and with so little success as the Jewish people. The Temple, in which Christ disputed with those learned in the Scriptures, was destroyed by fire. The candlestick was among the booty. It is probable that this magnificent piece, made of pure gold, was an actual relic of the treasures of Solomon's Temple which had been saved from the sack of Jerusalem by King Nebuchadnezzar of Babylon. On account of its great value the candlestick was long preserved in Rome, but finally disappeared when the City was plundered by the Vandals.

The first church built by Constantine the Great in Rome was St John Lateran. It was erected in the grounds of an imperial palace. In this palace, in the house of 'Fausta in Lateran' (Fausta was the Empress) the Council of Rome was held, in A.D. 313. From meetings in secret the bishops had now come out into the full light of publicity. They now met, as recognised dignitaries of the Church, in the imperial palace.

The church had been so lavishly decorated by Constantine that it was popularly nicknamed the 'Basilica Aurea' – Church of Gold. During the period of the barbarian invasions it was several times plundered. The Visigoths carried off and melted down the solid silver canopy of the altar. The church was several times damaged by fire and earthquake. Despite all these disasters St John Lateran has retained the ground plan of the original basilica, though the interior of the church today dates only from the seventeenth century, and the façade from as late as the eighteenth. A wooden table, which according to tradition was used by St Peter as an altar, is still preserved there, and this Roman mosaic floor (left) was recently found underneath the church.

St John Lateran was for a thousand years the seat of the popes and is today still the Episcopal Church of the Bishop of Rome. There is an inscription on the basilica describing it as 'Mother and Chief of all the Churches in the World'.

under Constantine the Great had something triumphal about it. Within a generation, in many parts of the Empire, many splendid churches were erected. Forces so long held under restraint and now released gave rise to an outburst of artistic fervour. The most creative minds and finest craftsmen of the time were engaged on the construction and embellishment of places of Christian worship. Pope Sylvester I petitioned the Emperor Constantine to build a church over the grave of the Apostle Peter. Building was begun in the third decade of the fourth century. The site was the ancient cemetery in which it was thought that Peter lay buried. The cemetery was at this time still in use, by pagans as well as Christians. Some half million cubic yards of earth had to be piled up to make the platform for the church, the floor of which was in places twenty-three feet higher than the original ground level. It was a four-aisled basilica, of which the interior walls were supported by ancient columns. The architectural centre of the church was the shrine of the Apostle Peter. The façade was richly adorned with mosaics. The inscription, put there at the orders of Constantine the Great, ran as follows:

Quod duce te mundus surrexit in astra triumphans
Hanc Constantinus victor tibi condidit aula(m)!
(*'Because under thy leadership the world has raised itself in triumph to the stars, Constantine the Victorious has dedicated this hall to thee.'*)

In these words the Roman emperor associates the victories of his own armies with the triumph of Christianity and records a conviction that these events had ushered in a new epoch.

About the end of the fifth century Pope Symmachus made St Peter's his

TAB · VIII

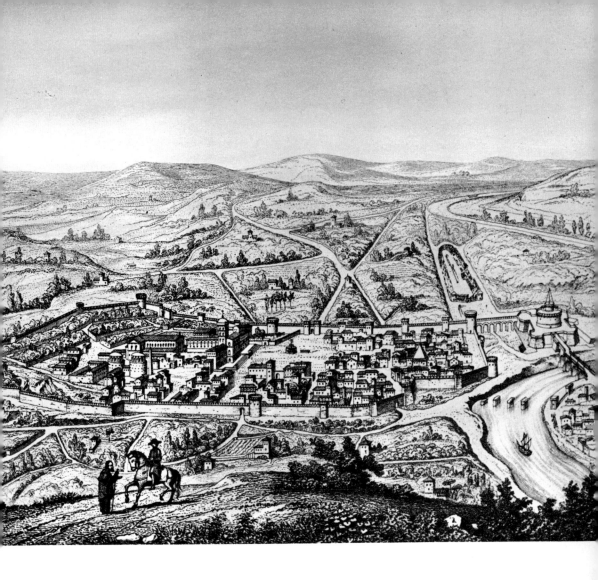

residence by building himself a palace next to the church. This palace, together with the old Church of St Peter, became the nucleus of the Vatican.

It was in this ancient Basilica of St Peter that at Christmas of the year 800 Charlemagne was crowned emperor by Pope Leo III. It is worth pausing to consider the historical panorama unfolded by this event. The basilica was founded over four and a half centuries earlier by Constantine, the first Christian to occupy the Roman imperial throne. The same Constantine transferred the capital of the Roman Empire to the East, to Constantinople. When Charlemagne was crowned, Jerusalem had been for a hundred years in the possession of the Arabs. Yet the ancient idea of the Roman Empire

had survived the migrations of peoples and the conquests of Islam. A Frank from the north received at the hands of the supreme head of the Christian Church in Rome his confirmation as successor of the Roman Emperors. And Charlemagne himself was long engaged upon a plan to reunite the West and the East under a single sceptre, by his own marriage with the Byzantine Empress Irene.

At the beginning of the sixteenth century the Basilica of Constantine was pulled down and in its place the new 'Basilica di San Pietro in Vaticano' was built, under Pope Julius II, by his architects Bramante and Michelangelo. St Peter's in Rome, built a thousand years later than the Hagia Sophia in Constantinople, is one of the great architectural creations of the West, a monument of faith from that rich epoch in which the Middle Ages were coming to an end and modern times were beginning.

Numerous reminders of the old basilica are preserved in St Peter's. In the Cathedra Petri there stands a wooden bishop's chair, which according to tradition is 'Peter's chair'. In the Capella della Pietà there stands an ancient bronze-gilt column of an unusual spiral form, the Colonna Santa. In style, it might be called a sort of 'late classical baroque'. It is the only survivor of a number of columns which Constantine gave for the embellishment of the first church. The Colonna Santa was taken by Bernini as a model for the columns of the baldachin, which today canopies the high altar of St Peter's.

The excavations under St Peters',

which were carried out on the instructions of the late Pope Pius XII during the years 1939 to 1949, produced exciting results.

The occasion for the excavations was some building operations in the Sacre Grotte, the crypt of St Peter's, to make room for a burial place for Pope Pius XI, whose wish it was to be buried in this crypt. In the course of these the workmen first of all came upon walls of the ancient Basilica of Constantine, then upon some sarcophagi, and finally upon a Roman mausoleum in a good state of preservation. This had been merely filled with earth by the builders of the older Church of St Peter. These finds thus first of all gave substance to the old tradition that a pagan cemetery lay underneath the ancient Church of St Peter. The plan, overleaf, shows the extent of the burial places so far excavated under the church, in comparison with the ground plan of Constantine's church. The letters denote tombs. The passage marked *Clivus* in the plan is reproduced in the picture, above. The mosaic 'Christ as Helios' adorns the cupola of the tomb M. Near the *Aedicula* was found a graffito – the first three letters of the name Peter – scratched on the wall.

The real surprise of the excavation was the discovery of parts of a shrine,

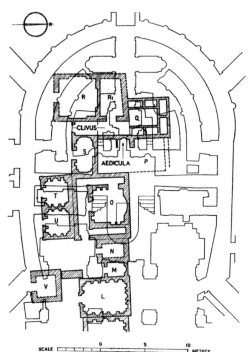

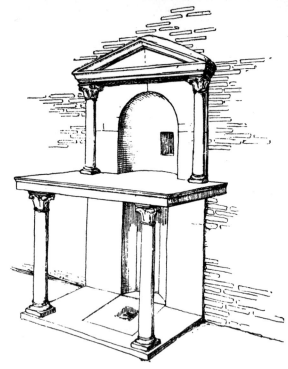

which in the plan is designated *Aedicula*. The drawing, made by the archaeologist Dr G. U. S. Corbett, shows what the shrine in all probability originally looked like.

The excavations are a great technical and scientific achievement. They go down to thirty feet under the floor of today's church, and had to be so conducted as not to endanger the church. Careful calculations had to be made and ingenious auxiliary structures provided by the engineers throughout the operation. In the surroundings of the *Aedicula* every stone was registered. As in a piece of detective work conclusions were drawn, hypotheses formulated, proofs looked for, found, or rejected. Jocelyn Toynbee, University Professor of Classical Ar-

chaeology at Cambridge, and John Ward Perkins, Director of the British School in Rome, have compiled from the detailed reports of those engaged on the site a book on the results of the excavations, with the title, *The Shrine of St Peter and the Vatican Excavations*.

The excavations have shown that the *Aedicula*, near which was found this marble portrait bust of a young woman, stood in front of a small open courtyard. Its erection can be dated with considerable certainty to about A.D. 160. There can be little doubt that this excavated monument is the same as that seen by the priest Gaius near the

end of the second century and described by him in a letter handed down by Eusebius. The shrine was dedicated to the Apostle Peter. It is for various reasons rather unlikely that it represents the place of his martyrdom. That it was his grave cannot be proved archaeologically, but at least there are no archaeological finds to suggest the contrary. Under the *Aedicula*, rather to one side, some bones have been found. All that is so far known about these bones is that they are the skeletal remains of a powerful, elderly man, and that the skull is missing.

A tradition deriving from earliest times has it that the grave of St Peter lies in the spot where the *Aedicula* has now been excavated. The shrine was built only about a hundred years after his death. This time span is not so long as to lend much weight to the objection that all knowledge of the site of his grave could meanwhile have been lost. After Nero's pogrom the Christians of Rome were left in peace for twenty years. They could not foresee the further oppressions that were to come. So they may well have found it possible to build a memorial on the apostle's grave, which could then have been replaced by the *Aedicula* in A.D. 160.

Directly above the *Aedicula*, under Bernini's canopy, stands the high altar of St Peter's.

The earliest gospel,
in the view of most Bible scholars, was the Gospel according to St Mark. In his first Epistle Peter affectionately calls Mark his son. In all probability Mark wrote his gospel in Rome. Papias, Bishop of Hierapolis in the second century, relates that Mark wrote down what Peter remembered of the deeds and words of Jesus Christ. On this ivory relief of the eleventh century, which comes from southern Italy, Peter is shown dictating to Mark while an angel watches over the truth of what is being written down.

The great dome of the Pantheon

is a meeting place of pagan and Christian traditions. The original building was put up by Marcus Agrippa, the son-in-law of the Emperor Augustus, in 27 B.C. After its destruction by lightning, the Pantheon was rebuilt by the Emperor Hadrian in the beginning of the second century A.D. And so it stands today under the Roman sky, the only ancient building of the former imperial capital which has been preserved to us in its entirety. The name means 'Sanctuary of all the gods'. It was a temple dedicated to the gods of the seven planets. Its dome was for half a millennium the greatest in the world. It was not dedicated as a church till the year 609 by Pope Boniface IV, by which time an even larger dome had been built in the Hagia Sophia in Constantinople. The Pope dedicated the old pagan temple to the Holy Virgin and all the martyrs under the name 'Sancta Maria ad Martyres'.

After the centuries of mysterious silence surrounding the person of Mary after the descent of the Holy Ghost, she began in the fifth century to be venerated in the Greek Orient, where the primeval image of the Asiatic mother-goddess had never been completely erased from people's minds. Only one and a half centuries after the destruction of the Temple of Artemis at Ephe-sus, a Council of the Church was held there and established the dogma that Mary was θεότοχος (theotokos) the Mother of God. The veneration of the Virgin Mary, too, first grew up in the Orient.

T·PANTHEON VVLGO ROTVNDA

The field of faith

was strewn with the fallen, and after its victory, for which they had given their lives, the Church commemorated them with loving devotion. St Laurence was one of the seven archdeacons of Rome. Laurence was a Spaniard from Huesca in the Province of Aragon. From Bishop Ambrose of Milan, we have an exact account of his martyrdom. In the reign of the Emperor Valerian, in A.D. 258, Pope Sixtus II, who had occupied St Peter's throne for less than a year, was condemned to death. Laurence accompanied him to the place of execution. The episode is instructive. Evidently it could only be a Christian who undertook such a humanitarian service. It seems, however, not to have been attended with immediate danger. The Pope dried the tears and silenced the grief of his companion with the prophecy that Laurence would follow him in three days. Laurence received the prophecy with joy. The further course of events is somewhat reminiscent of many of the old oracles, whose predictions were fulfilled just because they had been predicted. Laurence, who appears to have been far from poor, gave away all his possessions. The Prefect of Rome heard about it. His greed was excited. He sent for Laurence and ordered him to hand over all the Church's wealth. Laurence collected from all over Rome all the sick, aged, orphans, and widows he knew of and marched them to the Prefect's Palace, where he asked for the Prefect to come out, and showed them to him as the 'wealth of the Church'. The Prefect, much angered, there and then condemned him to die by fire, over a slow flame on a gridiron. Laurence took the sentence with cheerful acquiescence. With composure he endured the frightful torment and while on the gridiron continued to pray for the conversion of Rome. No doubt the unshakable resolution of this Spaniard must have made a great impression on the spectators, and there may well have been a number who in subsequent reflection on the event became converts to Christianity.

Constantine caused a church to be put up over the saint's grave, and on its site today stands the church of San Laurenzo fuori le Mura. It is one of the seven 'patriarchal churches' of Rome.

In this church St Laurence himself is especially revered, and in his native Spain, too, he is highly regarded to this day. Philip II founded a monastery in his honour, the famous Real Monasterio di San Laurenzo del Escorial.

Sometimes it is only a few plain bricks dug out of the earth

that give us valuable information about things of which we should otherwise know nothing. It stands to reason that the modest meeting places in which the Christians held their divine services, as long as they did not dare to hold them in public, remained dear and precious to them even after they were at last allowed to build churches. So it was that the new places of worship were often put up on the sites of the older meeting places.

Under the Church of SS Giovanni e Paolo the remains of just such an ancient meeting place have been excavated. Four private houses have been identified. Three of them were built in the middle of the third century, the fourth in the fourth century. The houses were not at first used for liturgical purposes. On the lower storey they had a row of shops opening on the street. Later brickwork gives evidence of subsequent conversion. A meeting room lit by seven windows was constructed. The archaeological finds are sufficient to give us a picture of the whole. From outside the building had the appearance of an ordinary three-storeyed dwelling house. Evidently Christians were allowed, at least in more peaceful times, to own houses. Their meeting room had to look like a private house from outside.

From an inscription we even know the name of the donor, Pammachius. This man was thus the earliest known private individual to build a church. The houses belonged to two officials who were employed in the Palace of Constantia, the daughter of the Emperor Constantine. They perished as victims of the persecutions of Christians carried on in the reign of the Emperor Julian the Apostate.

The frescoes are quite well preserved and show an important advance in artistic accomplishment. The man at prayer is depicted against a spacious background.

The prayers of early Christians

are worthily commemorated by the Church of San Clemente. It is a particularly well preserved basilica, built upon Roman masonry dating back to the Republican period, at the spot where the house of St Clement once stood. Clement was the third in succession after St Peter as Bishop of Rome. Origen considers that he was identical with the Clement mentioned by St Paul in his Epistle to the Philippians (Philippians IV, 3) among the 'fellow labourers whose names are in the book of life'.

The ancient basilica, now below ground level, was excavated in 1858 by Father Mulooly. The entrance to the atrium is supported on four fine columns. The narthex leads to the chapel which was one of the earliest in Rome. A beggar by the name of Servulus passed his whole life in this narthex. St Cyril, the apostle of the Slavs, is buried in San Clemente.

The greatest surprise of the excavation was the discovery of a temple of Mithras in this basilica. How did a pagan shrine come to be put up inside the Christian basilica? The most plausible answer to this question is that soon after the death of Clement the building was taken away from the Christians and given back to them again only by Constantine, and during this period the Mithras shrine was put in.

The Mithras cult was of Persian origin. Its myth is the heroic struggle between Mithras, god of light, and the primeval bull, the symbol of life and fertility. On the altar relief, here illustrated, Mithras wears Persian clothing and the Phrygian cap, which seventeen hundred years later was to become the symbol of the French Revolution. Mithras

has overcome the bull and is calling heaven to witness his victory.

Plutarch relates that the Mithras cult had been brought to the West by Cilician pirates whom Pompey had defeated. Mithraism was a religion of extreme patriarchal tendencies. Women were not admitted to its cult. It was very popular in the Roman Army, and a number of Mithras temples have been excavated on the sites of Roman garrisons, among them the one which was recently found in the City of London.

For the Christians of the first century the Mithras cult was always a particular source of vexation. They considered it a work of Satan. Its adherents met together in similar fashion to the Christians. Mithras was usually represented as a member of a trinity, together with one youth holding a torch upwards as a symbol of light, and another youth holding a torch downwards as a symbol of darkness. There was some sort of sacrament with sanctified bread and wine. There were rites of initiation similar to baptism.

The Mithras cult was widely disseminated in the Roman Empire. It is quite possible that there were times when its adherents were more numerous than those of Christianity. It has now completely vanished from the world.

ways of thought can be seen at work throughout the early centuries of the Church. Some of its consequences were peculiar. The best examples are to be found in Christian art, and it is these that have been most often preserved.

In this Crucifixion the sun and moon appear with Christ. The sun and moon are an ancient pair of opposites – archetypes of polarity, as they are called. In Asia they have been since primeval times the symbols of light and darkness, of good and evil. The persistence of this idea can be followed as far as the Yin and Yang of the Taoist religion of China. The sculpture comes from the Balkans and dates from the seventh or eighth centuries. At this late date the old intuitions of Asia still haunted the western world.

The process of transition from paganism to Christianity was a slow one. Rome remained pagan for a much longer period of time than Constantinople. The pagan tradition in Rome was more strongly rooted. Not till A.D. 382, half a century after the death of Constantine the Great, was the altar of the goddess of Victory removed from the assembly hall of the Roman Senate. The pagan temples were not expropriated until the reign of the Emperor Honorius in A.D. 408. Similarly in Athens, where the spirit of scientific scepticism offered a particularly stubborn resistance to the

mysteries of the new faith, the Athenian schools of philosophy continued to be held in high esteem long after the victory of Christianity. It was as a student in Athens that the Emperor Julian the Apostate made his resolution to restore their rights to the old gods.

Santa Costanza

was erected by Constantine the Great as a memorial to his daughter. It did not become a church until 1256. A blue mosaic on a white ground shows a wine harvest, done in a light-hearted rococo manner, with blithe pagan spirits playing around among Christian symbols. The pleasant bucolic scene reminds one of Ovid, and is an example of the natural continuity between pagan and Christian life, especially in the countryside, where the old Roman spirit-gods lingered on long after the State religion had lost its appeal.

On all the roads which led to Rome there were Christians among the travellers. And every one of these, on reaching the Empire's capital, as a matter of course visited the grave of St Peter. We know of two unlucky pilgrims who were killed by soldiers at St Peter's grave, to which they had zealously and unsuspectingly repaired immediately on their arrival in Rome.

No date can be given for the first pilgrimage. The practice developed gradually. In the third century the pious expedition was already a regular custom. An inscription from the end of the second century has been preserved in which a bishop named Abercius from Hierapolis gives an account of his pilgrimage from Phrygia in Asia Minor to Rome. The map below shows the patriarchal churches of Rome, which every pilgrim had to visit. Originally they were five, St John Lateran, St Peter's, San Paolo, San Lorenzo, and Santa Maria Maggiore. Two others were added later, Santa Croce in Gerusalemme and San Sebastiano. One of the earliest of the innumerable customs which evolved on these pilgrimages was that of taking home some holy water in a little lead flask with a Christian emblem or the picture of a saint stamped on it. The illustration on page 131 shows four such lead flasks, similar to those which have been found in different widely separated parts of the ancient world. The pilgrims who journeyed to the Holy Land carried, as shown in the illustration, a pilgrim's staff and had the cross sewn on their robes.

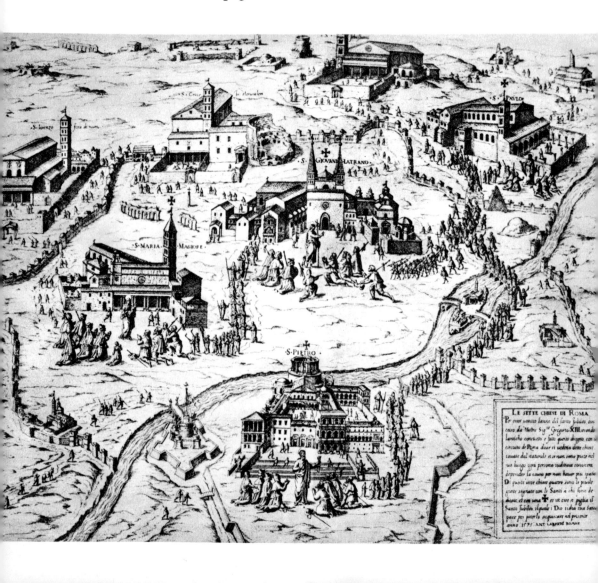

The great moment of history

in which the centuries of embittered conflict between the Roman Empire and Christianity came to an end is depicted symbolically on a fresco in the Santi Quattro Coronati in Rome. Constantine, the ruler of the secular Empire, accords recognition to Sylvester I, the supreme head of the Church, as Christ's vicar on earth, and receives his blessing. The painter shows a considerable degree of diplomatic finesse and a sound knowledge of historical fact. In the first picture the Emperor, on foot and without his crown, is visiting the Bishop of Rome, to present him with the papal tiara. In the second picture the Pope, high on horseback and wearing the tiara, is visiting the Emperor, who is now wearing his crown. Sylvester and his companions are mounted on greys. They were senators, who alone had this prerogative.

In the representation of this first meeting of an emperor with a pope there is already implied a conflict which throughout the entire Middle Ages was to give rise to controversy, and often bloodshed. This was the struggle between the imperial throne and the papacy. The Byzantine emperors regarded themselves as supreme heads of the Church. The Patriarch of Constantinople was appointed by them and was subordinate to them. In Italy, in the course of the collapse of the Western Roman Empire, many imperial powers, privileges, and possessions were taken over by the popes. The crowned heads of the newly arisen European States were expected by the popes to recognise their supremacy. The struggle was never finally decided. As late as the nineteenth century, His Apostolic Majesty the Emperor Franz Joseph I of Austria issued an effective veto against the election of a pope. But the conflict did ultimately cease to exist, for the crowned heads of the great Catholic kingdoms all lost their crowns.

VBIFVGIENSSPVSCOELAN ERELVERTITVR

Ambrose of Milan

was one of the 'Doctors of the Church'. *Doctor Ecclesiae* is a title of honour which has been conferred only on a few of the most important Christian theologians. Ambrose was the first holder of the title who lived and worked in that part of the world which today we call Europe.

Ambrose was Bishop of Milan from 374 to 397. He was a man of good family, his father being Prefect of Gaul. He himself lived in Milan as a lawyer. When he was elected bishop he had not yet been ordained a priest nor even baptised. It was a widespread custom to postpone baptism till the end of one's life, in order that as many as possible of one's sins, not only those already committed but those still to be committed, might be forgiven with the ceremony. This reckoning with Heaven failed to work, of course, if death came unexpectedly.

The picture on the left shows Ambrose being recalled to Milan by the Holy Ghost to take on the office of bishop. He was a likeable man of fine character, much loved by his flock and famous far and wide. To him it was that Augustine came for baptism.

One impressive event of his period of office was a dispute that he had with the Emperor Theodosius. The Emperor, after a revolt in Thessalonica, in which the commander of the garrison was murdered, had seven thousand of the city's inhabitants massacred. The Emperor then came to Milan, and wanted to attend divine service as usual. Ambrose met him at the church door and forbade him to enter the house of God. Even the imperial dignity did not permit the commission of crimes, and no one might pray with blood-stained hands. It is less a proof of the power of the Church than of the radiant force of the new faith that the Emperor submitted to the learned doctor's ruling. Not until Theodosius had made a public repentance of his crime was he readmitted by Ambrose to the congregation of the faithful.

A saint much beloved of the people

was Christina of Bolsena. Her martyrdom has been decked out by the imagi-nation of her admirers with countless miraculous details. Christina was born in the little town of Tiro, which has since sunk under the waters of Lake Bolsena. Her father Urban, the prefect of Bolsena, was regrettably lacking in urbanity of character. One day, so the legend goes, Christina saw

135

from the window of her father's palace a crowd of poor people begging for alms. She hastened down and, taking some golden and silver statues of gods which belonged to her father, broke them in pieces and distributed them among the waiting poor. Her father was so enraged that he had his daughter whipped and put in a dark dungeon. There an angel came to comfort her. Her father then had her thrown into the lake with a millstone around her neck. She swam to land. She was thrust in a red-hot oven, and next exposed to poisonous snakes; and when these methods did not succeed, her father had her sacrificed to Apollo. When she looked upon the statue of Apollo, the god tumbled from his pedestal, and her father was struck dead. Finally, the unhappy woman was shot to death with arrows.

It is unnecessary to speculate how much truth there may be in the story of this legendary martyrdom. In those days belief in miracles was not confined to any particular group of people; it was widespread, and of Christianity in particular it was believed that there were no limits to the wonders it could perform. The idea that the whole world can be rationally explained is one we have inherited from the ancient Greeks and their Roman pupils, but it was to be a long time before it got the hold that it has upon us today. St Christina is buried in a cave which was once dedicated to Apollo. In the catacombs which were entered from this cave Etruscan, Roman, and Greek inscriptions have been found.

The marble sculpture of St Christina on her tomb at Bolsena (previous page) is the work of Giovanni della Robbia. The face is chiselled with a soft beauty and innocence which make it easy to believe that it is the face of a saint.

It was of course Rome that played the dominant part in the evolution of Italian, no less than Eastern, Christianity. For one thing, it was easier in the capital for the persecuted to escape notice and when necessary to hide themselves. None-the-less, we find Christian traces from these early times scattered over the whole of Italy. In southern Italy this is only to be expected, since its cities, those of Magna Graecia, were Greek, and the Christianity of the two first centuries still stands entirely under the influence of its Eastern origin. Even in Rome till 200 the language of the Church was Greek. Ravenna for centuries after that belonged to eastern Byzantium and not to western Rome. Latin Christianity did not become important until it began to produce such commanding figures as Tertullian, Ambrose, and Augustine. It was Tertullian who wrote the *Apologeticum,* the great Latin treatise in defence of the new faith. Ambrose and Augustine were the first great divines of Latin theology.

More remarkable still was the expansion of Christianity in northern Italy. Here there lived Celts and Lombards, who had been long enough under the influence of Roman civilisation to be no longer barbarians, but not long enough to have lost all memories of barbarism. Here we see the beginning of a development that was to determine the later history of Christianity. Christianity began in one of the world's primordial culture zones, the Near East. It was taken over by the highly developed civilisation of the Graeco-Roman world. Its future lay with the barbarians.

In Aquileia, according to a tradition from the seventh century, the Apostle Mark preached, before he went to Alexandria. His bones today rest not far from this city, in the Church of St Mark in Venice, where they were brought from Alexandria. Under Bishop Theodore, who took part in the Council of Arles in 314, Aquileia already had a large Christian congregation. The delicate mosaic with the fishes comes from Theodore's church. We see time and again how mistaken it is to suppose that the Christians of these early centuries were opposed to the gaiety of classical art.

In A.D. 381 a council was held in this church and presided over by Bishop Ambrose. Its theme was the Arian heresy, which had been condemned at Nicaea.

The silver medallion of the Madonna enthroned with her child is of the fifth century and comes from Grado on the northern Adriatic coast. It is an early example of the process, seen so often in history, of the fertilisation of the West by the East. The influence of Byzantine art, which was in such magnificent flower at this period, is unmistakable.

In 452, Pope Leo the Great hastened from Rome to northern Italy to stop Attila, the King of the Huns, from continuing his march of conquest through Italy. By the power of his personality and the dignity of his office this formidable man accomplished the miracle, inducing the unconquered prince to turn and retrace his steps. Their dramatic encounter is shown in this painting by Raphael.

THE REALISATION of Europe's debt to Byzantine civilisation is of comparatively recent date. In earlier centuries Byzantium was scarcely recognised, at
least in Western Europe, as having had any share in its cultural heritage.
This indifference to Byzantium was reinforced in the nineteenth century by
prejudices inherited from the eighteenth. The 'Age of Enlightenment', with
its admiration for Greek and Roman art, letters, ideas, and institutions, its
cult of the classical, was very particular about what was to be called by that
name. The range of what it regarded as classical was strictly limited, and
nothing Christian was included in it. Associating itself with the old Roman
view that Roman decadence began with the Empire, the eighteenth century
found itself almost automatically looking on Christianity as an accompaniment of that decadence. So we have Edward Gibbon trying to prove at
great length that Christianity was responsible for the decline and fall of
the Roman Empire. Gibbon in his theological chapters lets it be seen
that if he had had to choose between Christianity and the Roman Empire he would have preferred the latter.

To an age which thus narrowly defined and so much admired the classical,
the civilisation of Byzantium was not only not classical, it was not even
original. The fact that it was Christian was nothing in its favour. The view
became prevalent that Byzantine art was static and its culture fossilised.

There was, of course, some truth in the idea that Christianity was responsible for the decline of the classical world. It was no doubt among the causes
of that decline. But it was Christianity, too, which for so long preserved the
classical heritage, until Europe was capable of taking it over. That is one of
the great historical achievements of Christianity, and it was due predominantly to Byzantium, which for seven long centuries defended the West
against Islam. The struggle between the cross and the crescent had already
begun when the Apostle Boniface set out to convert the Germans to
Christianity. Yet not until after the conquest of Constantinople in 1453
were the Turks in a position to make their last great assault on the West.
In the meantime Europe, through the defence of Vienna and the sea battle
of Lepanto, had become strong enough to beat back the armed forces of
Islam.

Yet until recently these services were almost unrecognised in the West, so
that here it was more a question of discovering Byzantium than of re-
discovering it. It was a case of exploring the unknown rather than of recalling the known. For while the Roman Empire, which was pagan until the

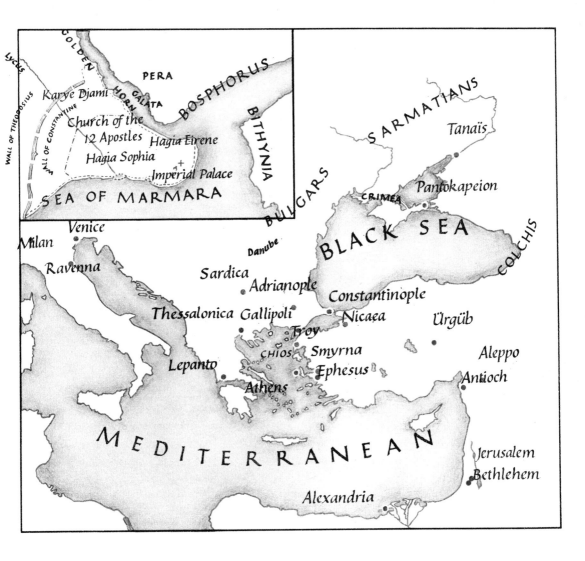

The map includes the following labels:

LYCUS, GOLDEN HORN, PERA, BOSPHORUS, GALATA, BITHYNIA, Karye Djami, WALL OF THEODOSIUS, WALL OF CONSTANTINE, Church of the 12 Apostles, Hagia Eirene, Hagia Sophia, Imperial Palace, SEA OF MARMARA

SARMATIANS, Tanaïs, Pantokapeion, CRIMEA, BULGARS, Danube, BLACK SEA, COLCHIS, Venice, Milan, Ravenna, Sardica, Adrianople, Constantinople, Ürgüb, Aleppo, Thessalonica, Gallipoli, Nicaea, Troy, CHIOS, Smyrna, Antioch, Lepanto, Ephesus, Athens, Jerusalem, Bethlehem, MEDITERRANEAN, Alexandria

fourth century A.D., has its place in our historical consciousness as part of our own European and Christian past, we have no such feelings about the Empire of Byzantium, which was Christian from its beginning. Few of us realise that the Hagia Sophia, the Church of the Holy Wisdom in Constantinople, is one of the most magnificent monuments of all Christian art. Few of us have the feeling that the history of Constantinople is part of European history, or that for centuries our own past was being enacted there.

The main reasons for this contrast of attitudes are to be found in the course of history itself. An entirely different feeling about Byzantium would be found, for instance, in Russia or among other peoples of Eastern Europe who owed their civilisation and their Christianity directly to the Eastern

Roman Empire. When the Roman Empire was divided into an eastern and a western half, the subsequent history not only of its own peoples, but of many others not belonging to it, was cut in two. The Empire of the West did not long survive the division, but was invaded and destroyed. The Empire of the East maintained itself for another thousand years.

Yet in the West, though Roman power collapsed, the Christian Church lived on, providing some continuity of culture and even of administration during the centuries of violent change. Amid the ruins of Roman power and in the tumult of barbarian invasions Europe was born.

For Europe, as we know from our own experience, is not a geographical entity. It is a cultural entity which evolved out of a compound of classical civilisation and Christianity. But it derived both these ingredients from the West, through Rome. As the *de facto* separation of the Latin and Greek halves of the Christian Church hardened into a complete schism, there was never any question to which half this new spiritual 'Europe' owed allegiance. Even the Irish Celtic Church, which for a period maintained an independent existence in Western Europe, did not forget its Roman parentage or deny the primacy of the Pope. Similarly, when after several centuries one of the new barbarian kings sought to restore the Roman Empire, and even felt the need of recognition from Byzantium, it was as Emperor of the West, on terms of parity with the Byzantine rulers, that he did so.

By the time of the Crusades, the schism between the Roman Catholic and Greek Orthodox Churches was possibly the most important fact about Byzantium in Western eyes. Byzantium was indeed an outpost of Christendom, but a schismatic one, whose rulers were in open disobedience to Christ's vicar on earth. Some of the crusading princes felt as much hostility for the Byzantine emperors as for the Saracens, and were as ready to go to war with the one as with the other, ostensibly on religious grounds.

This later picture of a Byzantium schismatic and corrupt has obscured the true nature of the Eastern Empire's part in the formation of a Christian Europe. The Roman Empire had brought about a happy union of the statesmanlike capacities of the Romans with the intellectual and artistic capacities of the Greeks. From the beginning of the imperial epoch this world was transformed by countless influences from the East. The Mithras cult swept Italy and the provinces. Persian gnosticism penetrated Greek philosophy. The triumph of the Orient was complete on the day when Elagabal, a high priest of Baal from the Syrian town of Emesa, mounted the Roman imperial throne. Had Christianity not made its appearance, the whole Roman world empire would have succumbed to Asia, not in a military sense, but in the field of ideas. Asia, with its ceaseless generation of new creeds and new philosophies, would in the long run have swamped those very attributes of classicism which for us are essential ingredients of the European mind – the clarity of Roman law, the scientific outlook of Greek philosophy, and the humanity inherent in ancient art.

This, it might be said, was our European past at its moment of greatest danger, and it was invaded and saved by Christianity. The fascinating thing about this development is that the new religion, though itself completely oriental in origin, was not destined to orientalise the ancient world. Although coming from the East, Christianity took possession, with remarkable assurance, of all those elements in the ancient world which were essentially European. For in the end it is not enough to say that Europe evolved out of a compound of classical civilisation and Christianity. Europe emerged because Christianity absorbed into itself and kept alive all those elements in classical antiquity that were European in their essence. The idea of Europe existed before Europe itself. Christianity realised this idea. Rome and Byzantium were the two halves of the stage on which this world drama was enacted.

The new religion, though oriental in its origin, came from a world which for centuries had been exposed to Greek influences. For Judaism was dispersed all over the ancient world and could not, despite the conservatism of the Hebrew spirit, isolate itself from its Graeco-Roman environment. Long before the time of Christ there was a Jewish hellenism, with its centre not in Jerusalem but in Alexandria.

The language of the young Christian religion was, almost from the very beginning, Greek. This was far from being a matter of course. Christ spoke Aramaic. From information we possess, it is known that at least the Gospel according to St Matthew existed in Aramaic. Scholars are also of the opinion that the Greek New Testament is not a continuation of the Hebrew Old Testament but a continuation of the Septuagint: that is, of the Greek translation of the Old Testament which King Ptolemy Philadelphus caused to be made in Alexandria in the third century B.C.

The peculiar sureness with which Christianity made its choice from the cultural treasures of antiquity and then transformed and assimilated what it had chosen, so as to make it European, is particularly well demonstrated by Byzantine art. The elements that contributed to the evolution of Byzantine art included, as David Talbot Rice has shown, the architecture of Asia Minor, the painting of Egypt, and the ornamental sculpture of Syria. But these elements were no longer, at the times of their absorption, purely Syrian,

143

purely Egyptian, or purely of Asia Minor. They had been hellenised for many centuries. Hellenism had numerous facets. There was not only a Jewish, but also an Asiatic, an Egyptian, and a Syrian hellenism. In Byzantium these hellenised oriental traditions were forged, by the creative piety and the fresh thinking of a newly emergent world, under a heaven which had become transcendent, into an entirely new art with an independent character of its own. Outstanding monuments of this new art have been preserved to us in the early mosaics of Ravenna, Rome, and Salonica. If one compares Byzantine mosaics of this period with ancient mosaics, one at once realises the creative power of the new faith. It is not just that the subjects of these mosaics are almost exclusively religious. They are works of art of the highest order, of a transparent spirituality which was not to be attained by Western Europe till centuries later.

Once more the achievement was a Greek one, covering the two hundred years between the reigns of the Emperors Constantine and Justinian. The dedication of the Hagia Sophia was the culmination of this development. It was a great moment for the faith and for art. The Emperor Justinian stepped out alone from the glittering assembly, and standing at the altar, lifted up his hands and cried out: 'Honour and glory to the All-Highest who has counted me worthy to complete such a work! Solomon, I have surpassed thee!'

At the beginning of the first millennium B.C. King Solomon dedicated the Temple in Jerusalem. It was the first House of God. Half a millennium later the Greeks erected the Parthenon. It is still, as a ruin today, the most perfect expression of the tranquillity to be found in this world. A millennium later Christianity gave mankind the Hagia Sophia. It is the most transcendent vision of the peace of God known to the history of architecture.

'HOLY! HOLY! HOLY!'

is inscribed on the banners which the two angels on this seventh-century Byzantine mosaic are carrying. Over the head of one angel stands the word ΑΡΧΕ (for ΑΡΧΗ – *arche*) and over that of the other, the word ΔΥΝΑΜΙC (*dynamis*). The words designate two of the nine choirs into which angels are divided. ΑΡΧΗ is in this context to be translated 'dominion', ΔΥΝΑΜΙC, 'power'. The writing at the angels' feet: 'And may all the angels adore him'.

Like a seventeenth-century air photograph,

Grelot's drawing, with a somewhat foreshortened perspective, gives a clear picture of the geographical situation of Constantinople. The country to the right is the north-west corner of Anatolia. Behind the mountains lies Troy. The land to the left is the Gallipoli Peninsula, which became famous in the first World War. Jason with his Argonauts passed through these straits to fetch the Golden Fleece from Colchis on the east coast of the Black Sea. To the right of the city, which is just visible in the background, the Bosporus begins, leading to the Black Sea. Constantinople lies wholly on European soil.

Constantine the Great chose the site for his capital with remarkable political, geographical, and military acumen. From the point of view both of commerce and of sea and land strategy it is a key position of the first importance. The illustration on the opposite page, copied from a sketch map of Christophorus de Bondelmontibus, a thirteenth-century Florentine traveller, shows very well what a powerful fortress the Christian city of Constantinople was.

146

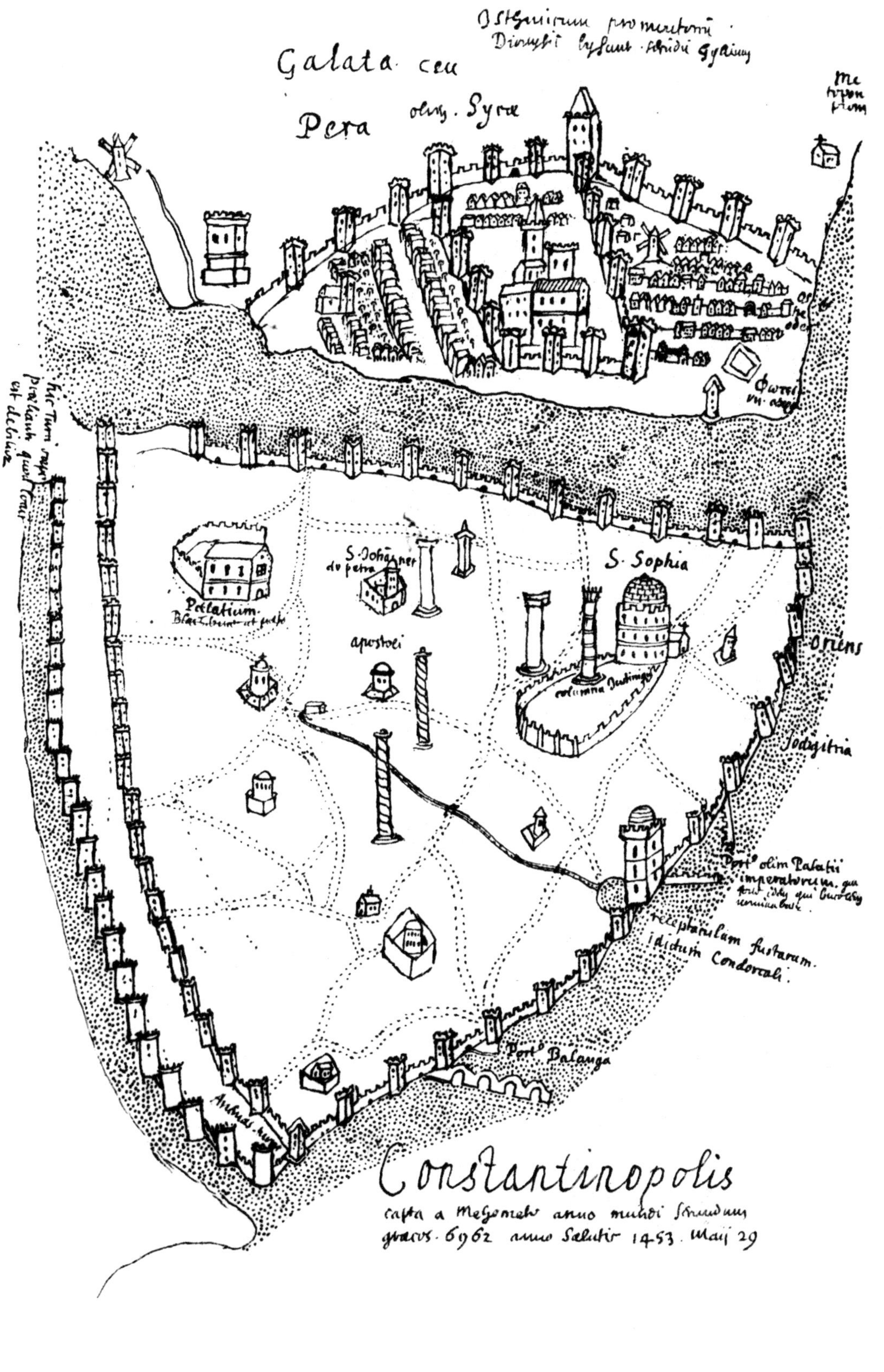

Galata ceu

Pera olim Syca

Osteuirum promontorii
Dionysii byzant schidi gyaium

metropolim

Palatium
Blach...

S. Johannes
de petra

apostoei

S. Sophia

columna Justinigi

Oriens

Jodigitria

Pori olim Palatii
imperatorum...

...lam Justarum
i dictus in Condocali

Porti Balanga

Constantinopolis

capta a Mahomete anno mundi secundum
graecos 6962 anno Salutis 1453. Maij 29

The drawing above is a view from Pera across the Golden Horn, with its busy maritime traffic, to the little peninsula which has played such an important part in history. At the point of this peninsula the town of Byzantium was founded in the year 660 B.C. by Doric Greeks. The ancient *Polis* already had as its city badge the crescent moon with the star.

Within the site of the ancient Byzantium stands the Seraglio, the former residence of the Sultana. In the background to the right rises the Hagia Sophia, with its four Turkish minarets. The coastal strip to the left of the picture, dotted with the houses of Scutari, is part of Asia.

After the Emperor Constantine had conquered all his enemies, by the Edict of Milan issued in A.D. 313, he brought to an end the great historical debate between Christianity and the Roman Empire. Christianity was recognised as a religion tolerated by the State.

The Gospel had had to endure nearly three hundred years of repression. As happens again and again in history, it was in the end the weaker which overcame the stronger, by the power of an idea. Sufferings and sacrifices made the first three hundred years of the new religion into a heroic age. These years, with their countless examples of spiritual heroism, are a treasure-house of memories from which the faith has been able to draw strength and comfort right up to our own day.

The importance of Constantine's reign can hardly be overestimated. By making peace with Christianity he decisively influenced the course of history. While he was on the throne the Empire enjoyed a respite from turbulent struggles for power inside, and a period of military security outside, its frontiers. By his bold decision to found a new capital in the East he gave the

148

Empire a structure that was to impose itself with enduring effect on subsequent ages. In its early days his city was not yet called after him. The name Constantinople was coined by the people. The city's official name was *Nea Rome*, 'New Rome'. To this day the Patriarch of Constantinople bears on his seal the title of 'Archbishop of New Rome'. The Greek text on the seal, above, no longer completely legible, should read:

ALEXIOS ARCHIEPISK (opos) KONSTANTINOUPOL (eos)

NEAS ROMES

With his many magnificently decorated buildings Constantine ushered in a
new period of late classical art. An excellent historical portrait of this epoch
has been given us by Jacob Burckhardt in his *Age of Constantine the Great*.
The personal character of Constantine was not quite as unexceptionable as
his historical achievement. Though he treated his mother with great respect,
he ruled despotically and was unscrupulous in procuring the death of
members of his own family when policy seemed to require it. It is recorded,
however, that at the end of his life his conscience awoke and he repented of
his misdeeds. He is said also to have been baptised not long before his death,
but probably regarded himself as a Christian before that. The Greek Church
not only considers Constantine a saint, but has even revered him at times
as a 'thirteenth apostle'. The Roman Church has contented itself with
awarding him the title of 'the Great'.

The Imperial Palace,

which Constantine erected in his new capital, must have been, from the
descriptions we still possess, an imposing array of buildings. From the fourth
to the eleventh century it was repeatedly extended and altered. At one time
the palace had an area of over 400,000 square yards, with ten residential
buildings, audience halls, several churches, libraries, baths, and a riding
school. So it certainly afforded scope for intrigues. Every trace of this

agglomeration was lost until in 1912, after a fire, some remains of masonry came to light again.

Constantinople, *Nea Rome*, like old Rome, lies on seven hills, though the seventh of these, it is true, was a very modest one. The constructional plan of the city was determined by this ground formation, so that the important buildings were erected again and again on the same sites. Some of the city's great boulevards still follow the same course as in antiquity. Even the seraglio of the Turkish sultana was built on the same little peninsula on which, a little further to the west, the Palace of the Emperor had stood.

The excavation of the Imperial Palace has been begun. Among the first finds encountered by the archaeologists are some mosaics of the fifth century. Every colour occurring in marble or in other hard stones was made use of in these mosaics. For blue, green and yellow glass was employed. The eagle fighting with a snake, left, gives an idea of the beauty and high standard attained by the art of this period. The frieze with a young man's head is of rather later date. Since stylistically similar representations are known from the art of the Sarmatians and Parthians, the portrait is taken to be that of a barbarian prince.

AD MAJOREM DEI GLORIAM – *to the greater glory of God –*
many fine churches were dedicated by Constantine in his new capital. They
were all destined to make way for the even more splendid buildings of his
successors. There was one of his churches, however, of the beauty of which,
even though it no longer exists, we can still convince ourselves with our own
eyes. This was the Church of the Twelve Apostles. Procopius has given a
description of it, and from this we know that St Mark's in Venice was built
to the same plan. Besides this, by a lucky chance a miniature (above) has
been preserved, depicting the transfer of the body of St Chrysostom, in the
background of which the five cupolas of the church appear. Constantine
had his mausoleum built on to the Apostles' church. The mausoleum was
a rotunda roofed with a cupola, and in it stood the sarcophagus of Constantine, with cenotaphs of the Twelve Apostles in a half-circle round it. It must
be admitted that this first emperor on a Christian throne had an exalted idea
of his own imperial dignity.
When after the Turkish conquest Mohammed II decided to convert the
Hagia Sophia into a mosque, he first of all ordered that the Church of the
Twelve Apostles should be left to the Christians as a patriarchal church.

In 1456, however, he did after all put a mosque of his own in its place. On the spot where for over a thousand years the sarcophagus of the Christian emperor had lain, there stands today the Türbé, the tomb of the Moslem conqueror of his city.

Hagia Eirene, the Church of the Holy Peace, was already a Christian sanctuary in ancient Byzantium. Constantine built a church on the site. This was destroyed in the Nika revolt of the year 532, but restored by Justinian. Its empty interior today no longer gives any idea of how magnificently Justinian decorated it. According to Procopius, it was excelled only by the Hagia Sophia itself. The Turks for a long time used the Church of the Holy Peace as an arsenal. In front of it stands the Plane Tree of the Janissaries, under which the soldiers of this privileged corps were accustomed to gather, to cheer the Sultan or to mutiny against him.

The photograph, below, is taken from the Hagia Sophia. The shadow of two of its minarets falls on the shining white wall of the Hagia Eirene. The view sweeps over the gardens of the Seraglio and the Bosporus, far across to the coast of Anatolia. In the interior of the church a portion of an old mosaic from the time of Constantine has been excavated.

The ancient Hagia Sophia is also attributed to Constantine, but probably

it was erected by his son Constantius. It was adorned with numerous pagan statues. It too was destroyed in the Nika revolt, and then obliterated when the new Hagia Sophia was built. Some remains of the older building, which was known to the people simply as 'The Great Church', have been excavated by archaeologists. Here the Lamb symbol turns up again. The

Basilican 'Great Church' still had a wooden roof. Two hundred years later there arose in its place one of the greatest domes ever built.

Obedience to the Fourth Commandment

can seldom have had more momentous consequences in history than in the case of Constantine the Great and his mother Helena. It seems probable that

Helena was an innkeeper's daughter from Drepanum in Nicomedia, though another popular account has it that she was British. It is at any rate very likely that in her youth she was extremely good-looking. She married the Roman general Constantius Chlorus. Born in a cottage, she died in a palace. After her death she was canonised. She was a woman of importance.

After Constantius Chlorus had become emperor, he divorced his wife. He

then married the step-daughter of the Emperor Maximianus Heraclius. But Constantius' son Constantine remained loyal to his mother Helena, and when he himself ascended the throne, by way of amends for his father's treatment of her, conferred on her the title 'Augusta' and had coins struck bearing her effigy.

The Empress's devotion to Christianity was such a prominent trait in her character that Eusebius, the historian of the age of Constantine, thinks she must have been a follower of Christianity from childhood. He relates that she attended divine service every day and there mingled, in modest attire, with the other women at prayer.

The Emperor put great sums of money at his mother's disposal. With this money Helena built churches from Germany to Palestine. At an advanced age she travelled to Jerusalem to search for the Holy Places, which at this period were lost beneath the Roman buildings of Aelia Capitolina, the city that the Emperor Hadrian had founded on the ruins of Jerusalem after the Jewish rebellion under Bar Kochba. The tradition is that Helena rediscovered the Holy Sepulchre, and found the Cross of Christ. The 'Discovery of the Cross' has stirred the imagination of Christians all over the world in every century ever since. Again and again artists have rendered this subject. The relief of the Empress Helena, left, comes from a representation of the scene on a stone cross from Kelloe in the north of England. The fresco, on the facing page, comes from a cave church near Ürgüb, in the interior of Anatolia. The Empress Helena and the Emperor Constantine hold the Cross between them.

There are numberless legends about the 'True Cross of Christ', its finding, and its subsequent fate. They are, like so many legends, a mixture of truth, piety, and myth.

The rediscovery of the Holy Places was among the more stirring consequences of the encouragement given to Christianity by Constantine the Great. It was also in keeping with the new orientation of the imperial outlook, which had found expression in the creation of a new capital in the East, and the expansion of imperial patronage which accompanied it. Constantinople, with its Christian sympathies, began to assume the heritage of the great hellenistic cities of the Orient. Alexandria, Antioch, and Ephesus now looked not to Rome but to the Byzantine court, where Constantine gave impartial welcome to philosophers, theologians, and artists. Greek and Latin literature, philosophy, the art of rhetoric, and the science of law were taught there. The Emperor brought people from all parts of the far-flung empire to populate his rapidly rising city. In such an atmosphere it was natural for Christians to concern themselves with Christian origins, and the revival of Jerusalem, after two hundred years as a pagan shrine, followed the identification of the sites of the main events in the New Testament narrative.

The seventeenth-century painter Danielo Hersio attempted to reconstruct a panorama of Jerusalem according to the Bible, and though his imaginative drawing reproduces the archaeological facts only at isolated points, its general effect of magnificence does justice to ancient accounts of Zion. It also suggests the impression that must have been made on the pilgrim when he first sighted the walled city in its mountain setting, from the top of the pass by the Mount of Olives, as he came up from the Dead Sea. Another

view of Jerusalem, above, contains a reconstruction of the Temple of Solomon that probably gives a fair enough idea of the imposing effect of the
actual building.

The photograph shows the Dome of the Rock, the famous mosque erected
towards the end of the seventh century by the Omayyad Caliph Abd al-
Malik. It is the work of Greek architects, Byzantine in style. The first dome
collapsed and was replaced by the Caliph Hakim in the eleventh century.
The rock over which it was built has a long history of religious associations.
It was traditionally the place where Abraham was ready to sacrifice his son
Isaac, and it is the probable site of the first Jewish Temple and of Hadrian's
Temple of Aelia Capitolina.

Around the gallery under the dome there runs a broad blue band, on
which a verse of the Koran is written in gold. It contains the words: 'Jesus
the Messiah is only the son of Mary, the emissary of God and of his Word,
that he laid in Mary.'

Constantine erected a basilica and alongside it a building to house the

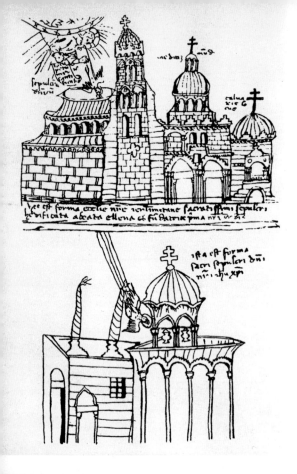

Holy Sepulchre. The rock of Golgotha lay 'only a stone's throw away', in a courtyard open to the south, adjoining the church, and adorned with colonnades. The fifth-century mosaic in Santa Pudenziana in Rome is an almost contemporary representation of the arrangement of buildings at that date. It shows Christ seated before a rock on which stands a large cross adorned with jewels. This way of depicting the Saviour corresponds to a ceremony then in use, in which the Bishop of Jerusalem sat on his bishop's throne at the foot of the rock of Golgotha. The buildings on the left–hand side of the mosaic are said to represent the Basilica of Constantine.

Constantine's basilica was destroyed by the Persians in A.D. 614. It was afterwards rebuilt, and much later still the Crusaders gave the Church of the Holy Sepulchre its present form by incorporating the chapels on the several holy sites in one new church. Despite subsequent rebuilding, the latest and most thorough after a disastrous fire in 1808, the church still retains many of its original Crusader features. The drawing, top left, depicts the Crusader church of the fourteenth century. The print below, right, shows the appearance of the church at the Renaissance. The photograph, left, is of today's building.

162

Thus in the Church of the Holy Sepulchre, which is called by the Eastern Christians the Church of the Resurrection, the Tomb of Christ and the Hill of Golgotha are covered by a single roof. The location of these sites has sometimes been disputed, but modern opinion is on the whole content to accept them as traditionally handed down.

'And she brought forth her first-born son,

and wrapped him in swaddling clothes, and laid him in a manger, because there was no room for them in the inn.' The inn referred to by Luke (II, 7) was in all probability a cave. To this day caves like this are used as lodgings in the Bethlehem region. A reference to Bethlehem as the birthplace of Jesus Christ is to be found in Justin the Martyr, about A.D. 160. Eighty years later Origen writes that even the enemies of the faith did not doubt the fact that Jesus was born in the place revered by Christians as his birthplace. The Emperor Hadrian, who reigned from 117 to 138, through his painstaking hostility to the holy places revered by the Christians made their identification a hundred and eighty years later much more probable. He put a statue of Jupiter over the Holy Sepulchre, and a portrait of Venus in marble on Golgotha. He made the cave in which Jesus was born into a sanctuary of Adonis, the lover of Venus.

The Empress Helena built a church over the birthplace. In the drawing, the cave of the Nativity can be clearly recognised underneath the church. The architectural history of this basilica is disputed. It is certain that Justinian added the choir, but it is possible that the nave goes back to the time of Constantine. The church has several times in history been miraculously saved and has never been destroyed. Many pilgrim accounts confirm that the Church of the Nativity has hardly changed in the course of centuries.

The Crusaders found it undamaged. Here, on Christmas Eve of the year 1101, three hundred years after Charlemagne had become Roman Emperor, Duke Baldwin was crowned first King of Jerusalem. The last man to hold

the title of King of Jerusalem was the Emperor Francis Joseph of Austria. From outside, the building of grey stone has a fortress-like appearance. The ancient atrium has vanished. The doorway through which the church is entered today has been walled up except for a narrow opening, and so the spaciousness of the interior comes as a surprise. It is of great simplicity and

harmoniously proportioned. The only conqueror to destroy any part of this church was British. We must be grateful to him. In the nineteenth century the Greek monks had separated the chancel from the nave by a dividing wall that was rather unfortunate from the architectural point of view. Nothing would induce them to remove it. After the conquest of Bethlehem by the British in the first World War, the commanding officer used his first few days of unrestricted authority in the town to have this wall pulled down by his men. Thanks to his energy and knowledge of archaeology we can today admire this interior in all its ancient beauty.

The figures in the bottom row of the mosaic are the ancestors of Christ. In the row above them the places where the Councils of the Church were held are represented by their church buildings. One of these is the Church of Antioch, another the Church of Sardica, the modern Sofia. Neither of these churches exists today. On the altars lie volumes of the Gospels. A Greek inscription refers to the Council of Constantinople of A.D. 381, in which the divinity of the Holy Ghost was proclaimed a dogma of the Church.

At the sides of the high altar two flights of steps lead down to the Grotto of the Nativity, which is today richly adorned with marble. The birthplace itself, which lies exactly under the high altar, is designated by a silver star carrying the inscription: HIC DE VIRGINE MARIA JESUS CHRISTUS NATUS EST – 'Here of the Virgin Mary Jesus Christ was born.'

(the woodcut shows the town in the fifteenth century) was an event of the greatest importance for the faith, for the Church, and for imperial policy.

At the very moment when the new religion had finally prevailed, it was shaken to its foundations by internal discords caused by two heresies that had sprung up simultaneously in widely distant places. One of these had a relatively trivial cause. Donatus, a fanatical African Christian, supported by a Bishop of Carthage of the same name, demanded that bishops who in the most recent persecutions had shown themselves weak, denied the faith, or handed over the holy scriptures to the police, should be relieved of their offices. The movement, known to history as Donatism, very soon took on a political character. When the Donatists failed to gain acceptance for their demands, they in many places appointed opposition bishops. Constantine had already convened a council of bishops at Arles in A.D. 314, in an attempt to dispose of the issue, but Donatism persisted in North Africa until its conquest by the Arabs.

The other dispute had a much deeper-lying cause. It took its name from Arius, a priest in Egypt, who declared that Christ the Son was not consubstantial (of identical substance) with God the Father. Christ, he said, as the divine Logos, the Word, was only a created being. This question gave rise to passionate controversies, for such points of doctrine were felt at that early formative period to be of burning importance.

Constantine summoned a universal council of all bishops, the first Ecu-
menical Council of Christendom. It met in the Imperial Palace in
Nicaea. The Emperor himself presided. His deputy was the Spanish Bishop
Hosius of Cordoba. The chief opponent of Arius was Athanasius, later
to become Patriarch of Alexandria. The doctrine of Arius was condemned.
The picture on the right shows Arius under the feet of the assembly and
draped with the *Anathema*. The resolution of the Council embodied a
statement of belief known as the *Symbolum Nicaenum*, or Nicene Creed.
The form of words that goes by this name today, and is used as a confession of faith throughout Christendom, has been supposed to be a version
of the original text made in A.D. 381, but may in fact be of different origin.
By its resolution, however worded, the Council of Nicaea saved the unity
of the main body of the Church at the cost of excluding those populations
which had embraced Arianism. These were later to play an important part
in history and it was some centuries before the heresy was extinguished.
Nicaea lies some sixty miles south-west of Constantinople. It is today a
small Turkish village, of barely five hundred inhabitants, in a forsaken and
not easily accessible corner of Anatolia. In former times the great trade route
to Syria passed through here, and the lake along which Nicaea picturesquely
straggles was connected with the sea by a channel through which ships could
pass. The city in Roman times was an imperial residence. Later, the Seljuk
princes ruled here. In the first crusade Nicaea was won back from the

Seljuks by Godfrey de Bouillon. When the Crusaders conquered Constantinople a hundred years later and made it the capital of the Latin Empire,
Nicaea became the capital of the Greek Emperor and the patriarchal seat.
Nothing of ancient times has been preserved except the tremendous city wall,
which a dozen emperors had a hand in building.

All that remains from a later period is the ruin of another Hagia Sophia,
in which the Second Council of Nicaea met in A.D. 787. This Council
was convened by the Empress Irene against iconoclasm. Ever since the
beginning of the eighth century the question of image worship had been one
of the main issues of Byzantine politics. The controversy concerned the
adoration in churches of pictures of Jesus Christ, the Virgin Mary, and the
saints, which the opponents of image worship, the image-breakers, or iconoclasts, condemned as idolatry. The iconoclastic movement, which caused
the destruction of an untold number of artistic treasures, may have been
influenced by Eastern religions such as Manichaeism and Islam, and the
emperors who supported iconoclasm were in fact of Eastern origin.

The Empress Irene was a vigorous opponent of iconoclasm and at the
Nicene Council of 787 all the theological arguments in favour of the worship
of images were produced.

The miniature, above, shows the theologians discussing the question before
the throne. The Council's resolution in favour of the veneration of images
proved, however, to be only a temporary set-back for the iconoclasts, who
were not finally disposed of for another fifty years.

The spirit of the new faith

brought a breath of renewal to outworn classical forms. Soon after its establishment, the Roman Empire had undergone a process of hellenisation lasting for centuries. During further centuries the Orient transformed and gave back to the West the Hellenic culture it had received. Hellenism was orientalised. The great achievement of Byzantium was to form a new culture from the fusion of this late Oriental-hellenist classicism with Christianity.

The great variety of artistic expression to which this culture gave rise is shown by the three objects pictured here. The silver-gilt liturgical fan, below, is an example of perfected craftsmanship and mature artistic technique. Its archangel with the wheels of fire and border decoration of peacock's feathers

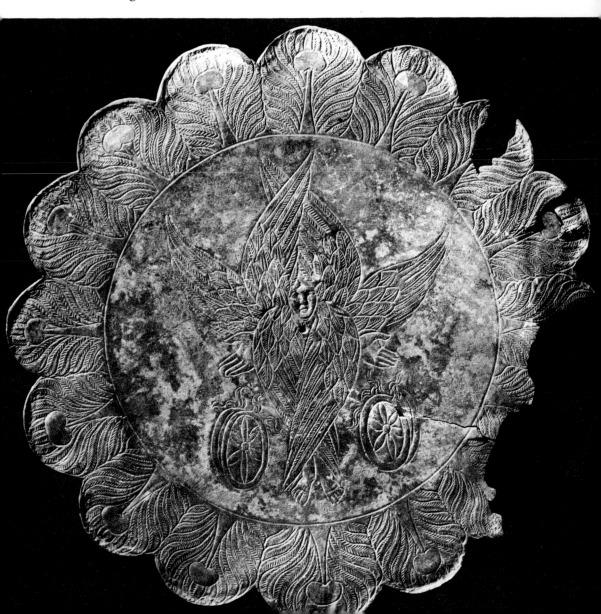

are thoroughly Byzantine. This fine piece was found in 1908, in the Syrian desert near Aleppo. The medallion, left, with the Crucifixion, is strange as well as rare. Christ is shown standing on a rectangular pedestal, a very unusual mode of representation. Moreover, His body has been merged with the cross in an extraordinary way, the head alone being distinct. This peculiar stylisation was due to a widespread reluctance in the early period to represent the passion of Christ pictorially. The small crosses to right and left of the figure represent the starry heavens. This quaint piece was found in the Crimea, and was obviously the work of a minor provincial craftsman.

Of more sophisticated workmanship is the fish, carved from a single piece of rock crystal. The fish symbol was, of course, in frequent use among the early Christians. This piece has been assigned to the sixth century and probably comes from Egypt.

With the realisation in modern times of the truly original character of Byzantine civilisation, there has come a new appreciation of Byzantine art, an appreciation that has found expression in the great exhibitions which have been held in many European cities in recent years. Byzantine art had drawn from Christianity a creative strength that outlasted the thousand years of Byzantine history and profoundly influenced the art of Western Europe.

VEUE DE TMPLE DE S.^{TE} SOPHIE MIDI

Two hundred years elapsed

between the day when Constantine the Great laid the foundation stone of St Peter's in Rome and the day when the Emperor Justinian dedicated the Hagia Sophia, Constantinople, seen in the drawing above. During this span of time new names had come into history, names that must have fallen uncouthly on Mediterranean ears. Armanarich founded the kingdom of the Ostrogoths in southern Russia. Shapur II, King of Persia, won a bloody victory over the Huns, thus saving the Mediterranean lands from being overrun. Alaric, King of the Visigoths, conquered Rome. Gaiseric, King of the Vandals, conquered North Africa. The Merovingian Clovis founded the Kingdom of the Franks.

Under Justinian, who reigned from A.D. 527 to 565 and died three years before the Prophet Mohammed was born in the deserts of Arabia, Byzantium once more attained a peak of power and achievement. The range of Justinian's activities was extraordinary, and his imperial record was almost equally eventful in the military, administrative, and cultural spheres. His generals Belisarius and Narses won back North Africa from the Vandals and destroyed the Ostrogothic kingdom in Italy. Of more permanent effect than either of these was the codification of the Roman Law carried out under Justinians's direction by Tribonian; this profoundly influenced the development of subsequent legal systems. Justinian promoted the advancement of science and engaged in theological controversy. His extensive public works included the building of numerous churches and hospitals in Constantinople, Jerusalem, and other places. He extended the Imperial Palace, erected a senate house, ordered the construction of an aqueduct for Alexandria, and dredged out a harbour at Constantinople. But the zenith of his creative enthusiasm, the culmination of his life and reign, was the consecration of

Hagia Sophia, the Church of the Holy Wisdom. It happens very rarely in history that a civilisation at the peak of its development can display itself so effectively and with such pride and splendour as Byzantium did in this masterpiece of world architecture.

Christianity's new view of life was determined by the belief in another world connected with this one by faith in one almighty, invisible, and unimaginable God. The incarnate son of God was the mediator between God and the faithful. In the Church of the Holy Wisdom this view of life has been expressed with miraculous clarity. The Church was revolutionary both in its conception and in the architectural techniques employed in it. The great dome, 184 feet high and 102 feet in diameter, is supported on the rectangular body with its buttressing half-domes in such a way as to give almost no impression of weight. As the visitor looks up into the huge golden vault, he has the feeling that earthly and heavenly space are merging into one another. No building before or since has so perfectly embodied a spiritual conception in a masonry hell. Early writers indeed could find words for their astonishment only by saying that the hands of angels had helped to build it.

The drawing on page 173 shows the exterior, the photograph, left, the interior of the church, the height of which can be gauged by the size of the man silhouetted against the sunlight.

The Hagia Sophia was decorated with unexampled splendour. The building cost 320,000 pounds of gold. The walls were covered with the most wonderful mosaics. After the ravages of the iconoclasts, the church was provided with new mosaics. The archangel, above, is among these, dating from the ninth century. From all parts of the Empire the finest marble was brought. The altar, richly ornamented with precious stones, was of pure gold. The whole of Christendom, at that time still united in its faith, looked to this building as a proud assertion of that faith.

Byzantium in its golden age

was the product of a culture that in its deepest origins was always Greek, and it remained Greek to the end. From this came the characteristic unity of style that it preserved until its collapse. In the continuity of this Greek environment the classical tradition was kept alive throughout the upheavals of the migration of peoples and of our own Middle Ages.

After the storms of the iconoclastic controversy, which in large measure accounted for the estrangement between Byzantium and Rome, there followed a period that is described as the second golden age. It is the same period in which Romanesque art evolved in Europe. Irreplaceable treasures had been destroyed by the iconoclasts, but the inexhaustible vitality of the late Greek world produced new ones. A particularly fine piece is the Veroli shrine (below)

from the tenth century. On the ivory panels surrounding the shrine, cheerful scenes from classical mythology are depicted.

From the same century comes the ivory ikon (facing page) which represents
the coronation of the Emperor Romanos and the Empress Eudoxia at the
hands of Christ. At the time of this coronation Otto the Great was ruling
in Germany. Ottonian art is an offspring of Byzantine art. The German
Emperor married his son to a Byzantine princess. While Byzantium under
Romanos was paying tribute to the Empire of Kiev, the Turkish Khan Kara
Bochra with his subjects was embracing Islam.

The enamel plaques belong to a crown of the time of Constantine IX
Monomachus, 1042–1055, which has been preserved intact. The crown is
today in possession of the National Museum in Budapest. It probably reached Hungary as a present to King Andreas I from his friend the Emperor.
The figures on the two outside plaques represent Humility and Truth re-
spectively, while the two middle ones are dancers.

Splendid as the art of this epoch was, the dissolution of the Empire had
begun. Lower Italy was lost to the Normans. The greater part of Asia Minor
was conquered by the Seljuks. In 1054 occurred the final separation of the
Roman Catholic from the Greek Orthodox Church.

The influence of a ruler's wife won a whole people over to Christianity and laid the foundations of the greatest and most enduring extension of Byzantine civilisation far beyond its frontiers. As early as the second half of the ninth century the Patriarch Photios had sent missionaries to Russia. The Grand Duchess Olga of Kiev, during a visit to Byzantium, was instructed in the Christian faith by the Patriarch and baptised by the Emperor himself. But despite her proselytising efforts her son Sviatoslav, a military conqueror who had extended the boundaries of his Grand Duchy to the Volga and the Danube, remained pagan. Her faith was rewarded, however, after her

death, when her grandson Vladimir I accepted baptism himself and made Christianity the State religion.

The Byzantine Emperor Basil II had asked the ruler of Kiev for help in putting down an insurrection, and as reward had promised him the hand in marriage of Princess Anna, his beautiful daughter. After Vladimir had given the required help, the Emperor changed his mind about the match, and the Grand Duke indignantly took up arms again, this time against the Emperor, and conquered the Crimea. The Emperor was now ready to keep his promise. But of course a princess of Byzantium, which had been Christian for six and a half centuries, could not be expected to marry a pagan.

In the Chronicle of Nestor, the first Russian historian, who wrote about these events at the beginning of the twelfth century, it is recorded that the Grand Duke sent out an embassy to sample the rites of worship among the Moslems, the Jews, the Germans, and the Greeks. Their report makes entertaining reading. Evidently the Byzantines put on for them the full splendour of a festival service in Hagia Sophia, and the envoys reported to their master in Kiev: 'We did not know whether we were in Heaven or Earth... God lives among these people. Their divine service is more beautiful than that of other nations. We cannot forget this magnificence.'

Grand Duke Vladimir had himself baptised and married Anna. It was the first time in history that a princess born in the purple became the wife of a barbarian prince. The wedding was celebrated in A.D. 989, with Byzantine and Russian pageantry, at Korsum, in the Crimea.

In Kiev, the 'Mother of Russian Cities', Yaroslav the Wise in A.D. 1018 put in hand the building of the Hagia Sophia, which was completed in 1061. The central structure still dates from this period. The drawing gives an idea of the decoration of the original church. The architects and artists of these first Russian churches were Greeks. Yaroslav can be regarded as a European ruler; he was related by marriage to the royal houses of Sweden, Norway, Denmark, Hungary, Poland, and France.

The sarcophagus of Yaroslav the Wise has been preserved. It is of such pure Byzantine style that we can assume it was made in Constantinople.

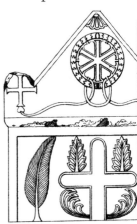

One glance inside the cathedral of Novgorod, built between 1045 and 1052, shows in how precise a sense the Russian Church is a daughter of Byzantium. Later, the Russians liked to call Moscow the Third Rome. In the East as in the West it was the young barbarian nations that took over the heritage of Christianity from the dying civilisations of Rome and Greece and carried it to new heights.

In a lonely mountain valley on the island of Chios,

opening on the sea, lies the monastery of Nea Moni. It can be reached only
by some hours' walk on foot or on muleback. It is situated in a landscape
of profound peace and idyllic beauty. The nearest signs of human activity
are the ships that pass, far out on the blue Aegean, on their way from
Smyrna to Piraeus, the port of Athens.

The monastery was founded in 1042 by the Emperor Constantine Monomachus, and was once wealthy. At the beginning of the present century it
still had twenty monks, who have all since died. Today two old nuns, in
charge of the keys of the church, are the only inhabitants of this once splendid
complex of buildings.

The Emperor sent his best craftsman from the capital to work on Nea Moni.
The mosaics have been preserved. One of them shows the 'Anastasis', the
resurrection on the Day of Judgment. Christ, with the stigmata, first wakes

Adam and Eve from the dead. In the picture below, one of the two figures is King Solomon, the other probably King David. The colour of his halo is a particularly rare kind of shining red. The mosaic art had a new, and final, peak of development under the Macedonian emperors. Mosaics of this period are to be found in the Hagia Sophia and Kariye Cami in Constantinople, the Church of the Koimesis in Nicaea, the Hagia Sophia in Salonica, and in this abandoned monastery of Nea Moni on Chios.

The nuns gathered in prayer

and portrayed in this manuscript, the original of which is now at Oxford,
lived about A.D. 1400, when the last Byzantine imperial house, that of the
Palaeologues, was already in power. If any of the younger nuns in this
gathering reached the age of seventy, she must have lived through the horrors
of the Turkish conquest. The Ottomans had already set foot on European
soil near Gallipoli and conquered the Balkans. It is extraordinary how,

despite the steady approach of catastrophe, the Byzantium of this period never tired of producing the finest works of art. These works do not perhaps rank as high as those of the first or second golden ages. But they do show an extraordinary refinement, the elegance of a period of cultivated decadence. At the same time there was one more revival of scholarship. A lively interest was awakened in the study of the classics. So, right at the end of its fluctuating history, Byzantium in its death throes contrived to hand over to Europe the torch which in Italy was to kindle the Renaissance. This was Byzantium's parting gift to Europe, which already owed so much to the city on the Bosporus, and yet so basely betrayed and abandoned it. And the heritage of Byzantium was even rich enough to be shared between West and East. Up to the time of Peter the Great the spirit of Byzantium gave life to the art and culture of Russia during its period of growth.

On the ramparts of Constantinople for ten long centuries Christianity was defended against one besieger after another. The wall, which runs from the Sea of Marmora to the Golden Horn, four miles long, is today preserved throughout its whole length. As early as the year 413 the Regent Anthemius, during the minority of the Emperor Theodosius II, installed a fortification line provided with towers. It was this first rampart that saved Constantinople from capture by Attila. After this fortification line had been largely destroyed by an earthquake in A.D. 447, a wall was built, with a ditch outside it and then a second wall outside that. From inside to outside this whole girdle of fortification measured nearly two hundred feet. From the floor of the ditch to the top of the wall was a height of a hundred feet, and there were nearly a hundred towers.

In its massive construction this ruin resembles that of the Great Wall of China, which, however, is of immensely greater length, running for 1,200

miles half across Asia. The building of the Wall of China in the second century B.C. by the Emperor Shi Huang-ti, the founder of the Ts'in dynasty, provided a reason why in the course of subsequent history the peoples of Central Asia, Huns, Seljuks, Turks, Mongols, again and again moved down on the West. In consequence of these movements, the ancient stones of the walls of Constantinople have witnessed innumerable deeds of bravery and endurance. At the Gate of St Romanos the last Emperor of Byzantium, Constantine XI of the house of Palaeologue, abandoned by the Christian powers of Europe, fell in battle against the Moslems on 31 May 1453.

Mohammed II, surnamed Fehti, the Conqueror, marched victoriously into Constantinople. On the morning of his victory he made the conquered city the capital of the new world empire of the Ottomans.

Gentile Bellini painted this Sultan, and was invested with the rank of a Pasha for doing so. The man he portrays is by no means the type of a brutal warlord, but a man of refined features, with a cast of melancholy. After three days of plunder and murder Mohammed was able to regain control of his soldiery and restore order. He promised the Christians life and freedom and appointed a new Orthodox Patriarch, whose successor today still resides in Istanbul.

HOWEVER MUCH WE MAY KNOW about the world of antiquity, it is not altogether easy to picture to ourselves what antiquity knew about the world. Ancient geography begins with the legend of the voyage of Jason and his Argonauts to Colchis. Undoubtedly this legend must be based on a historical voyage of exploration, in the course of which the adventurous Greek mariners discovered the Black Sea. The Voyage of the Argonauts is placed by scholars between the years 1150 and 1000 B.C. King Solomon's oversea expedition to the land of Ophir is to be dated to the year 945 or thereabouts. His ships put out from the Gulf of Aqaba, but where Ophir lay is a still unsolved problem.

The Canary Islands and Madeira had already been discovered by the Phoenicians before 800 B.C. Two hundred years later Phoenician ships carried out a circumnavigation of Africa. They began their voyage in the Red Sea and returned to Egypt by way of the 'Pillars of Hercules'–the Straits of Gibraltar. Towards the end of the sixth century the Carthaginian Himilco got as far as Ireland or Britain, perhaps both.

Darius' campaign into the country of the Scythians, which had taken place in the year 514 B.C., brought the Persian army as far as Bessarabia. A part of Darius' forces, which had entered the estuary of the Don with a fleet, may possibly have reached the Volga. Even at that early date there was a lively traffic on the ancient caravan trails leading to eastern Russia and Siberia. However, the great merchants who knew and controlled these trade routes generally preferred to keep quiet about them. Their geographical knowledge, the source of their wealth, was a monopoly.

In the fourth century Alexander the Great's march across Asia extended the horizons of the classical world to the Aral Sea, the Hindu Kush, and the boundaries of India.

About the year 100 B.C., Hippalos discovered the possibility of sailing with the help of the monsoon from the mouth of the Red Sea over the open sea to India and back. A lively maritime traffic developed. The voyage from the Red Sea to India lasted forty days. In the Indian seaports the Roman and Egyptian merchants met with dealers from far-distant, mysterious China.

The story of the ancient silk road, which led from north-west China across the Tarim Basin to Persia, is full of vicissitudes. For long periods it carried a regular caravan traffic, and for centuries in between it was deserted. While the *Imperium Romanum* was at its highest point, during the two first centuries

A.D., the silk road was open. We know that the Phoenician city of Tyre not only imported silk from China, but also re-exported to China textiles of high artistic quality manufactured from the raw silk. It seems that at that time, among the ladies of the imperial Chinese court, the patterns of Tyre were in demand.

The first visit of Romans to China recorded in the Chinese annals took place in A.D. 120. These, however, were not official envoys of the Roman emperor but jugglers and musicians. Somewhat later than this, in the Hou-Han Shu, the annals of the later Han Dynasty, we find a report of an embassy which arrived in China in A.D. 166 from the Emperor Marcus Aurelius.

The horizon of the ancients was broader than we think. Their knowledge of the world extended considerably beyond the frontiers of the Roman Empire. Great scholars like Polybius, Strabo, Pliny, and the most important of all, Claudius Ptolemaeus, brought together the geographical knowledge of their day in works which have in part been preserved to us. It can at least be said, therefore, that this knowledge was common to educated Greeks and Romans of the first centuries A.D.

We know of a grandiose strategic plan of Julius Caesar's to rid the Roman Empire once and for all of the Germanic threat to its existence. He wanted to launch a large-scale campaign westwards from the Caspian Sea. This idea, which in boldness of conception rivalled the plans of Alexander the Great, was extinguished by the assassin's dagger. Had it been carried out it would have changed the world no less than the campaigns of the Macedonian conqueror.

The notion of such a campaign may perhaps be said to align Caesar more with the modern age than with his own contemporaries. The peculiar passion of modern man for getting to know the globe right to its uttermost corners was then to be found only in individuals. On the whole, the men of antiquity lived within the secure confines of a civilisation rooted firmly in itself. They had neither the wish nor the need to overstep these bounds.

For the apostles and the early Christian missionaries the situation was quite a different one. The demands of knowledge and the requirements of their mission were for them the same. For them the world did not consist only of the classical civilisation. The message of Christ was not destined for the men of this civilisation alone but for all men. Indeed, the conviction that there was such a thing as *mankind* was from the beginning one of Christianity's most modern characteristics. It was in great part this idea that enabled Christianity to survive the downfall of the classical world. So it is no coincidence that the Christian tradition should be so insistent on this point: it was the apostles themselves who translated the idea of mankind into fact. Almost everywhere in the world, from Gaul to Ethiopia, from Spain to India, the Christians believe that it was an apostle who was the first to bring the Gospel to their country.

The Thomasite Christians in India have a tradition going back to very early times that their Church was founded by the Apostle Thomas and that he suffered martyrdom in India.

A great deal has been written to prove or disprove the truth of this tradition. There are no historical documents to support it. But we have already seen that a journey from Palestine to India at that period was nothing unusual. And at all periods of history emigrants have always been on the move, here today and gone tomorrow. After the destruction of Jerusalem in A.D. 70 we know that Jewish emigrants settled on the Malabar coast of India.

The first reports about the Thomasite Christians date from the fourth century. Theophilus travelled in the year 354 to Arabia Felix and Ethiopia as the ambassador of the Emperor Constantine, and returned home by way of India. In India he reformed the Christian Church ceremonial by bringing it into line with that which had become customary in the Roman Empire.

At the end of the sixth century a pilgrim named Theodore, who was passing through Gaul, told Gregory of Tours that in Mylapore on the Malabar coast there was a monastery and a church in which the bones of the Apostle Thomas had first been buried. They had later been moved to Edessa in Mesopotamia. A Syrian calendar of the ninth century gives under the third of July: 'St Thomas. He was bored through by a lance in India. His bones rest in Urhai... A great Holy Day.' Urhai is the SyrianArmenian name for Edessa.

The Christians in India have preserved numerous memories of St Thomas,

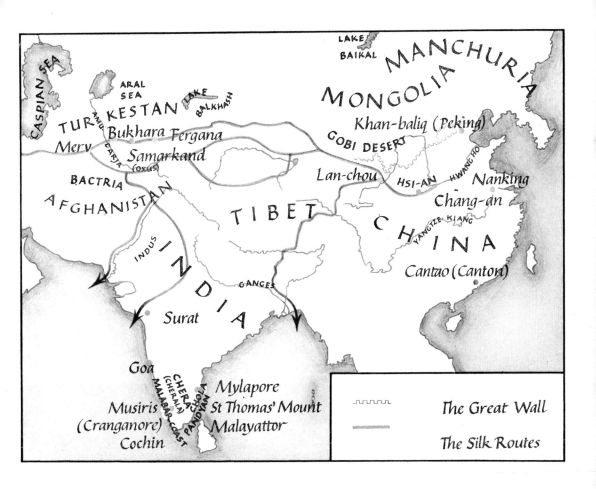

passing them on from mouth to mouth. Such oral traditions have not the same standing as written documents, but the memorials of the Apostle Thomas to be found in India and the stories about him can scarcely have sprung up without any reason at all. Moreover the traditions are linked with contemporary personages who are known historically to have existed. As with so many other legends, it does seem that there must be a core of historical truth in those about the Apostle Thomas.

In China, too, there were early Christian missions, though all knowledge of them was lost in Europe until the beginning of the seventeenth century. But in the year 1623 it became known that a stone tablet of the year 781 had been found in north-west China with an inscription in Chinese and Syriac recording in detail the wide prevalence of Christianity in China about the middle of the seventh century. This discovery caused as much sensation among the scholars of that day as the discovery of the Dead Sea Scrolls in our own day. In fact, from what we now know, it seems that China on three separate occasions was on the point of becoming Christian.

Among the records of Christianity in China, the oldest of all say that the Apostle Thomas visited this country too. St Francis Xavier, the apostle of India at the beginning of modern times, confirms this tradition in a letter from Amboina, dated 10 May 1546. He writes: 'Many people say that the Apostle Thomas was in China.' But the most informative report is that of Caspar da Cruz, a Dominican, who went to China in the year 1554. In his *Tractado da China* he writes: 'While I was in the country in which the Apostle St Thomas suffered martyrdom' (on the Malabar coast, that is) '…I learned that the Apostle had been in China before that, to preach the Gospel there, and that after he had been there some time and seen that he could bear no fruit among them, he returned to Moleapor, leaving three or four disciples there behind him… In the city of Canton… I saw a chapel …in which was the figure of a very finely clothed woman with a child on her arm, and before it a lamp was burning. As I suspected that here was something Christian, I asked one of the lay brothers and also some of the heathen priests what was the significance of this woman. But nobody could tell me or give me an explanation of any kind. It may well be an image of our Mother of God, fashioned by the ancient Christians, or left behind there by St Thomas… But one comes in the end to the conclusion that everything is forgotten. It might just as well be a heathen image.'

In the East as in the West, history and myth are so intimately intertwined in the Christian tradition that it is not always easy to be sure which is which. And for Christians it is not necessarily important, since both are valid.

This page from the Codex Sinaiticus, the famous Bible manuscript from the Monastery of St Catherine on Mount Sinai, shows a portion of the Epistle of St Paul to the Galatians. In the third column, lines 7 to 9, are the words:

ΟΤΕΔΕΗΛΘ(ΕΝ)
ΤΟΠΛΗΡΩΜΑΤΟΥ
ΧΡΟΝΟΥ…

'hote de elth(en) to pleroma tou chronou …' – 'But when the fulness of the time was come …'

ΙϹΝΝ MENOCZWOΠOII ΛΧΡΙΤΗϹΠΡΟΘΕϹϹΜ
ΔϹΛ ϹΛΙΟΝΤWϹΕΚΝΟ ΛϹΤΟΥΠΛΙΡΟϹ
ΛΛΝ ΜΟΥΗΝΛΝΗΛΙΚ ΟΥΤWϹΚΛΙΗΜΙϹΟΤ
ΤWΟ ΟϹΥΝΗΛΛΛϹΥΝΕ ΗΜΕΝΝΗΠΙΟΙΥΠ
ΟΠΟΙ ΚΛΙϹΕΝΗΓΡΛΦΗ ΤΛϹΤΟΙΧΙΧΙΟΥΚΟϹΗ
ΝΗΝ ΤΛΙΛΝΤΛΥΠΟΛΜΗ ΗΜΕΘΛΛϹΛΟΥΛW
ΟΥΔΙ ΤΙΛΝΙΝΛΗΕΠΛΓΓ ΜΕΝΟΙΟΤΕΛΕΗΛΘ
ΝΙΛΤΛ ΛΙΛΕΚΠΙϹΤΕWϹΙΥ ΙΟΠΛΙΡWΜΛΧΙΟΥ
ΒΡΛΛΙ ΧΥΛΟΘΗΤΟΙϹΙΠΙ ΧΡΟΝΟΥΕΞΛΠΕϹΤΙ
ΛΕΠΙΝ ΟΥϹΙΝ ΧΕΝΟΘϹΤΟΝΥΝΛΥ
ΔϹΙΠ ΠΡΟΤΟΥΛΕΕΛΘΙΝΤΗ ΙΟΥΙϹΝΟΜΕΝΟΝ·Κ
ΟΥΛΕΙ ΠΙϹΤΙΝΥΠΟΝΟΜ ΓΥΝΛΙΚΟϹΓΕΝΟΜ
ΡΜΛΙ ΕΦΡΟΥΡΟΥΜΕΘΛΜ ΝΟΝΥΠΟΝΟΜΟΝ
ΛΩΝ ΚΛΙΟΜΕΝΟΙΕΙϹΤΗ ΙΝΛΤΟΥϹΥΠΟΝΟ
ΝΟϹ ΜΕΛΛΟΥϹΛΝΠΙϹΤΙ ΜΟΝΕΞΛΟΡΛϹΗ
ΜΛΤΙ ΛΠΟΚΛΛΥΦΘΗΝΛΙ ΝΛΤΗΝΥΙΟΘΕϹΙΛΝ
ΧϹϹ WϹΤΕΟΝΟΜΟϹΠΛΙ ΛΠΟΛΛΒWΜΕΝ
ϹΔΛΙ ΛΝΩΓΟϹΗΜWΝΓ ΟΤΙΔΕΕϹΤΕΥΙΟΙϹΛ
ΟΚϹ ΓΟΝΕΝΕΙϹΧΝΙΝΛ ΠΕϹΤΙΛΕΝΘΟΘϹΙΟ
ΙΝΥΠ ΕΚΠΙϹΤΕWϹΛΙΚΝ ΠΝΛΧΙΟΥΥΙΟΥΛΥΤ
ΛΤΕ WΘWΜΕΛΟΟΥ ΕΙϹΤΛϹΚΛΡΔΙΛϹΗ
ΙΤΡΙΛ ϹΗϹΛΕΠΙϹΠΙϹΙΕ ΜWΝΚΡΑΖΟΝΛΒΒΛ
ΕΤΟ WϹΟΥΚΕΤΙΥΠΟΠΝ ΟΠΛΤΗΡWϹΤΕΟΥΚΕ
ϹΟΥ ΛΝΩΓΟΝΕϹΜΕΝ ΤΙΕΙΛΟΥΛΟϹΛΛΛΛ
ΤΟΚΛ ΠΛΝΤΕϹΓΛΡΥΙΟΙΟΙ ΥΙΟϹΕΙΛΕΥΙΟϹΚΛΙ
ΝϹΙΝ ΘΥΕϹΤΕΛΙΛΤΗϹΠΙ ΚΛΗΡΟΝΟΜΟϹΔΙΛΘΥ
ΡΕΚ WϹΕΝΧWΙΥ ΛΛΥ
ΗΡΟ ΟϹΟΙΓΛΡΕΙϹΧΝΕΒΛ ΛΛΛΛΤΟΤΕΜΕΝΟΥ
ΕΠΕ ΠΤΙϹΘΗΙϹΧΝΕΝΛ ΚΕΙΛΟΤΕϹΘΝΕΛΥ
ϹΙW ϹΛϹΘΟΟΥΚΕΝΙΠΟΥ ΛΕΥϹΛΤΕΤΟΙϹΦΥϹΕΙ
ΕΠΝ ΛΛΙΟϹΟΥΔΕΕΛΛΙΝ ΜΗΟΥϹΙΘΕΟΙϹΝΥ
ΡΙϹΙΝ ΟΥΚΕΝΙΛΟΥΛΟϹ ΛΕΓΝΟΝΤΕϹΘΝ
ΛΕΕΛΕΥΘΕΡΟϹΟΥ ΜΛΛΛΟΝΛΕΓΝWϹ
ΟϹΙW ΚΕΝΙΛΡϹΝΚΛΙΘΗ ΘΕΝΤΕϹΥΠΟΘΥ
ΝΧΛ ΛΥΛΠΛΝΤΕϹΓΛΡ ΠWϹΕΠΙϹΤΡΕΦΕ
ΡΟΗΛ ΜΕΙϹΕϹΤΕΕΝΧWΙΥ ΤΕΠΛΛΙΝΕΠΙΤΛΛϹ
ΤΟϹΙΠ ΕΙΛΕΥΜΕΙϹΧΥΓΛΡ ΘΕΝΗΚΛΙΠΤWΧΛ
ΕΧΙΝ ΤΟΥΛΒΡΛΛΜϹΙΠΕΡ ϹΤΟΙΧΙΛΟΙϹΠΛΛΙ
ΛΤΤΕ ΜΛΕϹΤΕΚΛΤΛϹΤΙΝ ΛΝWΘΕΝΛΟΥΛΕΥ
ΜΕΙ ΓΕΛΙΛΝΚΛΗΡΟΝΛΜ ϹΕΘΕΛΕΤΕΗΜΕΡΛ
ΤΗϹ ΛΕΓWΛϹϹΨΟϹΟΝ ΠΛΡΛΤΗΡΕΙϹΘΚΛΙ
ΙΝΟ ΧΡΟΝΟΝΟΚΛΗΡΟ ΜΗΝΛϹΚΛΙΚΛΙΡ
ΙΝ ΝΟΜΟϹΝΗΠΙΟϹ ΚΛΙΕΝΙΛΥΤΟΥϹΦ
ϹΚΛ ΕϹΤΙΝΟΥΛΕΝΔΙΛ ΒΟΥΜΛΙΥΜΛϹΜΗ
ΤϹΙ ΦΕΡΙΛΟΥΛΟΥΚϹΠΛ ΠWϹΕΙΚΗΚΕΚΟΠΙ
ΜΗΕ ΤΟ... ...ΛΚΛϹΙΟ Υ...ΛϹ

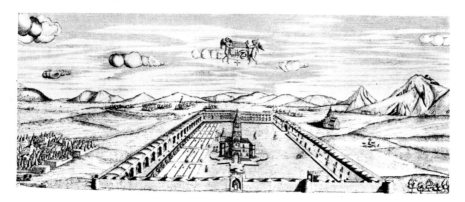

In a critical border region,

through every vicissitude of war and peace, freedom and subjection, the Armenians have preserved their national identity intact from pre-Christian to modern times. Their country lies in north-east Asia Minor, and through its fertile valleys ran the trade routes connecting the Iranian highlands with the Asia Minor seaports and the Black Sea with Mesopotamia. Therefore Armenia from the earliest times was coveted and attacked by all its neighbours. It was conquered again and again. Again and again the Armenians had to fight to win back their freedom. Some few times in its history Armenia itself was a great power. From 94 to 56 B.C. Tigranes I ruled over Asia Minor and a great part of Syria and Mesopotamia. He had residences in Tarsus and Antioch, and was the father-in-law of one of Rome's greatest and most dangerous enemies, King Mithradates of Pontus. A later ruler, Tiridates I, was formally recognised King of Armenia by Nero in the year 66. Christian Armenia was later allied with Byzantium and won many victories against Sassanid Persia.

After Persia had become Moslem, the Armenian kings of the house of Bagration contrived by skilful diplomacy to obtain recognition from the Caliph in Baghdad as well as from the Emperor in Byzantium. The Prince Bagration of Tolstoy's *War and Peace* was a prince of this royal house. The long period during which the Bagratids reigned over Armenia was one of the happiest in its history. In 980 King Ashot III built the celebrated Cathedral of Ani, a wonderful fusion of the Persian and Byzantine styles of architecture. Such was the fame of this masterpiece that, when in the year 989 the Hagia Sophia in Constantinople had collapsed in an earthquake, Tiridates, the architect of the Cathedral of Ani, was called to Constantinople to restore the fallen dome.

Armenia lost its freedom after forty years of fighting against the Seljuks, but in the year 1080 the Rupenid dynasty founded yet another Armenian empire in Cilicia on the south coast of Anatolia. This Armenia played an important political part in the Crusades. Since that time there has never again been a free Armenia.

After the conquest of Constantinople in 1453 the Sultan Mohammed II appointed Bishop Hovakim as Armenian patriarch. With the exception of those matters regulated by Moslem law, he was invested under the Millet system with full legal powers over the Armenian Christians in the Ottoman Empire, similar to those exercised over the Orthodox Christians by the new Greek Orthodox patriarch Gennadius.

Today there are five Armenian patriarchates. The most exalted, that of the Catholicos, has its seat in Etchmiadzin in the Soviet Armenian Republic. A second has its seat in Istanbul, a third in Jerusalem. This distribution reflects the fate of the Armenian people, dispersed over almost as much of

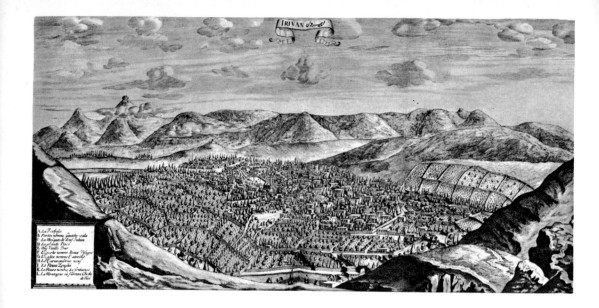

the world today as the Jews. In 1605 Shah Abbas invited thousands of
Armenians to settle in Persia, and they there founded at Julpa, near Isfahan,
a flourishing colony. There were Armenian colonies in India and the Far
East long before Europeans were able to settle in these countries.

Armenia has the oldest Biblical tradition in the world. It relates that the
spot where Noah's Ark grounded after the Flood was the peak of Mount
Ararat, near Erivan. Traces of the Ark, too, have been found more than
once by imaginative travellers, but no confirmation of their stories has ever
been forthcoming. As the Ark was made of pinewood, it could scarcely have
been preserved except in fossil form. But Jean Chardin, who was in Erivan
in the second half of the seventeenth century, in his drawing of the city,
above, could not resist including, besides the Seljuk minarets, a picture of
the Ark itself on top of Mount Ararat.

Christianity reached Armenia very early. There were already Christians in
Melitene, in Southern Armenia, in the time of the Emperor Marcus Aurelius, at the end of the second century. Eusebius mentions a letter written by
Dionysius of Alexandria about the year 200 'to the Bishop Maruzanes and
the brethren in Armenia'. Maruzanes was probably Bishop of Sebaste. At
the Council of Nicaea Armenia was represented by the two bishops Aris-
takes and Akrites.

Armenian is an independent member of the Indo-European group of
languages. At the beginning of the fifth century Bishop Mesrob created a
new Armenian alphabet of thirty-six letters, and used it to start an Armenian translation of the Bible. Much of the Greek Church fathers' works

has also been translated into Armenian. As happened later with Luther's translation of the Bible into German, a rich literature has grown out of Bishop Mesrob's creation of an Armenian written language. And this literature has helped the Armenians to preserve their national identity through all the persecutions of later centuries. On the other hand the Armenian Bible did contribute to the separation of the Armenian Church from the rest of Christendom. The Armenian language has not the same clarity as Greek, and it became increasingly hard to understand the difficult distinctions drawn by the later Councils of the Church when they were translated into Armenian. So the Armenian Church drifted apart and has remained independent to this day. The Armenian Bible manuscripts are particularly fine and richly illuminated. Among the most famous are some very early ones which are of great importance for Bible scholarship.

The great missionary of Armenia was St Gregory the Illuminator. He was a prince of the royal house of the Arsacids and so a Parthian. The portrait on the right comes from an Armenian New Testament. After the Armenians had driven out the invading Persians in 286, Gregory persuaded King Tiridates III to turn Christian. Not content with accepting baptism

himself, the king declared the conversion of his whole people to Christianity, and sealed it by the destruction of the pagan sanctuary in Ashtishat and the erection of a church in its place. Gregory founded twelve bishoprics. Thus Armenia can claim to be the first country in which Christianity was recognised by the State and became the dominant religion. The martyrdom of St Gregory, for which no historical evidence has so far been forthcoming, is depicted above in a twelfth-century Greek manuscript. Since the time of King Tiridates the Armenians have remained a pious Christian people. As early as the fifth century they possessed a monastery on the Mount of Olives outside Jerusalem, and to this day the Armenian monks play an important part in looking after the holy places in Palestine.

At the patriarchal residence of Etchmiadzin there are three ninth-century churches. The basilica form is not usual among Armenian churches, which are mostly built to a rectangular ground plan with four apses. The outside walls of the Church of Achtamar by Lake Van are entirely covered with sculptures, mostly Old Testament scenes.

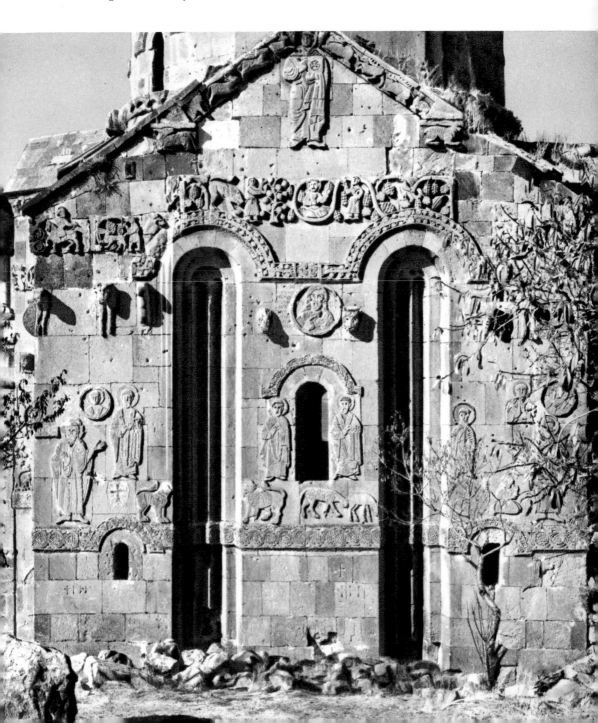

The relief shows an archangel. The supernatural being with four wings is a very ancient Asiatic *motif*, as may be seen in the sculptured watcher on the gate of the Palace of the Achaemenids in Pasargadae, from the end of the sixth century B. C.

The ivory relief depicts the martyrdom of the forty martyrs of Sebaste, a grim and dramatic episode of the beginning of the fourth century A.D. They were forty Roman legionaries, Christians who could be induced neither by command nor by persuasion nor by torture to renounce their faith. They were exposed naked on a frozen lake, and on the shore great fires were lit

and hot baths prepared. A pardon was promised to any of the forty who would forswear Christ and exchange the ice for warmth and comfort. Forty is one of the old sacred numbers and the martyrs prayed that not one of them might weaken and accept the offer. But one of them did do so. He rushed ashore and sprang into one of the baths, but the sudden warmth after exposure was too much for his heart. He died on the spot and so 'lost earthly and heavenly life at one and the same instant'.

But the sacred complement of forty was after all made up in the end. One Christian legionary, who was not on duty and so had escaped the ordeal, had a dream. He saw angels floating down from heaven with robes and crowns for the Martyrs. He knew his comrades numbered forty, but could count only thirty-nine crowns. He woke up, hastened to the lake, threw off his clothes, and ran out on to the ice. Death did not come quickly to the forty: it was three days and three nights before the last of them was dead. The miniature below is an illustration to Psalm LXVI, 12: 'we went through fire and through water; but thou broughtest us out into a wealthy place.' It shows the remains of the forty martyrs being recovered from the lake and transferred to a reliquary. The story of this martyrdom was a favourite one and has often been illustrated in Christian art.

The earliest legend of Christendom

is commemorated in a royal coat of arms, that of the Kings of Georgia. Under the crown of the royal house it bears a medallion, with a picture of the coat of Christ for which the Roman sol-diers cast lots under the cross on Golgotha. The medallion is supported by two lions and rests on a mountain peak. The illustration is from a Georgian bible of the eighteenth century. Accord-ing to tradition the coat of Christ found its way to Georgia. The first King of Georgia to be converted to Christianity was King Mirian, who reigned from 300 to 342. The picture of this King is reproduced from a woodcut, after a fresco in the Georgian Monastery of the Holy Cross in Jerusalem. King Mirian was converted by a wo-man who had fallen into his hands as a captive. She was St Nino. Highly honoured in Georgia, she is the first woman missionary in Christian history.

Georgia is situated in Transcaucasia between the

Black Sea and the Caspian Sea. Its Georgian name is Sakhartvelo, derived from that of the legendary hero of Georgian pre-history and founder of the Kingdom of Georgia, Khartles, who is credited also with many other great exploits.

Georgia's history contains a record of sufferings and catastrophes similar to that of its southern neighbour, Armenia. The country was a perpetual battlefield, first in the fighting between the Romans and the Persians, later in the centuries of warfare between Byzantium and Islam. In the eighth century there was an Arab emirate in Tiflis. One of Georgia's great ages of prosperity was the period of its union with Armenia under the Bagration princes. In the fourteenth century Tiflis was conquered by Timur Khan, and it was at this time that St Demetrius, second after St Nino in the catalogue of Georgian saints, suffered martyrdom. Georgian literature, which was particularly productive during the sixteenth, seventeenth and eighteenth centuries, is known to the west chiefly for its great heroic epics. Among others, Schiller was inspired by them.

On the north Georgia is bounded by the great central *massif* of the Caucasian mountains, but this did not in the long run prevent its occupation

by Russia. Czar Paul I brought Georgia under his rule as a result of internal faction, When the German Caucasus Corps occupied Tiflis in 1918 it instituted for itself a new Order, the medal of which has a portrait of St Nino on one face. Subsequently Georgia became the Grusinian Soviet Republic, but before that, in the Czarist province of Tiflis, there was born one Joseph Vissarionovitch Djugashvili, who later took the revolutionary surname 'Stalin' – 'Man of Steel'.

It is surprising to discover that in this distant corner of the world very ancient Christian traditions have been preserved for more than two thou-sand years. The first to preach the gospel in Georgia, according to Georgian tradition, was the Apostle Andrew. It is indeed quite conceivable that Andrew did reach Georgia, in his wanderings from Syria through Asia Minor and Armenia. There stood in Pitzounda a church which was said to have been put up originally by St Andrew himself and which was later enlarged by Justinian. This picture of it was sketched in the middle of the nineteenth century by a French traveller.

The story of the coming of the coat of Christ to Georgia is of considerable historical interest. The tradition is that it was rescued by some Georgian Jews who were present at the crucifixion of Jesus in Jerusalem and brought home by them.

We know that there were many Jews who, in consequence of the events at the Crucifixion, recognised Jesus as the Son of God. Joseph of Arimathea begged the body of Christ of Pontius Pilate. It almost goes without saying that attempts would be made by some of these pious Jews to buy the coat of Christ from the Roman soldier who had won it by lot.

It may be objected that the Christian conception of a holy relic did not yet exist, but it would have been no more than a natural human impulse to want to save from profanation the sole remaining earthly possession of the innocently crucified one, the Son of God. And it would also be a matter of course that the Jews who had bought the coat from the Roman soldier should take it home with them. We see from this tradition how a legend may very well be true, even when it lacks histo-rical confirmation.

This golden medallion is a reliquary of the twelfth century. On one side is a portrait of St George in enamel, with his name. On the other there is a portrait of St Demetrius in the centre and on the gold border round it a Georgian inscription referring by name to Ketaven, a Georgian saint, and saying that the reliquary contains a piece of wood from the Holy Cross. When the rectangular enamel plate with St Demetrius' portrait is folded back, the holy relic becomes visible. The Greek inscription which begins on the obverse and runs on round the edge of the medallion may be translated:

(Thy servant) prays that he may be Thy zealous defender in his battles, anointed with Thy blood and with balm.

St Ketaven was Queen of Georgia. She was wearing the reliquary about her neck when in the year 1624, at the reconquest of her country by the Persians, she died a martyr's death.

PERSIA

Far back in apostolic times

the Christian mission had already reached Persia. The first missionary to Mesopotamia, according to the tradition, was Mari, a pupil of Adais, who was one of the seventy chosen by Jesus himself. At that time the dominant people beyond the Euphrates were the Parthians, who were tolerant in religious matters. Between the Euphrates and the Tigris in the year 225, when the empire of the Parthians was destroyed by the Persians, there was a chain of twenty Christian bishoprics extending from the Caspian Sea to the Persian Gulf. We have already given an account of the Christian community in Dura Europus, and in the second century there were isolated Christian communities in Bactria in eastern Persia. One of the bishops at the Council of Nicaea signed himself 'John of the Persians. Bishop of all Persia and Greater India'.

The further development of Christianity in Persia was influenced by three factors. First, that of language: the Christian mission with its starting point in Edessa was based on Syrian Christianity and used the Syriac language, then widespread in the Orient. Secondly, the Persian State, far from being tolerant, was hostile to the new faith. Thirdly, Nestorianism: in the fifth century the teaching of Nestorius conquered the whole Persian Church.

The fact that Persian Christianity was Syrian in its orientation caused it to become increasingly estranged in course of time from the Greek-orientated Christianity of the Roman Empire. The Syrian Church had been the first to create a liturgy in a language understood by the non-Greek-speaking common people. The hostility of the Persian Empire, which had its own State religion, led to severe persecutions of Christians in Persia long after they had ceased in the Roman Empire. Finally, the conversion of the Persian Church to the heretical doctrines of Nestorianism finally severed the Christians of the East from those of the West.

The Persians are a people with one of the most ancient civilisations known to history. After an intervening period of subjugation and hellenisation, they reacted powerfully to the great invasion of Alexander the Great, and at the beginning of the third century A. D. the Sassanids founded a new Persian Empire. Shapur II made Zoroastrianism, the old Persian religion, into a State religion. Ruins of the Zoroastrian towers of fire, seen in the nineteenth-century lithograph above, are still to be found in Persia.

Constantine the Great wrote a letter to Shapur II in which he begged the King of the Persians to protect the Christians in his kingdom. But King Shapur regarded the letter as a provocation. The Zoroastrian priests per-

suaded him that every Christian was a friend of the Romans and therefore an enemy of Persia. As a result there were violent persecutions, in which 16,000 people are said to have lost their lives.

The drawing is a reproduction of a relief, in which the left-hand figure is King Shapur II in his Persian royal robes. King Shapur reigned no less than seventy years, from 309 to 379, a timespan not exceeded by any other ruler known to history. The sardonyx below, from the third century, shows a fight between a Roman and a Persian, a formal representation of a scene which might have occurred in any of their innumerable wars.

Despite all persecutions, militant Christianity in Persia lived on, though it was never to gain the upper hand there. In the fifth century there were bishops in Herat and Merv, in the remote province of Bactria, which borders on India. The first Turkish converts to Christianity were made by monks who had moved eastwards from Bactria into Central Asia, where the ancestors of later Turkish conquerors had their homeland.

In A.D. 410 a Council of the Persian Church was held at Seleucia-Ctesi-

phon and attended by forty Persian bishops, who there formally recognised the confession of Christian faith laid down by the Council of Nicaea.

And though it was forbidden by Persian law, the Christians began to make converts among the Zoroastrians. The result was a new wave of persecution, just about the same time that a new war broke out between Persia and the Roman Empire. When the persecutions and the war were over, a synod of Persian bishops resolved to sever all connections with the Western Church. The reasons for this step were not theological but political in character. The Persian patriarch declared his independence of Rome on the ground that his obedience was to Christ alone, and the Persian State accorded recognition to the Patriarch.

In the course of the fifth century the Persian Church was conquered by the doctrines of Nestorianism. Nestorius, who was Bishop of Constantinople from 428 to 431, had taught that Christ not only had two natures, one divine and one human, but also consisted of two persons, inseparable yet distinct. The idea that Mary was the mother of God was rejected by Nestorius as pagan. His teaching was condemned as a heresy in 431, by the Synod of Ephesus. It lived on, however, for centuries after its condemnation, just like Arianism.

Nestorian Christianity spread far into Asia from the Syrian and Persian Churches. Relatively recent documentary evidence of its existence there is given by a sixteenth-century Persian codex which is kept in the Medici Library in Florence. The illustration here shown is of the Magi receiving the prophecy of the immaculate conception.

SINAI

For fifteen hundred million years

this mountain has been reaching towards the sky above the Sinai Peninsula. It is the Jebel Musa, the Mount of Moses, 7,700 feet high, and capped with snow in winter. It is composed of quartz and granite and belongs to the early history of the earth.

From the year 3200 B.C. onward the Egyptian Pharaohs exploited the turquoise deposits in this desert region, and the names of thirty-nine Pharaohs have been found in inscriptions still surviving here. A Phoenician stone inscription, discovered on this peninsula, is the oldest known example of an inscribed alphabet.

It is here, in the Sinai Desert, that the people of Israel, according to the Old Testament story, wandered for forty years after their exodus from Egypt, and a mountain in the south of the peninsula is the spot in which Moses is said to have received the Law.

At the foot of Jebel Musa lies the Monastery of St Catherine. This may be called a fortress of God in this wilderness, since the original building was actually a stronghold and sanctuary for the protection of Christian hermits from attack by marauding Bedouin. Hermits have lived in this neighbourhood since the third century A.D., and in the fourth century their numbers must have been considerable. On Mount Serbal the remains of a monastery of this period have been discovered, and in the Pharan Oasis about this time there was already a bishop. Towards the end of the fourth century we hear of two massacres carried out by Bedouin among the Christian monks and hermits.

It was not till 530, however, that the Emperor Justinian built a fortress for their protection, on the spot where, according to tradition, Moses heard the voice of the Lord from the burning bush, and it was this building which evolved into the Monastery of St Catherine. In the plan the small rectangular room behind the apse of the church is the Chapel of the Burning Bush.

Justinian gave the monastery a hundred Roman and a hundred Egyptian slaves with women and children. The descendants of this slave population, the Jebeliyeh, to this day act as servants to the monks, though they have all been

A PLAN of the Convent, and Church of Mount Sinai. To the Most Rev. Father in God, John L. Archbishop of Canterbury Primate of all ENGLAND and Metropolitan.

converted to Islam. The prophet Mohammed once visited the monastery and commanded the Bedouin to leave its pious inmates in peace. In return the monks built next door to the monastery church a mosque for the followers of the Prophet. This mosque, which must be a unique instance of toleration within the walls of a place of Christian retreat, is today in ruins.

The bishopric of Sinai was elevated to an archbishopric by the Council of Chalcedon, and the monastery is today still one of the most important foundations of the Greek Orthodox Church, a place of sanctuary in the desert and a Christian outpost in the world of Islam. It contains a valuable library, but its most famous volume is no longer on its shelves. This is the Codex Sinaiticus, after the Codex Vaticanus the oldest known Bible manuscript. It was discovered in the library in the middle of the nineteenth century by the German scholar Constantin von Tischendorf.

The Codex was written about the year 400 in a wonderfully fine Greek script. One small portion of it is in the library of Leipzig Univerity, but the main portion, formerly in the possession of the Czar of Russia, was sold by the Soviet Government in 1933 to the British Museum for £ 100,000 – the highest price ever paid for a manuscript.

Outside one of the monastery walls is a small projecting structure from which in earlier times a basket was let down to bring up the pilgrims, this being the only means of access. When the rope began to fray, the monks would utter a prayer before hauling up each pilgrim. For some time now the monastery has had a small entrance at the side for people, but the basket lift is still used for goods. As a further reminder of more troubled times, there are still a few old cannon standing on the encircling wall of St Catherine's.

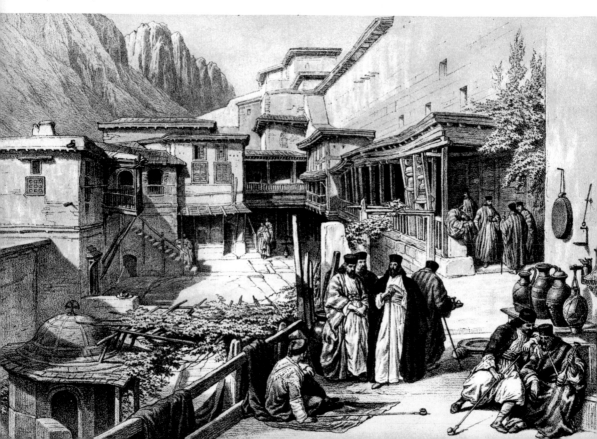

Sheltered from the desert

in south-western Arabia there were already flourishing civilisations a thousand years before the birth of Christ. Queen Bilqis of Sheba appears in the
Bible as a mysterious figure whose visit to King Solomon from her remote
kingdom was an occasion of fabulous splendour; she gave and received
presents on a scale never equalled by any two historical heads of State. The
Queen was long considered a fairy tale character. Today, however, it is
known that Sheba exists and is in South Arabia. It will probably not be
long before the Queen's palace is excavated by archaeologists. Many inscriptions have already been found, and their decipherment is gradually
building up an outline of the early history of Arabia. The photograph
shows some of the inscriptions at Sammat al-Nadhun.

South-western Arabia, called by the Romans *Arabia Felix* ('Happy Arabia')
in contrast to the deserts by which it is bounded, is a well-watered mountain

country with hilly pastures for cattle. The early Arabian kings had a highly developed irrigation system, by the help of which they cultivated extensive areas that have now reverted to desert. Their most famous achievement was the Marib Dam, a work of engineering that would be considered remark-able even today. A few ruins are all that is now left to remind us how this country must once have looked.

Arabia is possibly the only country on earth of which the question is never asked, 'Where did its population come from?' For it is generally considered to be the homeland of the Semites, who are thus of all modern peoples the one which has roamed most widely about the world and at the same time the only one which really knows its land of origin.

None of the great conquering nations in the history of the Near East has ever entirely succeeded in subduing Arabia. Yet there was plenty to excite their covetousness in the land out of which came incense and myrrh, cinnamon and spikenard, pepper, gold, and precious stones. Some of these products came from overseas. The Arabs, with their command of the passage from the Red Sea to the Indian Ocean, for centuries enjoyed a monopoly of sea traffic with India and Africa, a monopoly which they jealously defended.

In the year 24 B. C. the Romans tried to conquer Arabia Felix. But their general, Aelius Gallus, was completely unsuccessful. Sand, heat, and thirst were stronger than the Roman arms. Christianity entered Arabia from all sides. The Jews had had considerable settlements in the peninsula since ancient times, and it is probable that here, as elsewhere, small Jewish-Christian communities were formed. In the third century we hear of Chris-tian communities in northern Arabia, on the Persian Gulf coast, and on the isles of Bahrain. As early as A. D. 244 Bostra, the capital of the Roman province of Arabia, to the north-west of the peninsula, had its own bishop.

The Roman Emperor Philip (top right), who reigned from A.D. 244 to 249, was an Arab, born in Bostra, and probably also a Christian. Nothing of any great importance is known about his reign except that, by a stroke of historical irony, it was he, an Arab, who celebrated with great pomp the thousandth anniversary of the foundation of Rome.

There were Christian communities, too, in the Red Sea ports. Yet it cannot be said that the Arabian peninsula was ever thoroughly penetrated by the Christian faith. The colonies in the great cities remained small and the Gospel did not reach the roaming Bedouins. Only in Arabia Felix did Christianity for a time prevail in the sixth century. The story is told in documents of the Himyarite Dynasty, which had ruled in Arabia Felix

from the second century B. C. At the beginning of the sixth century there were Christian churches in Nadj- ran, Hadhramaut, and Marib. But As'ad Kamil, a king who with his whole tribe, the T'ubba, had been converted to the Jewish faith, ferociously attacked the Christians and put them cruelly to death. The Ethiopian Emperor Caleb of Axum thereupon took the field against him and defeated him. For two generations there- after, in what is today the Yemen, there was a Christian Arabia under the protection of the throne of Axum. The cities of Arabia Felix, where the style of building has not changed much, probably did not look very different from this picture of Saana.

Two great disasters, coming on top of one another, put an end to the story of Christian Arabia. The great Marib Dam broke. It must have been an appalling catas- trophe, and the impression it made on people's minds can be judged from the fact that the event was mentioned some decades later in the Koran. Then the country was conquered by the Persians, and what was left of Christianity after that was swept away by Islam. Only Jesus Christ Himself was taken over into the new teaching of Mohammed. For Moslems, how- ever, he is no longer the Son of God, but only a prophet.

A Chancellor of the Exchequer reading the Prophet Isaiah

as he journeys through the country in his carriage conjures up an unusual picture. The Acts of the Apostles relates how this man of Ethiopia, an eunuch of great authority under Candace, Queen of the Ethiopians, who had charge of all her treasure, on his journey home from Jerusalem met the Apostle Philip. He invited him into his 'chariot' to discuss with him a passage from Isaiah. The Apostle interpreted it as a prophecy. In a wayside brook the Chancellor was baptised by Philip. The whole history of Christianity in Ethiopia is as unusual as this story of the first Ethiopian to be baptised.

Homer, in the *Odyssey*, called the Ethiopians 'the most remote of peoples'. Ethiopia has been an independent state since the eleventh century B.C. In the eighth century the Ethiopians conquered Egypt. In the seventh century Semitic tribes from southern Arabia entered Ethiopia and settled there. Herodotus distinguishes two races there, one with long hair and one with wooly hair. Its religion and civilisation were extensively influenced by Egypt. In the third century King Ergamenes, a contemporary of the Egyptian king,

Ptolemy Philadelphus, overthrew in Ethiopia a priestly government whose authority was such that it could order the king's death.

The capital of ancient Ethiopia was Axum, in the north of what is now Abyssinia, and it is in the Church at Axum that the kings and emperors have been crowned up to our own times. Here too stands a famous group of granite monoliths dating from the pre-Christian period, the tallest of which is seventy feet high. For fifteen centuries they have stood witness to innumerable coronations.

While its remoteness and inaccessibility have preserved Ethiopia through much of its history from foreign conquest, it has at all times been open to foreign influences. Even Greek civilisation penetrated it through the trading ports on the Red Sea coast, which were regularly visited by ships voyaging to and from India and Africa.

The Ptolemies were accustomed to recruit Ethiopians for the defence of the various military bases which they had established on this coast. So it was that ordinary Ethiopians came in contact with the officers of the Hellenistic Egyptian Empire, and took back home with them to their villages the knowledge and experience that they had thus gained as soldiers. Beside Lake Tana there are colonies of Jews who, like the Samaritans, recognise only the Pentateuch, the five books of Moses, as Holy Scripture. According to their own tradition they came to Ethiopia in the time of King Solomon.

The Emperor of Ethiopia calls himself the 'Lion of Judah'. The ruling house claims descent from the ancient emperors of Axum, who in turn claimed descent from Menelik, the legendary son of King Solomon and the Queen of Sheba, according to this version an Ethiopian queen. The source of this legend is the *Kebra-Nagast* or *Fame of Kings*, a historical romance in Gheez, the classical Ethiopian language.

The *Kebra-Nagast*, which in its present form dates from the fourteenth century, has an entertaining story about the trick by which Solomon in his wisdom contrived to seduce the Queen of Sheba. He gave her several banquets one after another, with rare and delicious, but sharply seasoned, dishes. When the Queen showed signs of exhaustion, he invited her to sleep in his palace. She accepted on condition that he would swear not to touch her. Solomon swore, but made her swear in return not to touch any of the precious things in his palace. In the night the Queen was thirsty and drank a glass of water. Solomon, who had not slept, came to her with a smile and reproached her with having broken her word. 'But it was only a glass of water.' 'Well', said Solomon, 'is water not the most precious thing on earth?'

The son who was the outcome of this glass of water was born to the Queen on her return to Ethiopia and was there brought up. Later she sent him to the court of King Solomon, who received him with great honour. When he departed from home, Solomon gave the young prince some of his friends as companions, among them a young man named Azarius, who was a son of the high priest Zadok. Through this young man the Ethiopian priesthood claims descent from Aaron. The prince became the first emperor Menelik of Ethiopia. The tradition further relates that Azarius and his friends stole the Ark of the Covenant, from which they could not bear to be parted, from the Temple in Jerusalem and took it to Ethiopia with them. The people believe that the Ark is still hidden in their country.

The *Kebra-Nagast* contains so many preposterous stories that it would not be difficult to dismiss the whole of it as a fairy tale. It has, however, been believed in Ethiopia for centuries and is still believed there today. No people in the whole history of Christendom has so strongly felt the need to ground its past in Old Testament tradition. And the very antiquity of this legend has enabled it to survive the vicissitudes of later history, and also to be one of the principal factors in keeping Christianity alive in such churches as Ganetta Mariam, or the 'Garden of Mary', shown opposite.

The story of the introduction of Christianity into Ethiopia has more historical substance than that of the country's origins as told in *Kebra-Nagast*, but it has much of the same fairy tale quality.

In the middle of the fourth century Meropius, a philosopher of Tyre,

accompanied by two boys, the brothers Frumentius and Ardesius, undertook a voyage of exploration to far countries. On their way home their ship put in at an Abyssinian harbour, and there, a little while after making fast, it was boarded and everyone on it was massacred. But the two boys were not on board. They were sitting under a palm tree on shore, learning their lessons. When they were later found there, no one could bear to kill them, and they were sent as captives to the King. The King was delighted with the two

boys and had them educated at his court. In course of time Frumentius became his confidential adviser, and after his death was appointed by the Queen Mother as regent and tutor of her son Ezana. Some years later Frumentius made a journey to Alexandria, where he was consecrated bishop, and on his return to Ethiopia baptised the young King Ezana, introduced the Christian religion, and became the first Metropolitan of the Ethiopian Church.

In the sixth century A.D. nine monks came to Ethiopia and there founded the first monasteries. They are known as the 'Nine Saints'.

From the fourth to the seventh centuries the Ethiopian Church was under Greek influence. Diplomatic relations between the Kingdom of Axum and Byzantium were close and friendly, but the conquests of Islam cut off Ethiopia completely from the Christian world, and it came under Arab and Turkish influence. Only with the Coptic Church in Egypt were some superficial relations maintained. The trade in the Red Sea ports came to a stop, and their harbours fell into disuse. For centuries Ethiopia was isolated by the same course of events which cut India and China completely off from Europe. But Christianity nevertheless survived and flourished. The Ethiopian Church is closer in its beliefs to the Egyptian Coptic Church than to any other, but a great deal of its doctrine, liturgy, and church ceremonial is peculiar to itself. Many of its practices are clearly Judaic in origin. Stories of battles and more or less miraculous events from Ethiopian history are mixed in with Bible stories in the readings that form part of its church services, and the brightly coloured paintings that are displayed to the congregation show a similar variety of sacred and secular subjects.

Similar peculiarities are found in Ethiopian church buildings, which with their inner and outer precincts and their inmost sanctuary recall the arrangement of the Jewish Temple. Their architecture is varied. King Lallibela of the Zague Dynasty had ten churches hewn out of solid rock. Of the two churches in the village of Lallibela that are here illustrated the Church of St George has a cross on its flat roof, concealing a finely vaulted dome. In this church swarms of 'holy bess' live in niches under the roof of rock. The oldest church building in Ethiopia is the Imraha Christos. It

is not a monolithic structure but is a prototype for the Church of Emmanuel at Lallibela. Imraha Christos dates from the twelfth century, and is remarkable for its richly decorated coffered ceiling. The Ethiopians, like the American fathers, founded a city called Bethlehem. Its church dates from the thirteenth century, the same in which the Spaniards built the Cathedral of Burgos, the Germans Strasbourg Minster, and the English Salisbury Cathedral. The Church of Bethlehem has a great deal in common with the early Christian buldings in Syria, Egypt, and Arabia Felix. The picture on the left tells the story of a monk who was climbing up to his monastery by rope, the only means of access, when the rope broke, but by God's grace he was enabled to grow wings as he fell and so save himself.

The picture on the left shows how a whole monastery was saved from an impending attack, the monks being carried away by boat.

The miniature below shows Alexander the Great riding to Heaven on a griffon. With a fine disregard of the order of time, the Macedonian conqueror has been canonised by the Ethiopian church.

In A.D. 1268, when Rudolf of Habsburg was not yet King of the Romans, the imperial Solomonic house, which still rules Ethiopia today, was restored to the throne after a period during which it had been displaced by the Zague dynasty. Today, nearly seven hundred years later, it has already survived the Habsburgs by half a century. The Lion of Judah still watches over the sources of the Blue Nile. The Ethiopians are the only African people who, apart from some short-lived invasions, have kept their freedom throughout their history. When the Negus Negesti Haile Selassie had to flee Addis Ababa before Mussolini's troops, his Empress Zauditu made a vow. If God should grant the Emperor to return to Addis Ababa he would dedicate his imperial crown to the Church of the Holy Sepulchre in Jerusalem. And when the Italian machine guns had been finally silenced in Abyssinia the Empress fulfilled her vow.

'The Son of God was with Thomas in all the places of India... and with all the preachers of the Gospel, wheresoever they came.'

St Jerome

'Doubting Thomas' is the nick-name by which he is known. For he had refused to believe in the resurrection of the Lord until he had put his finger in the print of the nails and thrust his hand into his side, and Jesus granted him his wish. None of the disciples had a longer or more difficult way to wander in this world than the Apostle Thomas. In fulfilment of Christ's command 'Go ye into all the world', he travelled to India and probably also as far as China. According to tradition the Apostle Thomas landed in Musiris in A.D. 52. Today the place is call-ed Cranganore. The bas-relief of the Apostle and the old stone cross were discovered by the Portuguese in the sixteenth century at the traditional site of his grave in Myla-pore, near Madras. Scholars are not agreed on the meaning of the inscription surrounding the cross, though the lettering of the script is in Pahlevi characteristic of the Sassanid period. The cross dates from the sixth or seventh cen-turies, and after its discovery was built into a chapel which was put up there.

223

Pearls, ivory, silk,

and the world-famous pepper of the Malabar coast were exported from India to the Roman Empire as early as the reign of the Emperor Augustus. The seventeenth-century engraving shows the harbour of Suratte, which, with the harbour of Cranganore, was from ancient times a principal centre of this export trade. The exchange of goods between Rome and India grew steadily in importance with the increase in the power and wealth of Rome, and the emergence there of a luxury-loving moneyed class. Pliny estimated the yearly expenditure on luxury imports at 55,000,000 sesterces. Rome carefully cultivated diplomatic relations with the Indian potentates, and Roman coins were legal tender in India, where they have been excavated in large quantities. The Kings of Pandyan maintained a bodyguard of Roman legionaries – 'silent Mleccas with long cloaks, short swords, and murderous hearts, who stood guard before the Palace gates.'

are still held in reverence in India today. In Malayatoor, where St Thomas
went into retreat and in meditation achieved a mystical union with God, a
church was built, and this is today a place of pilgrimage. Every year on the
first Sunday after Easter a great festival is held there and visited by thousands
of pilgrims from all over the country. Much the same customs have evolved
in this distant land as in the Christianity of the West. The picture shows
St Thomas preaching.

One of the pleasantest legends of St Thomas is the following. On a fine
spring morning the Apostle was watching some Brahmins performing ritual
ablutions in the water of a temple basin. As they repeatedly chanted their
ceremonial words they kept throwing water into the air with their hands.
The Apostle asked the meaning of this performance, and was told that the
water was thrown into the air as a sacrifice to the gods. 'If that is so,' said
St Thomas with a smile, 'your offering appears not to be very acceptable to
the gods, or else the water would not fall back into the basin.'

The astonished Brahmins asked him if he then could make the drops of
water stay up in the air. Thomas replied that he could indeed do so, but
that he would only do it if they promised to be baptised. The Brahmins
agreed to the bargain and St Thomas threw the holy water into the air.
There the drops stayed hanging, like glittering diamonds, where the saint
had thrown them.

Some of the Brahmins did not keep their promise and pronounced a curse on the spot. Strangely enough, the place to this day is called 'Chowgat', which means 'the accursed wood'.

The third of July in the year of our Lord 72,

when Jerusalem was already a heap of ruins strewn with the bones of the fallen, was the day when, after forty years of preaching, praying, and good works as he travelled about the countries of the Far East, St Thomas suffered martyrdom.

On the morning of this day he was passing on his way the mountain of Mylapore, on which stood the Temple of Kali. The priests, who knew the Apostle, came thronging towards him and barred his way. No one, they said, was permitted to pass this way without performing an act of worship to the goddess. 'If thou prayest to our goddess, thou mayest go on thy way unhindered. And more than that, thou mayest partake of our delicacies.'

The Apostle answered with dignified calm, 'Shall I barter my immortal soul for a dish of rice? But nay, if ye insist, I shall go to your temple, and there shall ye see how the goddess flies from it and the temple is destroyed with fire.'

And so it happened. As the saint was compelled by the priests to approach the temple, the goddess Kali fled from her sanctuary and the temple began to burn. The priests fell into a rage and one of them seized a lance and ran the Apostle through the heart.

Such is the description of the death of St Thomas given in the sixteenth century by Maliakkel Thomas of Malayalam, who drew on ancient traditions.

There is another tradition, according to which the body of the Apostle was transferred to Edessa, in Syria, but the Thomasite Christians in India insist that his bones are in the vault of the Cathedral of S. Tomé in Mylapore. The picture shows one of the many memorial buildings to St Thomas in India. One very remarkable document is a picture of the Apostle's grave in the *Livre des Merveilles*. The Saint's hand is reaching out of the tomb, while outside in front of the chapel a human sacrifice is being performed to a heathen idol.

The court of King Alfred the Great

in far-distant England knew the fame of the relics of St Thomas and their miracle-working power. Before King Alfred went into battle against the Danes, he made a vow promising rich gifts to various sanctuaries, among them the Church of St Thomas in India. After his victory Sighelm, Bishop of Shireburn and Aethelstan, brought the promised gifts to Rome and India. That was in 883, so that at that time the memory of St Thomas's Indian mission was still part of the common stock of Christian knowledge.

The story of Christianity in China

is as full of mysteries as China itself. In the seventh month of the twelfth Chêng-Kuan year – that is, in A.D. 638 – T'ai-tsung, the great Emperor of the T'ang dynasty, issued a proclamation with the following text:

'The Way has no unchangeable name. For the wise man no method is permanent. Doctrines exist to benefit the nation, and to protect the living. The Persian monk O-lo-pên has come from afar with writings and doctrines, to offer them in Shang-Ching. The meaning of the doctrines has been care-fully examined. They are full of mystery, wonder, and peace. They set forth the reality of life and of perfection. They signify the salvation and wealth of men. It is good that they should be disseminated about the Empire. To this end the local authorities are commanded to build a monastery for twenty-one monks in the I-ning district.'

The twelfth Chêng-Kuan year fell in a time of extraordinary political upheavals in the world at large. While T'ai-tsung was strengthening the power and extending the boundaries of the Chinese Empire to a point which they were never to reach again, the Arabs burst out of the Arabian

Desert and defeated the Empire of Byzantium in the battle of the Yarmuk. The land of Christ became Moslem, and Syria, from which the monk O-lo-pên had brought to China the 'shining doctrine of the West', was lost to Islam. The Ommayyad dynasty ruled in Damascus. The Arab general Musa set out along the African coast of the Mediterranean on that extraordinary march which was to end only in the Spanish city of Toledo. The Arabs conquered Turkestan, and about a generation later the armies of the ancient empire of China encountered those of the new Arab world power at Amu-Darja.

In this same period occurred an event on the opposite edge of the world, in a place far removed from all these great happenings and apparently quite unimportant. The Irish-Celtic Church renewed its submission to the Pope in Rome. This event in the far West was to have historical consequences no less important than those which flowed from what was happening at the same time in the East.

We no longer have any portrait of the great Emperor T'ai-tsung. But we do know the appearance of his horses. The picture shows his favourite horse, as portrayed in a relief carved on the wall of the imperial tomb. The relief is a masterpiece from a great period of Chinese art.

'Memorial of the Dissemination of the Shining Doctrine from Ta-ch'in in the Land of the Centre'

This is the meaning of the nine Chinese characters at the head of the stone table of Hsi-an. Ta-ch'in is a rather vague Chinese ex-pression for the Roman Orient. Here it probably means Syria.

The *stele* gives an account of the mission of a Syrian monk in China. His name is given as O-lo-pên. The Chinese language has no alphabet, but is made up of words of one syllable, and can give only an approximate rendering of names from other languages. O-lo-pên probably represents the Syriac word

229

Rabban, meaning master or teacher. We know nothing of the personality or fate of this man, who almost succeeded in converting the most populous country on earth to Nestorian Christianity.

The Nestorians today have almost died out. The last remaining hundred thousand who are still faithful to this doctrine live in Iraq, Syria, Persia, and also in the United States.

The coming of Nestorianism to China is commemorated by this stone table, which was put up in A.D. 781, and then came to light again in 1623 during the building of a house. Its importance was immediately recognised by the Jesuit father Trigault, and owing to the incredible nature of its contents many western scholars for a long time regarded it as a forgery. There is no longer any doubt about its genuineness today. It reads in part:

'When T'ai-tsung, the glorious emperor, began his happy reign in fame and splendour, illuminating and wisely ruling his people, there lived in the land of Ta-ch'in a man of great virtue, O-lo-pên by name, who, soothsaying from gleaming clouds, brought hither the holy scriptures and overcame difficulties and dangers by observing the harmony of the winds.

'In the ninth year Chêng-kuan he came to Chang-an. The Emperor sent his Minister of State Duke Fang Hsuan-ling at the head of an escort into the western suburb, to receive the visitor and conduct him. His scriptures were translated in the library. When the doctrines were examined in the private rooms, the Emperor recognised their correctness and truth and order-ed that they should be preached and disseminated.'

It is hard to guess what the consequences might have been if the 'glorious Emperor' T'ai-tsung had gone over to Christianity. It is not known why he did not, but it is certain that Christianity flourished exceedingly in the China of the T'ang period. There were churches in nearly every city. The monu-ments above were found in the seventeenth century. This time of prosperity for the Christian faith lasted nearly two hundred years.

After the discovery of the stone table, further archaeological remains with Christian symbols were found, and there is no doubt that systematic excavations would give us an entirely new picture of the hold that Christianity once had on the people of the Chinese Empire. After being dug up, the table of stone was taken to a monastery, which remarkably enough is situated very close to the spot where O⁄lo⁄pên built the first Christian church.

The light of the Gospel in the Land of the Centre
was extinguished in A.D. 845. A wave of violent and fanatical xenophobia swept the country. The fundamentally tolerant disposition of the people was strained by the uninterrupted hostilities between the Buddhists and the Confucians. Confucius had created in the second half of the sixth century B.C. his wonderfully mature doctrine of society, with its acute understanding of human nature. The picture below shows Confucian scholars in cheerful conversation. Buddhism did not begin to spread through China until the third or fourth century A.D. After a while the power of its monasteries became as dangerous and intolerable to the Chinese government as that of the Christian monasteries was becoming at about this same time to the imperial government in Byzantium. The Emperor Wu Tsung promulgated a decree against alien religions. According to the historian Chu t'ang⁄shu, 260,000 Buddhist monks and nuns were expelled from their monasteries and convents. Of the Christians Chu t'ang⁄shu says:
'Among the monks and nuns who were accused of having as foreigners disseminated alien religions, both Ta⁄ch'in [Christians] and Mu⁄lu⁄fu [Zoroastrians], altogether more than three thousand persons were compelled to return to civilian life and to cease corrupting the manners of China.'

Jenghiz Khan,

the great Mongolian conqueror, had among his most loyal vassals the Ongut Turks. These had received the Nestorian teaching from missionaries who had come from Syria to Central Asia through Persia and Bactria.

They at that time controlled the country which is today called Kuei-Sui and the territories to the north of the Great Wall on the frontier of Shansi. Jenghiz Khan gave his daughter in marriage to the Ongut king, and through the Ongut princes Christianity was for generations familiar to the Mongol rulers. It had its place near to the Mongol throne and returned to China once more with the Mongol conquest. Jenghiz Khan's grandson, the great Emperor of China, Kublai Khan, is known to us from the writings of Marco Polo, who served him for seventeen years. Kublai Khan was the son of a Nestorian Christian, Princess Sorghaktani, of the royal family of the Kereit, who came from Outer Mongolia. Kublai Khan, himself a Buddhist, was personally tolerant in matters of religion. In 1264 he founded a new capital which was called by the

Mongols 'Khan-balig', or the 'City of the Khan', now known as Peking. This view of the city was drawn by a Dutch artist in the seventeenth century. Kublai Khan had already given a very hospitable welcome to the brothers Nicolo and Matteo Polo. The picture on the left shows the brothers being received by the Emperor. He questioned them in detail about the Christian faith and the Western Church. Finally he sent the two Venetians as his envoys to Rome to convey to the Pope his request for a hundred missionaries to be sent to China, and also oil from the lamp of the Holy Sepulchre.

It is tempting to consider how things might have turned out if such a power-ful nucleus of Christian teachers had been able to preach the Gospel in China under the protection of the Emperor. It was the period when the Crusades were coming to an end, and the Christians, after two hundred years of fighting, were being forced to leave the Holy Land again. If at this moment a bond had been established, through a common Christian interest,

Das ist der edel Ritter Marcho polo von Venedig der grost landtfarer der uns beschreibt die grossen wunder der welt die er gesehen hat von dem auffgang bis zu dem nydergang der sunne der gleychē vor nicht meer gehort seyn

between the highly civilised Empire of China and a Europe which after centuries of darkness and confusion was just beginning to be civilised once more, the consequences might have been profound both for Europe and China, and also for the intervening Empire of Islam.

But the opportunity was let slip. When the brothers Polo arrived in Rome in 1269, the chair of St Peter was unoccupied. They waited two years in vain for a new Pope, and then embarked on the return journey. This time Nicolo took his seventeen-year-old son Marco with him. Marco Polo returned home to Venice after two decades with startling wealth and still more startling tales of his adventures in far 'Cathay'.

A generation later John of Monte Corvino and Andrew of Perugia arrived in China. Their missionary successes among the Mongol emperors were considerable, but when the powerful empire of Kublai Khan collapsed, Hung Wu, the founder of the Ming Dynasty, outlawed Christianity 'as one of the foreign doctrines' that had been favoured by the Mongols. At one stroke all sources of information, Western or Chinese, dry up, and until the arrival there of the Jesuit father Matteo Ricci in the year 1605 there is no further word of Christianity in China.

BETWEEN THE SEA AND THE MARSHES, at the western corner of the Nile
Delta, on a strip of sand only a few miles wide, the city of Alexandria was
founded in the year 331 B.C. by Alexander the Great. The Greeks had
always shown a touch of genius in their ability to pick out at a glance the
ideal sites for their settlements. As the physical and spiritual successor to
thirty dynasties of pharaohs, Alexander hoped to win over the Egyptians
for the Greek world empire that he was building, and the foundation of
the new capital was a means to this end. As it happened, it was Alexander's
empire that fell to pieces after his death, while Egypt, under a line of
Macedonian rulers, became Hellenised. For centuries Alexandria was the
spiritual world capital of Hellenism.

From the outset the city was laid out on grandiose lines as an imperial
residence. Ptolemy I Soter, one of Alexander's generals, mounted the throne
of the pharaohs. He and his successors fetched scholars and artists from all
over the world to their court. Apelles, the most famous painter of antiquity,
and Euclid, one of the greatest mathematicians the world has seen, were
summoned to Alexandria. Demetrius of Phaleron it was who suggested the
foundation of the famous library, which both because of its size and the
importance of its contents was to assume a unique position in the ancient
world.

Ptolemy II Philadelphus, who reigned from 285 to 247 B.C., founded the
'Museum' – the University of Alexandria. It was an entire city district
consisting of palaces devoted to the arts of poetry and rhetoric, and to the
sciences. The Alexandria School of Medicine, which propagated the teaching of Hippocrates, led the world. Among the many famous scientists and
philosophers who taught at this university was the greatest astronomer and
geographer of antiquity, Claudius Ptolemaeus. It was his model of the
universe that dominated medieval astronomy and was superseded only
by that of Copernicus and Galileo.

But the building of palaces was only the beginning of Ptolemy II's services
to scholarship, which he furthered in every way. The translation of the Old
Testament into Greek was undertaken at his orders.

Alexandria was the city in which people, religions, opinions and merchandise from all countries of the Mediterranean came into contact with the
riches and the cultural heritage of Egypt. Here Ethiopian met Gaul, Syrian
Spaniard, or Scythian Carthaginian. The city was filled with an intelligent,
open-minded, sceptical, pleasure-seeking populace that was capable of

being roused to as much excitement over a philosophical theory as over the result of a horse race. Revolts were frequent. Alexandria's industry outstripped all competitors, and the skilfulness of its craftsmen was proverbial. The night life of the city, with its moonlit canals along which gondolas passed to and fro by the light of torches, was world-famous. The bankers of Alexandria were international financiers. The port was a centre of worldwide trade and commerce.

The city contained also the Mausoleum, in which the body of Alexander the Great lay embalmed in honey in a glass coffin.

During the centuries in which Christianity was spreading through Egypt, the face of Alexandria was gradually transformed. Not only the peoples and merchandise of the Orient but also their ideas and customs and proverbial Eastern luxury poured into the city, which itself became more and more oriental. The Emperor Trajan ordered the restoration of the canal between the Nile and the Red Sea, 160 feet broad, which had first been constructed under the pharaohs. A merchant ship could then sail from Lyons on the Rhone to Ceylon in the Indian Ocean.

Egypt played its part in all three of the great heresies of early Christianity. Arius, who disputed the divine nature of Christ, first preached his doctrine in Alexandria. Nestorius, who taught that Mary was not the mother of God but only the mother of Jesus' human nature, was, indeed, Patriarch of Constantinople, but it was Cyril of Alexandria who took up the fight against him. Nestorius was later banished to an oasis in the Libyan Desert on the borders of the Fayûm, and there died, without the least inkling that his doctrine would one day spread as far as Peking.

The third of these heresies, which was to have the most important consequences for Egypt, was that of Eutyches. Eutyches was abbot of a monastery

237

near Constantinople in the early part of the fifth century. He taught that Christ did not have two natures, a human and a divine, as maintained by dogma, but that after the union of the two natures He had only one nature – μόνη φύσις (mone physis), that of the word become flesh. From these two Greek words the doctrine got its name – Monophysite.

The Christian Church in Egypt evolved into the Coptic Church, which was separated from the rest of the Christian world by this one fundamental dogma, and has maintained itself in isolation, through the Arab conquest of Egypt, down to the present day.

Under the Arabs Alexandria sank gradually into oblivion. Very little now remains of the past glories of this once wonderful city. When Napoleon arrived in Egypt, it was a small Arab provincial town of not more than five thousand inhabitants. Today, of course, it is again a great city with modern buildings and an important harbour.

North Africa, from the time of its first conquest by the Romans, beginning in 147 B.C. with the destruction of Carthage, until its conquest by the Arabs at the end of the seventh century, was one of the most flourishing provinces of the Roman Empire. Moreover, after the coming of Christianity, North Africa was the strongest bastion of the new faith in the West.

For the recognition of Christianity by the Emperor Constantine did not bring with it the extinction of all opposition to the new faith inside the Empire. Its enemies were placed on the defensive, and probably later driven underground, but the old pagan worship of Greece and Rome did not vanish overnight, and for generations, at least until the time of Justinian, the public debate between the Christians and the pagan die-hards was a main preoccupation of the fathers of the Church.

It is true that the attempted revival of paganism by Julian the Apostate, who became emperor only twenty-four years after Constantine's death, seems to have met with little success. But his reign was short – only two years – and he concentrated his efforts in the East, where Christianity was strongest. It was in the West that paganism was most tenacious, not least in Rome itself, where the aristocracy long remained loyal to a State religion with which many of their own privileges had been associated.

One of the strongest arguments in the armoury of Christianity's opponents was that the misfortunes which visited the Roman Empire at about this time were a punishment for neglect of the old gods. The conquest of Rome by Alaric, the King of the Goths, in A.D. 410 was not only a political and military, but above all a spiritual catastrophe. Rome had lasted a thousand years under its pagan gods. Less than a generation after the Emperor

Theodosius had proclaimed Christianity as the Roman State religion, the ancient and eternal city itself fell into the hands of the barbarians. It did not need much superstition to see in this unimaginable disaster the wrath of the gods of Olympus, whose annual games had been discontinued only sixteen years before.

This argument was of serious concern to the Church. St Augustine, seeking to prove that the fall of Rome had nothing to do with the Christian faith, pointed out that the Christian churches in Rome were spared in the sack of the city. This exemption was on the orders of King Alaric himself, who was a Christian even though of the Arian persuasion.

At the time of the Gothic invasion thousands of refugees fled from Italy into Africa, which was prosperous enough to absorb them, and which remained a bulwark of the faith and of Christian obedience.

Subsequently the Arab conquest completely extinguished Christianity in Africa, apart from Egypt. We know that Augustine himself spoke Punic; he very possibly appointed as his helpers only Punic-speaking priests. But it is probable that Christianity had not a firm enough hold on the native population by the time the Arabs came. It is clear that there was no Punic Bible nor any literature in this language. After the conquest the Roman Christians in the cities must have departed elsewhere, while in the coun- tryside Christianity quickly died out.

In Syria, Anatolia, and Africa Christianity lost its most populous pro- vinces to Islam at a time when the conversion of the peoples of the north was only just beginning. It is quite possible that there were fewer Christians in the world in A.D. 1000 than there had been in A.D. 500.

No other European nation has a culture as old as Spain's. No other European nation contains such a diverse mixture of races and peoples as the inhabitants of the Iberian Peninsula. No other has evolved such a char- acteristic and uniform national style as that which the Spaniards call 'Hispanidad'.

Gades, the modern Cadiz, situated beyond the Pillars of Hercules on the Atlantic southern coast of Spain, is the oldest city in Europe. It was founded by the Phoenicians about 1100 B.C. The port was famous for its trade in tin and amber. On Spain's northern Atlantic coast the Basques, to judge from the antiquity of their language, may well be descended from that Palaeolithic people which in the caves of Altamira 16,000 years ago created the first works of art on European soil. In the seventh and sixth centuries B.C. Celts pushed down into Spain from the north and mingled with the original Iberian population. About the same time Phocian Greeks from

Marseilles, an early Greek colony, began founding colonies in Spain. For three years Iberia came under the dominion and cultural influence of Carthage. Today the city of Segovia still bears its Carthaginian name. When in 202 B.C. the Romans came to Spain, after the end of the Second Punic War, they found a highly developed culture already in existence there, compounded of Celtic, Iberian, Phoenician, and Greek elements.

Few countries of the Mediterranean owe so much to Roman statesmanship as Spain. Caesar took Roman colonists there and conferred rights of Roman citizenship on certain cities. Augustus ordered the conquest of the Asturias and Cantabria, thus extending Roman rule to the Bay of Biscay. Gifted Spaniards were soon appearing in positions of prominence in Rome itself. Seneca, philosopher and statesman, Martial, the poet, and Quintilian, the critic, were Spaniards, and the Emperors Trajan and Hadrian, both Andalusians, were the first provincials to ascend the imperial throne. The Emperor Theodosius the Great, who made Christianity into the Roman State religion, came from Galicia in the extreme north-west of Spain.

Under later Roman rule the Christian Church became a powerful force in Spain, and the first barbarian invasions did not reverse this development, since the Visigoths, who conquered Spain at the beginning of the fifth century, entered the country as Arian Christians, and less than a century later, in A.D. 587, under their King Reccared, went over to orthodox Catholicism.

The Arabs, who were the next invaders, were never able to conquer Spain entirely. The North remained Christian, and from there it was that the Reconquest was launched. After a struggle lasting for centuries the followers of the Prophet were finally driven out of the whole Spanish Peninsula. Spain became the most powerful country in Europe and was also the first to plant Christianity in a new continent. Once more, for the first time since the days of Constantine and Justinian, a Christian world empire came into being, an empire on which, in the famous words of the Emperor Charles V, the sun never set.

The Maltese cross of the year 808

is the work of a Visigoth goldsmith in Spain. It is now in the treasure-house of the Cathedral of Oviedo. Beautifully executed in gold filigree studded with jewels, semi-precious stones, and cameos, it is remarkable evidence of the artistic capacities of the new Europe which was rising on the ruins of the classical world.

PHAROS

The Pharos of Alexandria

was one of the 'seven wonders of the world'. It was a lighthouse for shipping built by Ptolemy II Philadelphus, and was higher than the Great Pyramid. Nothing remains of it today except the name, which is still the word for lighthouse in several of the world's languages. The same King Ptolemy II, who is seen on this very fine and well-preserved coin with his Queen Antionoe, also founded the famous Museum.

The Macedonian dynasty of the Ptolemies gave Egypt a series of very able rulers. The dynasty ended with a Queen, Cleopatra, who as a historic personage must have exercised a good deal of the fascination ascribed to her by poets and dramatists. By Julius Caesar she had a son, Caesarion, who like his father was assassinated.

Along the magnificent avenues of Alexandria
there wandered in A.D. 43 through the milling crowds two plainly dressed men. They had come from Palestine. One of them tore his shoe and they went to a cobbler to have it mended. The cobbler fumbled and his awl slipped and wounded him in the hand. In the shock of the accident he did not swear but called out 'Praise be to God'.

The owner of the shoe thereupon resolved that he would stay on in this Sodom in which there was at least one righteous man and preach the word of God. He healed the cobbler's hand and baptised him. He was the Apostle Mark, and his companion, who went on to another city, was Peter. Mansueto painted this picture, below, of St Mark healing the cobbler.

And so the cobbler Annainos, according to this tradition of the Christian Church of Egypt, became Alexandria's first Christian. After the death of St Mark he was the second Bishop of the Egyptian Church. Alexandria, like Rome, possesses a list of all its bishops, beginning with an apostle.

The bones of St Mark were for a long time objects of reverence in Alexandria, but in A.D. 829 a Venetian brought them back with him to Venice, where they are preserved to this day.

The most famous theologian of the Alexandrian school, known as the Catechetic, which was already in existence towards the end of the second century, was Origen. He was a scholar of Hebrew and a man of very wide education. He was strongly influenced by Plato's doctrine of ideas, which regarded 'ideas' as the sole reality and contrasted them with the material world of appearances. He wrote excellent commentaries on the Bible, and was the first to give a systematic philosophical account of Christian doctrine. His library is said to have contained six thousand volumes. He had an enduring influence on Christian theology even though his own theology was later condemned by the Church.

Even more famous than Origen was St Catherine of Alexandria. According to legend she was a member of one of the city's aristocratic families, and was studying at the University when a vision of the Virgin Mary with the Child converted her to Christianity. When the Emperor Maxentius ordered a new persecution of Christians, she obtained an audience of him, since he happened to be visiting Alexandria. The Emperor was so struck by the beauty of the young girl student that he gave orders that she should defend her attacks upon his gods before fifty philosophers. The scene is shown in the picture above. But the philosophers, too, were overcome by her beauty and dialectical skill and declared with one voice that Catherine had convinced them. Maxentius then offered her honours and riches, but she refused them all. She was scourged and sentenced to be broken on the wheel but the instrument of execution shattered at her touch. It has been the emblem of St Catherine ever since. She was ultimately beheaded, and angels carried her body to Mount Sinai. Her bones were taken in charge by the monks of the monastery built there and named after her.

St Catherine of Alexandria has been greatly revered throughout the Christian world. Among the voices that summoned the Maid of Orleans to the liberation of France was the voice of St Catherine.

A hundred generations of farmers,
thirty dynasties of pharaohs, three millennia of
history made up the past heritage of Egyptian
civilisation when the Apostle Mark brought the
Gospel to the land of the Nile. The number and
variety of deities worshipped was bewildering.
The animal, the human, and the divine were
mingled in these deities in a manner as alien to the
Greek as to the Jewish mind. Yet at the same time
the Egyptian religion had its metaphysical side,
for the Egyptians believed in the immortality of
the human soul, and it is to this belief that we owe
the vast memorial tombs of the pharaohs, the
Pyramids. The idea of resurrection after death
found its religious symbolisation in the myth of
Isis and Osiris. The whole life of the ancient
Egyptian was regulated by strict rites and moral
prescriptions, so that the Gospel here encountered
a mind very receptive to the new doctrine. But
the Egyptian traditions were of such overwhelming antiquity and so deeply planted in the souls of
this religious people that they could never be
entirely forgotten.

In a grave in Alexandria there was found a unique
small clay flask, or ampulla. The relief shows a
man in the attitude of prayer, the same attitude as
is found elsewhere in early Christian art, but in
this case we find not Christian symbols, but to
right and left of the worshipper the ancient sacred
animal of Egypt and the Nile – two crocodiles.
Even more remarkable is the head, below, with
the cap adorned with a cross. It is a vessel in
which incense was burnt. Despite the cross and
the alpha and omega engraved in the metal, this
object belongs not to the Christian world but to
the Benin culture of West Africa. The south coast
of the Mediterranean is separated from Africa
proper by the Sahara. But Egypt was always linked with the interior of Africa by routes through

245

the Sudan and Ethiopia. The Benin censer, otherwise unexplained, may be evidence that Christian tokens, at least, reached the west coast of Africa by some such route.

Ruined masonry in the desert

bears witness to an ancient place of Christian pilgrimage. Not far from Alexandria the Church of St Menas of Maryut was excavated fifty years ago. St Menas was probably a simple camel herd who because of his Christian love of his neighbours and his devotion to the faith was revered by his small desert congregation. He can never have dreamed that Christ himself would one day put his arm about his shoulder, as here depicted in this sixth-century Coptic painting, which today hangs in the Louvre. After a life of simple piety, Menas died at the end of the third or beginning of the fourth century and was buried by his fellow herdsmen near a spring.

His posthumous fame was due to a sick sheep. The sheep wandered to this spot, drank from the spring, and was restored to health. It may be supposed that it needed some special miracle to persuade Egyptian peasants to overcome their traditional horror of herdsmen, who were subject to an age-old taboo. But the news of the healing powers of the spring spread quickly, and sick people began coming from far and near to drink its waters.

A small church was built, and in course of time the saint's grave became a

famous place of pilgrimage that attracted pilgrims from all over the world.
In A.D. 400 the Emperor Arcadius erected a splendid basilica, the ruins of
which are shown in the picture.

The ampulla, one of those in which the pilgrims would take home holy oil
from the lamp which burned in the church, shows St Menas in the attitude
of prayer between two camels.

247

To leave the world's pageant

and go into the desert, there to seek peace of soul in the solitude of contemplation, is a very ancient Egyptian tradition. There have been hermits in Egypt since the earliest times.

The first Christian hermit of whom we have record was Paul of Thebes. In the middle of the third century, during the persecutions under the Emperor Decius, he fled into the desert. The picture shows the monastic establishment that grew up later on the spot where the saint had lived.

His days were spent in prayer and repentance. The palm tree provided him with food and clothing, and every day a crow came and brought him bread.

The story of his life and death has been told us by St Jerome. When Paul of Thebes was 113 years old, he received a visit from St Anthony, who at that time was only ninety. During his visit the crow, under the instructions of its heavenly paymaster, brought a double ration of bread. The two aged and venerable hermits sat side by side, exchanging not a word, but saying their prayers. Eventually Paul of Thebes died in the arms of St Anthony.

But the old man was too weak to bury his dead companion unaided, and eventually two lions appeared and dug a grave with their paws.

These and many other incidents in the lives of St Paul and his fellow hermits are shown in this remarkable painting by Starnina, which hangs in the Uffizi. In his eagerness to depict as many scenes as possible the artist has peopled his desert with anchorites until it seems almost as crowded as the world which they have left behind.

The first monastery of Christendom

was founded by St Anthony. The son of wealthy parents, he was born in A.D. 252 in the neighbourhood of Heracleopolis Magna in the Fayûm. At twenty he inherited a great fortune. One day in church he heard a reading of the passage in the New Testament (Matthew XIX, 21) in which Jesus says to the rich young man: 'If thou wilt be perfect, go and sell that thou hast, and give to the poor, and thou shalt have treasure in heaven; and come and follow me.' Anthony did what the young man had not done. He gave away all his possessions and followed the Lord.

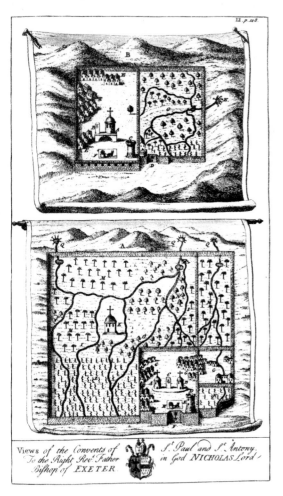

In these early centuries we frequently hear of a similar lightning stroke of illumination determining the whole future course of a person's life. Such an event can best be explained as having been the culmination of a long antecedent process of internal development. Anthony withdrew to a tomb on the edge of the desert and there lived in complete solitude for fifteen years. In the desert the stars shine more clearly, the sunsets and sunrises are of greater brilliance, and the vast emptiness of the landscape seems to bring God closer to man. It can scarcely be an accident that the idea of a unique transcendent God first grew up among a desert people. But the desert is filled, too, with wild beasts and is easily believed to be the home of demons, ghosts, and devils. And a throng of uncouth beings such as these are always represented as assisting at the famous temptations of St Anthony in his desert refuge, a subject that has inspired many artists.

The fame of the hermit began to spread. He was soon joined by others, who established themselves round about. Eventually Anthony acceded to the request of his brother hermits that he would take over the leadership of a small community. He gave up his solitary existence and devoted himself for five or six years to organising a communal way of life. The first community of monks, the first monastery of Christendom, was the result. In the life story of St Anthony as sketched out by Athanasius, the Patriarch of Alexandria, there is a reference to the surprise of the other hermits at finding the saint in such radiant bodily health. His mortifications and asceticism were not reflected in his appearance.

The picture shows the ground plan of the Monastery of St Anthony and that of the monastery which was founded on the grave of Paul of Thebes after that saint's death. St Anthony spent the second half of his life once

more in solitude. This time he built his hermitage by the Red Sea on a mountain that still bears his name today.

The saint on two subsequent occasions left his solitary cell, once in A. D. 311 to comfort some Christians condemned to martyrdom, and once again forty years later, to preach against the Arians. He lived on to see the triumph of the Christian faith.

It was not long before a number of other monasteries were founded in Egypt. St Pachomius of Tabennisi, which lies to the north of Luxor, drew up the first monastic rule, formulating the principles of asceticism.

St Macarius began his adult life as a sweet-merchant. He is the patron saint of pastrycooks. At forty years of age he withdrew from urban life and founded in the Libyan desert, at what is now Wadi Natrun, a monastery that still stands. The bare monastery walls, seen in the picture above, contain a church, the monks' cells, the working quarters, and a flourishing garden in the midst of these dusty salpetre wastes. There is something elevating in the thought that in this forsaken corner of earth, in this little church built of mud bricks, the praises of God have been chanted by the monks every day for the past fifteen hundred years, just as they are chanted today.

St Anthony died in A.D. 356 at the age of 104. In deference to the saint's own wishes, the site of his grave was kept secret.

A dominant personality

of Church life in Egypt in the middle of the fourth century was St Athanasius, Patriarch of Alexandria. It was he who at the Council of Nicaea was the great opponent of Arius. He was, moreover, the creator of hagiography, the writing of histories of the saints. Finally, it was he who, on a visit to Rome, brought to the West the first tidings of the foundation of the

monasteries in Egypt. The mosaic above, which bears his portrait, is to
be found in the Baptistery of St Mark's in Venice.

By the traditions of a unique civilisation stretching back to the dawn of
history the Egyptians, as we have already seen, were set apart from the other
peoples hellenised by the conquests of Alexander the Great. In religion, as
in politics, separatist tendencies began very early on to show themselves in
Christian Egypt, and in the long run these proved stronger than the orthodoxy even of such commanding figures as St Athanasius and of the Alexandrian school of theology. The monophysite heresy of Eutyches, who
preached the single nature of Christ, gained more and more adherents. The
resulting doctrinal controversies were of such bitterness that a new Catholic
bishop who mounted the pulpit one Good Friday to preach his inaugural
sermon was murdered in church. The Byzantine emperors exerted extraordinary efforts to restore religious peace to Egypt, the most valuable and
important part of their dominions. They were unsuccessful. Instead there
arose a sort of national Egyptian church, the Coptic Church. Though cut
off from the rest of Christendom by the rise of Islam, it has remained a
living force up to our own day.

The new piety,

which was the creation of the Gospel, that spirit of transcendence which gave a new other-worldly dimension to human life, generated in every people which received it a new art. The diversity of Christian art almost defies any attempt to give a unified account of it. For everywhere the artists worked with the old traditional forms, infusing into them the new spirit. Coptic Christianity has produced an abundance of artistic treasures. The fresco below is from the Wadi Sarga and shows St Cosmas and St Damian with their three younger brothers, each identified by name at his head. The picture in the centre, above the three younger brothers, is of earlier date. Its subject is the scene from the book of Daniel (III, 25), where the three Jewish administrators, Shadrach, Meshach, and Abed-nego, were thrown by Nebuchadnezzar into the burning fiery furnace because they had refused to worship the image of gold he had set up. All at once the king to his astonishment saw four men walking in the midst of the fire, without any hurt, and the form of the fourth was like a heavenly being, a guardian angel sent by the Lord to protect the three men. Of the martyrdom of Cosmas and Damian it is recorded that they, too, survived burning at the stake. Thus the painter, wishing to depict the two saints and their three brothers, incorporated the earlier wall painting in his own.

The capital with the eagle and the two ram's heads, above, is a particularly fine example of the high relief that is so characteristic of Coptic art. It comes from a church in Antinoe, the ancient Antinoupolis, the city founded by the Emperor Hadrian in A.D. 130 in honour of Antinous, the youth he so much loved who was drowned in the Nile near by.

The cross with the disk, below, is also fifth-century. This symbol was already known in Egypt in pre-Christian times and is here surrounded by two laurel branches signifying eternal life. The alpha and the omega, the first and last letters of the Greek alphabet, to the right and left of the cross, are the symbol of Christ as the beginning and end of all things, according to The Revelation (XXII, 13).

The fragment of a fifth-century linen curtain, above, is a particularly precious relic. Only the dryness of the Egyptian climate has made it possible for textile materials to be so long preserved. The fragment shows an annunciation. Mary, seated left, is spinning, and between her and the Archangel Gabriel, right, are the Greek letters MAPIA – Maria.

'*Let us stand up among the ruins*
and not lie on the ground with
those who are without hope!'
All the unshakable courage, the
joy of living, and confidence in the
future with which the Gospel
inspired the early Christians to
face the persecution of the State is
contained in this utterance of Cyprian, Bishop of Carthage, in the
middle of the third century.

Not many such testimonies have
been preserved to us, and we know
altogether too little about the beginnings of Christianity in Roman
Africa. In A.D. 180 or thereabouts we hear of some martyrs there, and towards the end of the second century there was a great Christian community
in Carthage, its capital. It was about this time that 'the fierce Tertullian'
wrote his 'Defence of Christianity', in which he warned the anti-Christian
governor that, if the Christians were to leave Carthage in a body, he would
be horrified to discover how forlorn and lonely he would then be.

Cyprian was a teacher of rhetoric. He was already forty-five years old when
he had himself baptised. Of the life that he led from that day on he himself
says that it brought him peace and happiness. He was the author of numerous writings on questions of Christian dogma and morals.

When he had been nearly ten years Bishop of Carthage, he was summoned
before the Proconsul Galerius Maximus. The laconic record of his exami-
nation has been preserved for us.

'You are Thascius Cyprianus?' the Proconsul asked him.
'I am he.'
'You have made yourself the leader of these sacrilegious persons?'
'I have.'
'The most holy Emperors have commanded you to offer sacrifice.'
'I shall not do so.'
'Consider well.'

'Do what you have been commanded to do. There is nothing to consider in this matter.' Galerius, who evidently felt esteem for the personality who stood before him and was impressed by the stoicism of his bearing, took counsel with his lawyers. Then he gave judgment: 'You have constituted yourself the enemy of the gods of Rome and of its holy laws. Since not even our holy Emperors have prevailed upon you to return to their worship, your blood shall be shed in witness of their laws. We command that Cyprianus be put to death by the sword.' Cyprian answered: 'Deo gratias!' He was executed. Later he was canonised by the Church. The picture opposite shows Cyprian before his baptism, surrounded by magic utensils and idols of the heathen gods. It is a miniature from a Greek manuscript of the ninth century. The oil lamp, above, is of fired clay and was found in Timgad. It bears a relief of Christ with two angels. He stands on a lion and a snake, in accordance with the words of the psalmist (Psalms XCI, 13): 'Thou shalt tread upon the lion and the adder . . .'

A completely preserved font of the sixth century was excavated in 1952 in Qelibia, east of Carthage. In the picture below the inscription on the upper edge can be clearly identified. It dedicates the font to the 'Most blessed Saint Cyprian' – STO. BEATISSIMO CYPRIANO

Doctor Ecclesiae,

Doctor of the Church, was the title of honour conferred on St Augustine by a grateful Christendom. Augustine spent the first half of his life in becoming a Christian, the second in being one. Fra Angelico has depicted, below, the moment of his conversion. With Augustine Christianity enters the Latin world, and does so, one might almost say, with a flourish of trumpets. It was he who breathed new life into the Latin language and put to new uses that refined instrument of expression which successive generations of writers and thinkers had made of it; and this although he was himself an African, descended from the ancient Carthaginian enemies of Rome.

Of course a Latin Christianity did exist in the West before the time of St Augustine. But it was in Africa, with Tertullian, that a Latin Christian literature first began. With St Augustine Latin Christianity attained the spiritual importance needed to place it on an equal footing with the Christianity of the Greek Orient.

From the earliest times the Gospel appealed to many different kinds of person. This universality of appeal enabled it to bring spiritual truth to people not only of widely differing race and culture and social position but also of varying temperament and intellect. As Christianity grew and prospered, so the claims on its universality increased. In the fourth century the Christian mind began to gain the upper hand over the pagan; the Christian writers began to write better Greek and better Latin; the works of Christian art begin to excel those still inspired by paganism.

Augustine was born in A.D. 354 at Tagaste, in Numidia. His father was well enough off to lead an eventful life. His mother, Monica, was a pious Christian. We know of her from Augustine's writings, and she must have been a remarkable woman. All her life she was praying for two wild souls, first for that of her big-hearted, reckless husband, then for that of her brilliant and wayward son. Her prayers were answered. Her husband was baptised on his death-bed, her son in the year in which she herself died. The halo surrounding her head is the reward for a lifetime of patient devotion.

An account of his life has been given us by Augustine himself in his *Confessions*. This first great autobiography of world literature is of such frankness that it deeply shocked his contemporaries. For us the *Confessions* is a document of inestimable value, and it still makes fascinating reading. The writings of St Augustine determined

the course of Christian theology for the next thousand years. Martin Luther himself claimed to be going back to St Augustine. The chief work of the *Doctor Ecclesia*, the *Civitas Dei – City of God* – was the foundation of Church policy in the Middle Ages.

For the last thirty-four years of his life Augustine was Bishop of Hippo, near his home town of Tagaste. He lived with his priests in poverty and prayer. Property was held in common. Thus Augustine became the founder of the first monastic order in the Latin world. Nearly four hundred of his sermons have been preserved. He was an untiring writer and his sharp tongue was much feared.

In Augustine's time the Donatists were strong in Africa. Donatist teaching at first consisted of only one point, that sacred offices performed by priests who had once been apostate were invalid. The Church, realising that even priests were not exempt from human frailty, condemned this doctrine. But the Donatists maintained their standpoint, and their heresy eventually grew into a social revolution which the emperors countered by every means at their disposal. The fanaticism of the Donatists, who often used violence, was of course attributed to Christians generally and did their reputation a great deal of harm.

Augustine challenged Fortunatus, the Donatist bishop, to a duel of words. For two days the two bishops disputed before all the people in public debate in the city baths. Fortunatus, whose abilities were no match for his opponent's, then departed from Hippo.

Augustine's life ended during a time of great trouble for his city, which was being besieged by the Vandals. He did not live to see the final catastrophe. One year after his death Hippo, after a siege lasting fourteen months, was captured and completely destroyed.

Among the objects excavated on the site of Hippo in modern times is a remarkable liturgical comb, a fine piece of craftsmanship. It dates from the beginning of the fifth century, that is, from the time of Augustine. One side shows Daniel in the lion's den, the other a soldier escorting two people. Combs of this kind were used by the priests at mass, so that it is not impossible that St Augustine himself once handled this one.

Buried in the desert sand

are many records of the past still awaiting discovery. From time to time the archaeologist's spade, guided by perseverance and inspired guesses, brings something important to light. At Apollonia in Cyrenaica, there has just recently been excavated, in the apse of the eastern church, a mosaic from the beginning of the fifth century. It shows symbolic animals with a cross in the centre. In Qasr-ul-Lebia, a little country town fifty miles west of Cyrene, the old Byzantine church has been preserved. In this very modest building a number of fine mosaics have been found. The cheerful pagan river god, above, represents the Tigris, one of the four rivers of Paradise. It seems that the early Christian worshippers did not find anything discordant in the inclusion of such a figure in their church decorations.

A special position

is occupied by Tripoli in the history of the African Church. The marble remains of Leptis Magna and Sabratha, which give an impression of magnificence even as ruins, show what important and populous cities they were.

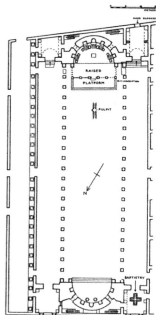

Archaeus was Bishop of Leptis Magna at the end of the second century. At the end of the third century there were bishops in Sabratha, Oea, and Gerba. We have no information, however, about the interior of the country, although there are many traces to indicate that Christianity was widespread among the mountain tribes. It had penetrated as far as Wadi Sofeggin on the borders of the Sahara, and Procopius records that in the reign of Justinian the inhabitants of Ghadames became converts. Ghadames is situated in the Fezzan, in the heart of the desert.

The security of the province was to a large extent dependent on the *limitanei,* frontier settlers organised on military lines, who were expected to defend the country against Bedouin raids from the desert. The authorities left these colonists in peace, since their own security depended on their loyalty. There were no martyrs in Tripolitania.

Donatism was widespread here, as in the whole of Roman Africa. In course of time the theological differences that gave rise to the movement were completely forgotten, but the Donatist Church, with its own bishops, became the native church. It lived on not through any theological opposition to the dogmas of the universal Christian Church but because of political opposition to its representatives, regarded as the agents also of colonial rule. So it came about that in the whole of Africa the coast was Catholic, the interior Donatist.

The picture above shows a pagan basilica that was built in Leptis Magna by the Emperor Severus and then converted into a Church by the Emperor Justinian. The existing ground plan was retained but at either end of the

main nave an apse was added to the basilica and in each of the four corners a chapel was built. The ruins are today still very impressive.

Sabratha had three periods of prosperity. At the end of the fifth century B.C. the Phoenicians had a great settlement here. At the end of the second century B.C. the Romans came, and in the middle of the fifth century A.D. the Vandals conquered the city and destroyed it so thoroughly that no stone remained standing on another. After the Vandals had been expelled again under Justinian, there was another short period of prosperity in a rebuilt Byzantine city. A church dating from this period, which has been excavated, was situated between the forum and the harbour.

Pieces of marble from ancient temples were used in the rather rough external structure of this church. But its floor, by contrast, was done in mosaic and is among the finest examples known to us anywhere. Two particularly charming details are the cock and the peacock under the bunches of grapes on the vine. This third period of prosperity was ended by the Arab invasion.

was one day to have its metropolis in Spain. But fifteen centuries were to elapse, from the first appearance of Christianity in that country, before this empire came into being and reached its peak of development, during the reigns of the Emperor Charles V and King Philip II. Perhaps it was the Apostle Paul himself who gave the first impulse to this long train of historical events. It is possible that he did carry out his intention of visiting Spain and was actually the first to preach the gospel in the far west as in so many other parts of the Roman Empire. However, there is no historical evidence for such a journey.

Otherwise we have almost no information about the beginnings of Christianity in Spain. But there are references to Christian churches there, by Irenaeus of Lyons in the second century, and by Tertullian in the third century.

The first certain record we possess is a letter of Cyprian, Bishop of Carthage, written to the brethren in Spain, and from this we learn that in his time there were bishops in Leon, Astorga, Merida, and Saragossa.

Fructuosus, Bishop of Tarragona, the capital of the Roman province of Spain, with two of his deacons suffered death by martyrdom in the city amphitheatre in A.D. 259. Fifty years later a synod was held in Elvira, the city that today is called Granada, and attended by bishops from all parts of Spain. On this occasion we learn that Christian usage in this land of many traditions was rather lax. The fact was mentioned at the synod that certain Christians were allowed with impunity to exercise the functions of pagan priests. The picture shows part of a fifth-century marble sarcophagus with the figures of Adam and Eve. It is one of the very few examples of early Christian art to be found in Spain.

One piece of architectural evidence

for the lively interchange of ideas among the Christians of the Roman world empire is San Miguel in Tarrasa. Tarrasa is the ancient Egara, and the Baptisterium of Egara, still extant today, is mentioned for the first time in A.D. 450.

It was not only theological disputes that travelled through the Christian communities of the Roman Empire, from Edessa in Mesopotamia to Egara in Spain, from one end of the Mediterranean to the other, but also artistic ideas. San Miguel in Tarrasa has a single central structure with a polygonal eastern apse, a ground plan unique in Spain. It was inspired by pagan Roman models and early Christian buildings based on them in Ravenna.

In the middle of the Baptisterium lies the ancient seven-sided font, in which the candidates for baptism were once completely immersed. They had to be naked, lest a demon might conceal itself in some piece of their clothing.

265

was the occupation of Spain by the Visigoths.

In A.D. 428 King Gaiseric with his Vandals invaded Spain. The whole of this wandering people numbered only eighty thousand men, women, and children. They were a warrior horde in whom the migratory urge and the lust for conquest were indistinguishable, and neither were satisfied for long by the concrete reality of what they had gained in Spain. They looked for fresh adventures, and thought they had found them when they heard in Spain of the legendary wealth of Africa. So when they were attacked in their turn by the Visigoths, they simply moved on, took ship across the Straits of Gibraltar, conquered Carthage, and founded their African kingdom.

Spain, which had been only superficially plundered in passing by the Vandals, was left without military protection for its wealth. So at the beginning of the fifth century the Visigoths started to move down into Spain from Aquitania, the south-western province of Gaul. They had to drive off some Suebi who had invaded the defenceless country, but encountered nothing in the way of more serious resistance. They demanded from every landowner the surrender of two-thirds of his cultivated land. This redistribution of land was called *Sortes Gothicae*, two words which must have struck terror into the hearts of Spanish landowners. But the Goths politely described the proprietors, whose land they thus confiscated, as *hospites* (hosts) and transfers of property seem to have proceeded in a more or less peaceful fashion. The 'hosts' came to some sort of terms with their unwelcome guests. Under King Athanagild, who reigned from A.D. 551 to 567, Toledo became the capital of the Visigoth kingdom.

The differences between Spaniards and Visigoths were more political than

religious, for the Visigoths were Arians. But they did not succeed in destroying the well-knit Catholic Church in Spain, and eventually the Visigoth King Reccared in 587 went over to Catholicism. His people followed his example, and the great heresy of Arius, which had continued to endanger Catholic orthodoxy for two and a half centuries after its condemnation by the Council of Nicaea, lost its last political support point and vanished from history.

The sarcophagus illustrated opposite was found in Briviescas. The wheel-like object in the centre is the Christian symbol said to have been devised by Constantine the Great for his imperial standard. But the workmanship is rough and what the figures mean is not known.

Some of the churches attributable to this period of Visigoth rule in Spain have been preserved, and the most important of them is San Juan Bautista de Baños. An inscription in this church records that it was built by King Recceswinth. The exterior is shown below.

Another well-preserved church is San Pedro de la Nave in Zamorra. The capital, above, shows the characteristic style of this pre-romanesque Catalan art. The artistic creations of the Visigoths had an important influence on the development of European architecture.

King Recceswinth's crown,
a marvellous example of the goldsmith's craft, is evidence of the love of display and the artistic appreciation of the Visigoth rulers. The crown is of gold, richly adorned with pearls and sapphires. The jewelled pendants round the rim are letters making up the name of the royal donor, for these crowns were dedicated by the Visigoth kings to the Church.

Though the northern invaders of the Roman Empire were technically barbarians, they not only had cultures of their own but the first-comers, at least, had been exposed for generations to the influence of the Roman civilisation. Living on the Roman borders, they had absorbed many elements of that civilisation and blended them with their own more primitive culture to make something new. Not all these cultural creations were destined to survive, and the Visigoth kingdom, for example, was of short duration. But it was ultimately the barbarians who built the new Christian Europe.

Under King Swinthila, who reigned from 611 to 636, the last bastions of the Byzantine Empire in Spain were destroyed. The Greeks, who for over a thousand years had contributed wealth, learning, science, and beauty to the life of Spain, were driven out. It was to be many centuries before Spain was again to know such well-being and freedom from fear as it had experienced under the rule of the Greek spirit and Roman law. King Recceswinth, who reigned from A.D. 649 to 672, introduced the Germanic law into Spain. Little more than a generation later the Arabs sailed across the Straits of Gibraltar. In the battle of Jerez de la Frontera King Roderick was killed and, bravely fighting, the Visigoth armies, and with them the first Visigoth empire, were overwhelmed.

The Arabs conquered Spain as far as Toledo. The mass of priceless treasures looted by the conquerors from the Toledo cathedral is said to have filled even the Caliph in Damascus with astonishment.

withdrew to the northern part of Spain. After a victory over the Moors at Covadonga in A.D. 722 King Pelayo founded a second Visigoth kingdom in the Asturias, the highland country in the north-west. The freedom-loving Goths took their piety and their artistic enthusiasm with them into their bleak mountain refuge. In A.D. 776 St Beatus of Libana published a commentary on The Revelation, of which some fine illuminated manu-scripts have been preserved from the ninth century. With this work St

que
e ap
lun
uccl
opá
duo
sat
hui
rpl
cut
ma
dep
obf
áro
ggc
apr
lud

NCIPIT EXPLANATIO SVPRASCRES

Beatus assured Gothic Spain of an honourable place in Christian literature.

In A.D. 830 a mysterious grave was discovered in Compostela, which is traditionally believed in Spain to be the grave of the Apostle James, San Jago in Spanish. Since the ninth century Santiago de Compostela has been one of the most important places of pilgrimage in Europe. A mystery play, 'The Miracle of St James', which has been performed for centuries, has given the Spanish people a picture of the Apostle as he appears in this late fifteenth-century Burgundian sculpture, a clever, kindly old man in the dress of a medieval pilgrim.

Though it no longer belongs to the early period, but to the Middle Ages, there is one famous object, the Arca Santa, which must be shown here on account of its historic importance. The Arca Santa is a shrine of cedarwood, encased in silver, and decorated with reliefs depicting scenes from the lives of Christ, the Virgin Mary, and the Apostles. The Shrine bears an inscription in Latin, and remarkably enough, also in Kufic (Arabic) script, according to which it was made in A.D. 1075. King Alfons the Great dedicated it to the Cathedral at Oviedo.

THANKS TO AN ACCIDENT of the earth's formation, Britain and Ireland both played a decisive part in one of the greatest cultural advances in human history. Bronze, the metal that gave its name to a whole age of man, is an alloy of copper and tin. The tin of almost all the Bronze-Age weapons, tools, and objects of art of the Mediterranean cultures came either from Ireland and Britain, or from Spain. At Falmouth there was traffic in tin at least as early as 1700 B.C., since a tin ingot of that date has been found there. It is cast in the same ox-hide shaped mould as ingots found in Crete.

The tin reached the Mediterranean by the sea route, calling at the ancient port of Tartessus on the south coast of Spain. About 525 B.C. the Carthaginian Admiral Himilko made a voyage to the 'Cassiterides', the mysterious tin islands, which must have been Britain and Ireland. Later on, the land route across Gaul was brought into use by Greek merchants in Marseilles for the transport of the precious metal. In the middle of the fourth century B.C. Pytheas of Marseilles made a famous voyage of exploration in which he sailed round the British Isles and found a sea route to Norway which was in use by the merchant ships of the seafaring northern peoples.

The oldest known population living in any part of the British Isles was related to the Iberians of ancient Spain. In the late Bronze Age Celts from the Continent moved across to the islands. Further Celtic invasions from about 500 B.C. onwards brought with them the iron culture of La Tène. But the first entry of the northern isles into history may be dated from Caesar's expedition to Britain in 55 B.C. A hundred years later, in A.D. 43, the whole southern half of Britain was dominated by the Romans. For three and a half centuries Britain was under their rule, with a protecting wall from coast to coast to keep out the Picts and Scots of the north, who were never conquered.

Roman Britain was a prosperous and peaceful country with numerous cities, good roads, and a flourishing trade with Gaul and the Mediterranean countries. Roman emperors were glad to visit Britain, and often did so. Yet this entire creation of Roman civilisation overseas was almost completely obliterated in the confusion of the Anglo-Saxon wars.

The raids on Britain by Saxon marauders had begun already in the middle of the fourth century A.D., at a time, that is, when it was still Roman. In the middle of the fifth century the ruling British monarch Vortigern had invited Saxons from the lower Elbe, so the story goes, to help him repel an invasion

by the ferocious Pictish tribes from the north.

The Saxons stayed, and having discovered that the land was undefended, sent the news back home. Hordes of Saxons, Angles, and Jutes began pouring into Britain, and the legendary kings Hengist and Horsa landed there from Schleswig-Holstein in A.D. 449. England has never been defended except by sea, and the Romans were the only conquerors who, having once set foot on the island, did not stay for good. Owing to this circumstance the population of Britain in time came to be made up of a mixture of races of which it can only be said that it proved its worth in history. In A.D. 577, in the battle of Deorham, the Germans finally defeated the Celtic Britons. Part of the defeated population fled to Wales, which has remained Celtic to this day. Others crossed the Channel to Gaul and there gave Brittany its name. The Christianisation of Britain, which had come about during the Roman period, was extinguished by these events, and the country had to be won over to Christianity all over again.

The second conquest of Britain by the Cross came from Ireland. In the middle of the fifth century St Patrick, a Celt from Wales, converted the Irish nation to Christianity. During his life, the monks of Ireland set out to win Anglo-Saxon Britain back to Christianity. The Irish mission had a rapid and thoroughgoing success, and within the next hundred years the whole of Britain became Christian. Soon Rome took a hand. In A.D. 590 Gregory the Great had become Pope, the first monk to ascend the throne of St Peter. He came from an old senatorial family, and as an aristocrat brought up in the Roman imperial tradition he may well have seen more clearly than others the importance for the future of Christianity of these vigorous and unsophisticated barbarian converts. Gregory had seriously considered going to Scotland himself as a missionary, but fortunately for Christianity he became Pope instead. He appointed a monk from his own monastery, Augustine by name, as papal legate and sent him to England.

273

In the course of the next fifty years there were violent disputes between the Irish-Celtic and the Roman Church in England. The feud was finally settled at the Synod of Whitby in A.D. 664. The majority of the Irish-Celtic bishops declared their readiness to accede to the Church of Rome, and the Irish-Celtic Church after some further centuries became completely assimilated.

The Roman Catholic Church of Anglo-Saxon Britain was almost immediately confronted by a great new task. At the end of the eighth century the Danes conquered the country, and the Church succeeded in converting the pagan conquerors to Christianity in only a few generations. When two hundred years later the Scandinavian Normans under William the Conqueror took possession of Britain, no further conversion was necessary, since the British had become Christian already. The British nation, which had come into being through the mixture of so many different peoples – Iberians, Celts, Angles, Jutes, Saxons, Danes, and Normans – was now launched on its eventful history.

During these centuries in which the new States of Europe were beginning to form, there were two outstanding historical achievements to the credit of the Irish. First, they sent a great number of missionaries to the continent, where large areas of central Europe were won over to Christianity. Secondly, while the continent was filled with the war cries of wandering barbarian hordes, on their quiet island they peacefully applied themselves to the arts and sciences. In the monasteries of this island on the edge of Europe a great deal of the classical heritage which would otherwise have been lost was preserved for later ages.

When Christian Europe had re-formed itself into its new national States, it could once more take up the classical tradition where it had been left off. The future of Christianity having been entrusted to the barbarians, the new peoples of Europe now also assumed the spiritual succession to the ancient Graeco-Roman civilisation of the Mediterranean. A classical-humanist Christian Europe was the result.

In the peace and stillness of a monastic cell in Jarrow from the end of the seventh till the middle of the eighth century, there lived a quiet, hard-working scholar. The Venerable Bede's great work was his Ecclesiastical History, which, fortunately for our knowledge of early Christianity in England, has been preserved.

A few drops of the blood of Christ,

according to an old legend, reached England. When Joseph of Arimathea and his son took the body of Christ from the Cross, it is related, some blood flowed and dripped on to the son's breast. Joseph caught it in two little flasks, which, according to the apocryphal 'Acta Pilati', he took with him when, in company with other Jews from Palestine, he accompanied the Apostle Philip to Gaul. In A.D. 63, the story continues, Joseph was put by Philip at the head of an expedition of twelve men who sailed to England. They landed on the coast of Wales and wandered inland till they came to the court of King Arviragus. The King, impressed by the great holiness of his guests, gave them the 'Isle of Glass' (Glastonbury). Here Joseph planted in the ground his staff, which, miraculously turning into a thorn-tree, blossomed ever after on Christmas Day. Later, at the command of the Archangel Gabriel, Joseph built a church of wattles, dedicated to the Virgin Mary, which is traditionally sited in the crypt of the Benedictine abbey shown in the picture. According to legend, Joseph was buried near the church, and the precious flasks were put into the grave with him.

Gildas, the British chronicler of the sixth century, says that the Gospel came to Britain in the last years of Tiberius's reign, that is, before A.D. 37.

The sower Arepo holds with care the wheels.

This rather nonsensical-sounding sentence is the translation of five Latin words arranged in the form of a word-square – reading the same across as down. The words, incised in plaster, were found in 1868 on the wall of a Roman house in Cirencester.

The house dates from the second half of the first century, and the word-square is a cryptogram, a coded message. It is in fact the earliest Christian inscription yet found in Britain. For the letters can be so ordered that they form a cross, which again reads the same across as down, giving the two words 'Pater Noster' – 'Our Father' – enclosed between the Alpha and the Omega, the symbols of Christ.

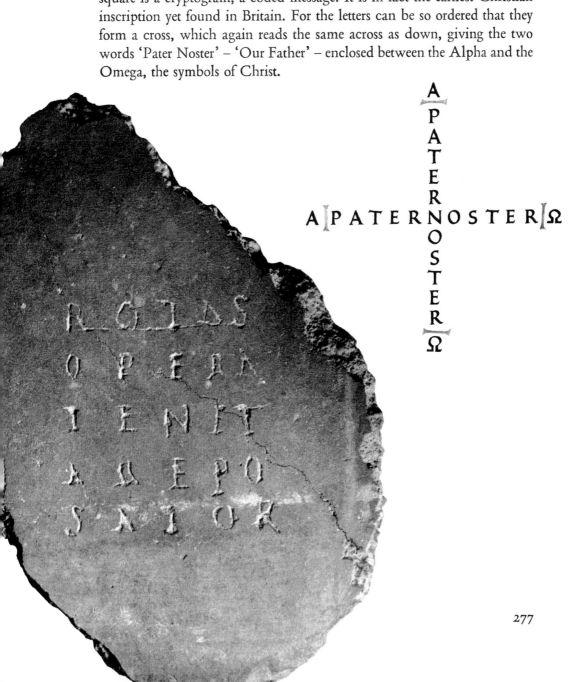

```
            A
            P
            A
            T
            E
            R
A P A T E R N O S T E R Ω
            O
            S
            T
            E
            R
            Ω
```

A British pewter bowl,

an ancient mosaic, and fragments of a fresco belong to the few archaeological evidences so far discovered in support of the literary tradition that Christianity made an early entry into Roman Britain. According to this tradition a Bishop of London attended the Council of Arles in A.D. 314, and the pewter bowl, which was excavated in London, does at least confirm that there were Christians there as early as this. For it is decorated with the monogram of Christ, the Christogram, made up of the first two letters of the name Christ in Greek, X (= Chi, ch) and P (= Rho, r). The mosaic from Frampton in Dorset, to judge from its outline, must have been the floor of a Christian chapel. Since its discovery less than a century ago, unfortunately, the mosaic has been destroyed. Fortunately an exact contemporary drawing of the find has been preserved, and shows that here too, as in all the countries of antiquity, pagan and Christian elements have been cheerfully associated. In Lullingstone, in the villa of a rich man, there was a room which was clearly a Christian chapel. The rich man of Lullingstone seems to have become Christian in the last years of the reign of the Emperor Constantius, who died in A.D. 361. From the rubble of his house the archaeologists have reconstructed

278

piece by piece a mural in one of the first-floor rooms. It is a fresco of seven columns alternating with six human figures, standing, with arms raised above their heads in what was at that time the attitude of prayer. The illustration, right, shows one of these figures, which is probably a portrait of a member of the family. The whole is the earliest instance yet found in England of a room which was used for Christian purposes.

The first British martyr

was St Alban. He was a soldier in one of the legions stationed in Britain, and his death occurred in the course of the last persecutions of Christians before the reign of Constantine the Great.

The place of execution to which St Alban was led lay on a hill. Bede, in his later account of this event, says that the hill was entirely overgrown with wild flowers and by reason of its beauty worthy to be consecrated with the blood of a blessed martyr.

The illustration, below, shows the building of the monastery that was founded in the martyr's honour in the ninth century, in the city named after him, St Albans.

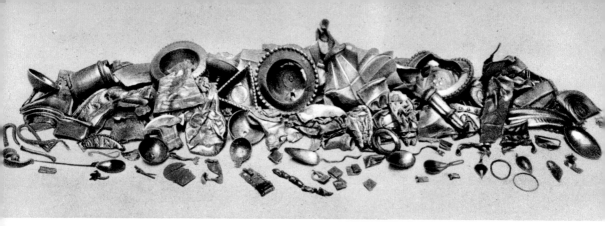

A buried treasure and three ancient stones

are evidence of the decline of Christianity in Roman Britain. In A.D. 325 the British Church gave its recognition to the resolutions of the Council of Nicaea. In 359 three British bishops took part in the Council of Ariminum, the modern Rimini. The Pax Romana was at that time still unbroken, allowing the journey to be made in perfect safety, but the three British bishops were so poor that the Emperor Constantius paid their expenses out of his own pocket.

As Britain was gradually denuded of Roman troops, the pagans began to assert themselves once more. Buried treasure is the only mark left to us of tragedies of which we shall never know the details. The illustration, above, shows a treasure of Roman silver of the fourth century, which was found in Traprain Law, a Scottish settlement south of the Forth. From the manner in which the treasure was divided it has been inferred that it was left by two robber bands, Picts or Britons, who were surprised before they could bring their plunder into safety. Among the objects in the treasure is a silver spoon with the Christogram (below). It was the custom among the Romans to present a child at birth with a silver spoon. This custom was taken over by the Christians and has been kept alive to this day. This charmingly graceful silver spoon is the oldest christening present known to us anywhere.

A similar treasure has been found in Mildenhall, in the south of England, where it must have been buried by a wealthy Roman during the first Saxon invasions. It also contains a silver spoon with a Christogram, to which the Alpha and Omega have been added. The Traprain Law spoon from the north has been preserved because it was carried off by robbers, the Mildenhall spoon from the south because it was hidden in time to prevent robbers getting it.

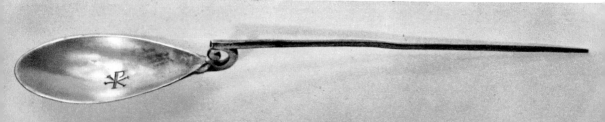

The three memorial stones come from Wales. In the inhospitable uplands, as they then were, of ancient Britain, Christianity was able to maintain itself after the withdrawal of the Romans.

The first stone, which comes from Penmachno in North Wales, is engraved with the Christogram, and belongs to the late fifth century. We do not know who the Carausius of the inscription below the Christogram is, but the name indicates a Roman ancestry. About the end of the third century a Roman admiral of this name rose up against Rome and established a brief sovereignty as 'Emperor of Britain' – a title that sounds as if it might have been invented by Bernard Shaw.

On the second stone the inscription is surmounted by a wheel-cross and refers to a King Voteporix, who is mentioned by the chronicler Gildas as a King of South Wales in the sixth century. He calls himself 'PROTICTOR', a title reserved for members of the imperial bodyguard. It seems clear that Voteporix must have travelled widely about the world before assuming the kingship in his Welsh home. Evidently, too, he made himself thoroughly conversant with the manners and customs of the barbarous age in which he lived, for Gildas says of him that he was full of trickery and committed many murders and many adulteries, the unworthy son of a good father, who even in his old age did not desist from his misdeeds. The Latin word should, of course, be spelt '*Protector*', but it seems that at this date the knowledge of Latin orthography in South Wales was no longer to be relied on.

The third stone is engraved with a Latin cross and comes from Llangadwaladr, on the Island of Anglesey. The inscription below it refers to a King Catanus, the 'wisest and most excellent of all kings', who died in A.D. 625. He built the first Christian church in this district.

The blessing of St Patrick and the curse of St Ruadhan

both rest together on the famous hill of Tara (below). Tara was for many centuries the capital of the kingdoms of Ireland. These were independent kingdoms, but their rulers always recognised one among their number as paramount – as 'High King'. Every March 25 the Irish gathered in Tara to celebrate the great spring festival, which began with the kindling of the holy fire by the white-robed Druids, who officiated at such ancient Celtic ceremonies.

In A.D. 432 there occurred at the spring festival such an unusual event that it is remembered in Irish folklore to this day. When the kings and chieftains under their High King Laoghaire were assembled about the hill of Tara and the holy fire had been kindled, it was discovered that another fire was burning on the distant mountains of Slane. It was St Patrick celebrating, with a few fellow believers, the Christian Easter festival. As the flames shot up to heaven St Patrick proclaimed to his companions that the fire he had kindled would never again be extinguished in Ireland. They were the proud words of a man who had nothing to set against the pagan warriors and the anger of their wise men but his faith in Christ and his own personal courage. This story has in course of time been enriched by the Celtic imagination with a number of picturesque details. There was a clamour of war cries among the pagans and of preparations for attack, but the sound of St Patrick's mighty voice scattered them like chaff before the wind, and so they called a truce. The Saint was invited to visit King Laoghaire. In a narrow valley some warriors laid an ambush for him, but as the Saint and his companions walked along the valley, all that the waiting warriors saw was a file of

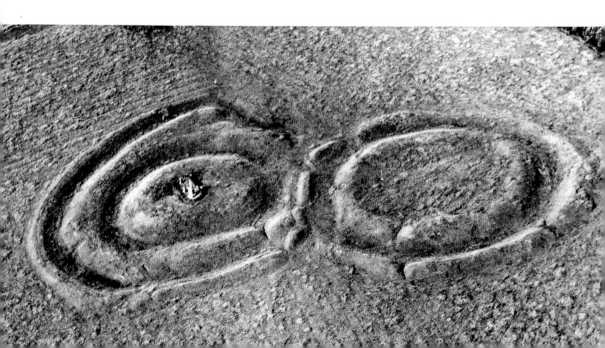

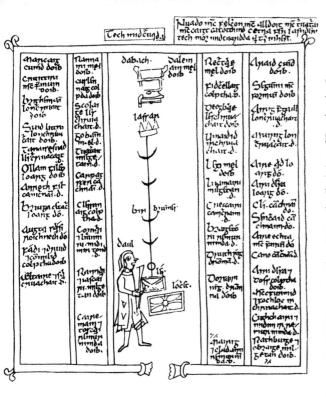

eight stags followed by a fawn with a bundle on its back. This was the Saint himself. The strangers advanced through the closed and guarded gates into the great hall of Tara. The foundations of this hall of assembly, built in the third century by King Cormac MacAirt, are still to be seen today. The story of these events is told in the Book of Leinster (left), a manuscript of the twelfth century.

The High King Laoghaire seems to have been an enlightened and benevolent monarch. True, he could never bring himself to give up the faith of his fathers, but he gave St Patrick permission to preach the Gospel among the Irish.

Christian life had been almost extinguished in the British Isles in the disorder that began after the departure of the Romans. The conversion of the Irish by Saint Patrick begins a new epoch – that of the Celtic Church in Ireland and England.

A hundred years after the Easter festival of 432 Christianity was so firmly rooted in Ireland that Saint Ruadhan was able to lay Tara, the ancient holy place of the Druid festivals, under a terrible curse.

Only rarely in the history of Christianity

has it happened that one man has succeeded in converting a whole country to the faith in the course of his own lifetime. St Patrick was born in 190 in a town in the west of the British Isles. His birthplace is not exactly known, but it may probably have been Caerwent in South Wales. So St Patrick was no doubt of Celtic origin. His father was a Roman decurion and a deacon of the Church. His childhood was passed under the protection of the Pax Romana. But then the last Roman legion left Britain. The good times were over.

When Patrick was sixteen, his peaceful schooldays were brought to an abrupt conclusion by a pirate raid and he was taken off to Ireland.

His Irish kidnappers had no inkling that the boy they had stolen would one day baptise their own grandchildren, nor can they have known what important consequences the few years he served them as a shepherd would one day have for Patrick and for Ireland. After a few years of captivity Patrick succeeded in escaping from his master and in getting away from Ireland on board a boat that was transporting Irish wolf-hounds to the Continent. On his return home, however, he could not forget his lonely watches on the Irish hills and came gradually to the conviction that it was his task to return there and preach the gospel to the Irish heathen.

He went first of all to the famous island monastery of Lerinum, off what is today Cannes, on the south coast of France. He visited St Martin of Tours. Then he spent a number of years with Bishop Germanus in Auxerre.

Finally he was consecrated bishop and returned to Ireland.

He travelled untiringly up hand down the country, and his work prospered. The tokens of a travelling bishop, a peculiarly Irish institution, were the crook and the bell. The stone figure of Lough Erne, left, which dates from the ninth century, shows a monk with a bell in his left hand and a crook in his right. The crook, illustrated on the opposite page, belonged to an unknown holy man from the Kells monastery in County Meath, and dates from the tenth century. Its ornamentation shows Scandinavian influences. The oldest surviving bell, shown beside it, is made of bronze, and belonged to Cumascach, the Prior of Armagh monastery. His death in 908 is recorded in the Annals of Ulster. St Patrick must have carried a crook and a bell similar to these as he travelled up and down Ireland.

He preached to kings, baptised far and wide, and ordained priests. He built churches and founded the first of the monasteries which in the course of the next few centuries were to play such an important part in the developing consciousness of Europe, not only because of their piety but even more perhaps because of their learning.

When St Patrick died in 461, much loved and venerated by the Irish, the island, as a whole, had become Christian. But the old pagan world of the Celts was never entirely forgotten there. The supernatural beings with which that world was peopled, the fairies, the trolls, the elves, and the rest, have lived on in Catholic Irish folklore. Many stories were woven about their encounters with the personages of Christian mythology, and these stories have continued to inspire Irish poets and playwrights up to our own day.

Fifteen hundred years of Cornish history have left this grey, moss-grown stone, the 'Mên Scryfys', standing alone in this wild moorland. The inscription on it, literally translated, reads: 'Of Realobranus, the son of Cunovalus'. The names are Celtic, with Latin endings. The stone dates from the last period of the decline of Roman civilisation in Britain.

On a small, flower-covered peninsula near Tintagel, almost an island, but connected with the mainland by a narrow spine of rock, about the year 500, St Juliot built a church and a hermitage, which gradually developed into a monastic community. The monastery had some small cells, whose remains can still be seen. Such monasteries were probably not bound together by a strict rule, but were rather a loosely organised community of men each serving God after his own fashion.

Material poverty and spiritual wealth

were combined in the lives of the early Christians in Ireland. The illustration above shows the reconstruction of a *Muinntir*, a small monastic settlement of the eighth century, of a kind that was characteristic of Irish Christianity. The settlement was situated on a rocky islet in the neighbourhood of Valencia on the coast of Country Kerry.

The monks in these coastal settlements earned a precarious living from sea fishing, with an additional meagre diet that must have consisted mostly of porridge. In this their way of life probably did not differ greatly from that of their pagan ancestors, whom they resembled also in their love for song and storytelling. One hero of monkish legend is St Brendan, whose adventures recalled those of Conall, the king's son, in the songs of the pagan bards of old. While Conall sailed out over the ocean in a skiff woven of gold thread, to seek the Happy Lands of the West, St Brendan was in some sense a historical figure, and was born about the beginning of the sixth century in what is now County Kerry. A hill, a bay, and a cape today bear his name. He entered the Monastery of Clonard, in Meath.

In 545, twenty years before St Columba founded the Monastery of Iona on the west coast of Scotland, St Brendan voyaged with three friends to the 'Dalriadic Isles' (Hebrides). But this did not content the lively and adventurous monk. Among the Celts of the Atlantic coasts of Europe there lived the legend of a western land far across the ocean, in which St Brendan, like Columbus after him, believed the Garden of Eden must lie. So one day, with a few courageous companions, he set out in search of 'the promised land of the Saints'. His first voyage was a failure, and he was roundly rebuked by the abbot of his monastery for his idle curiosity. But St Brendan was undeterred and set out on a second voyage.

After many adventures, so the story runs, the seafaring monks discovered, in the midst of the ocean, a tiny island. The monks landed. But suddenly the land began to move: the island was a great whale, a very friendly and accommodating whale at that. The creature was converted to Christianity and from then on followed St Brendan's boat, the saint even celebrating Easter mass on its back.

One day the whale took the monks on his back and brought them to a wonderful island, the Paradise of Birds. These birds were really angels who had fallen with Lucifer. As their sin had not been so great as Lucifer's, they were allowed to live on this island. St Brendan sailed on, and eventually reached a great land.

Having thus staked his claim to be, like Erik the Red, a forerunner of Columbus in discovering America, and after emerging unscathed from all his adventures, St Brendan returned to Ireland, where he died between 577 and 583. The adventures of St Brendan are an oft-told tale that incorporates elements of pagan Celtic folklore in the life of a Christian missionary. St Brendan today is a kind of patron saint of Irish fishermen. They think of him before they put out into the dangerous waters of their western coasts.

St Patrick was still alive

when St Ninian set out for the north and at Whithorn founded the first Scottish monastery. But information about St Ninian and the fate of his mission to Scotland is scanty. It is known only that he converted the southern Picts. The cave into which the saint was accustomed to retire for meditation was rediscovered in 1871, and in it were found some crosses and a stone with the inscription SANC (TO) NINIA (NO).

The period of Irish cultural ascendancy

in the West, which lasted for some five centuries, was due to the peculiarities of Irish-Celtic Christianity, which was more closely adapted to the way of life not only of the Celts, but also of other semi-barbarian peoples then occupying western Europe. It is probable that many of its institutions had been taken over more or less intact from pagan Celtic society.

The wandering habit of the Irish monks and bishops took them as missionaries all over western and northern Europe during the centuries when the

Roman Church had not yet recovered from the collapse of Roman civilisation in the West.

Manuscripts written by these Irish monks during Europe's dark ages are
among the greatest treasures in the possession of European libraries today.

The earliest extant Irish manuscript, the *Cathach* of St Columba, is a
Gospel manuscript, which was probably written as early as the sixth
century. Its script, above, is known as Celtic half-uncial. At this early date
the Irish had not only evolved a characteristic script of their own, and one
of great beauty at that, but had also begun to ornament initial letters.

Patient scholarship and restless wandering

were alike characteristic of the life of the Irish monasteries. Many of the
monks spent their whole lives in copying and annotating manuscripts, and
this studious tradition was kept alive in all the monasteries the Irish founded.
But other monks could not rest while such a great part of Europe, and
neighbouring Britain in particular, was still pagan. Leaving their studies
and copying behind, they set forth, amid perils and privations, to preach
the Gospel to the barbarians across the sea. In Britain it was the descendants
of these barbarian converts of the sixth and seventh centuries who were
destined, a millennium later, to carry the Christian tidings into the furthest
corners of the world.

St Columba, born in 521 in County Donegal, belonged to the family of
the High Kings of Ireland. He studied in the monastery of Moville, and
was himself the founder of three Irish monasteries, at Derry, Durrow, and

290

Kells. In 563, with twelve companions – a complement symbolic of Christ and his disciples – he set sail for Argyll in Scotland. Here, at the end of the fifth century, a group of his kinsmen from Dalriada, in County Antrim, had settled and founded a kingdom which they named after their homeland. King Conall of this new Dalriada welcomed Columba and allowed him to settle on a Hebridean islet west of Mull that afterwards became known as Iona. Here Columba founded the famous Monastery of Iona. The portrait of the saint, above, is from an Irish manuscript preserved in the library of the Monastery of St Gall, in Switzerland. Nothing, of course, has remained of the modest wattle huts that St Columba and his companions at first put up for themselves, but the old rampart and ditch, which walled off the monastery as a sanctuary from the outer world, are still extant. Similar ramparts had already been in use by the Irish kings to protect their palaces. It was from here that St Columba brought Christianity to the pagan North Picts.

The most famous Irish manuscript

is the ninth-century Book of Kells. It was probably begun in Iona and taken to Kells in Ireland in 804 when the monks had to flee from the Vikings. It was there completed. Today the manuscript is in Dublin. One of the miniatures in it, above, shows Christ being tempted to throw himself from the Temple. The artist has given the Temple the same form as the early churches of the *Muinntirs* with their steep-pitched roofs.

292

The small reliquary from Mony-musk in Scotland also follows the early church type. As the illustration shows, it has two eyelets through which a chain or string was passed so that it might be worn by the bishop about his neck on solemn occasions. The object dates from about the same period as that in which the Book of Kells was written.

The Shrine of St Rule, which is preserved in the Cathedral of St Andrews, is of somewhat later date. It shows a fine relief with a hunting scene, probably representing King David. The Celtic Church always buried its saints with elaborate ceremonial. We know from the chronicles of Adamnan, ninth abbot of Iona, that the services on the death of St Columba lasted three days and three nights, after which the saint was buried in or near the church which he himself had founded.

This ornate initial

is composed of the three letters 'L I B' that begin the title of St Matthew's Gospel in the 'Lindisfarne Gospels', or 'Book of Durham'. The title runs: '*Liber generationis Jesu Christi, filii David, filii Abraham*' ('Book of the Ancestry of Jesus Christ, son of David, son of Abraham'). The Lindisfarne Gospels consist of St Jerome's Latin version of the four gospels with some usual appendages and an Anglo-Saxon gloss that was added two centuries later. The monk who wrote this gloss also records that the manuscript was the work of Eadfrith, Bishop of Lindisfarne. The wonderful illuminations which give this manuscript its great celebrity are in the Irish-Celtic tradition (with elaborate initials and abstract designs) but show some Anglo-Saxon influences. They certainly prove Bishop Eadfrith to have been a master of his craft.

The monastery of Lindisfarne was an Irish foundation. Its founder, Aidan, came from the monastery of Iona, where King Oswald of Northumbria had spent some years in exile while Edwin, a prince of a rival dynasty, was on the throne. Edwin had favoured the Roman mission of St Augustine and received and been baptised by his bishop Paulinus. But he was killed in

battle with a pagan alliance of British from Wales and English from the Midlands. When Oswald, having fought his way back to the throne, set about restoring Christianity, he turned naturally not to Rome but to his fellow monks of the Irish Church.

In A.D. 633 at 'Heavenfield', near the old Roman Wall, we are told that he met in battle the pagan army commanded by his British enemy Cadwallon. Before the battle he had set up a great wooden cross and prayed to it with all his army. After winning the battle, he invited his friends of the Iona Monastery to found a monastery in his kingdom. The foundation was eventually undertaken by Aidan, a pupil of Columba, and the chosen site was

Lindisfarne, an island on the east coast that could be reached from the mainland at low tide on foot. It is today called Holy Island.

There are no traces left today of the first monastery of Lindisfarne and its church. After an eventful history the monastery was plundered by the Vikings in 875 and burnt to the ground. All but a handful of the monks were slaughtered. The Vikings were the last, and among the most savage, of the barbarian invaders of the former Roman lands of the West. It was their raids on Iceland and Scotland that in effect brought to an end the period of Irish Christian leadership in Europe. The Vikings were the last European people to be converted to Christianity.

As Papal Legate

St Augustine landed in A.D. 597 near Richborough, a Saxon fortress on the east Kent coast. Pope Gregory the Great had sent him to Britain to effect the reunion of the Irish-Celtic Church with Rome. Britain at this time was a medley of Anglo-Saxon and British, that is Welsh, Irish, or Pictish, principalities, part pagan, part Christian, and the Christians mostly followed the practices of the Irish Church that had converted them. The Irish Church, though owning the primacy of the Pope, went its own way in matters of organisation and ceremony.

On his arrival Augustine proceeded to the court of King Ethelbert of Kent, whose queen, Bertha, was a Catholic princess of the Merovingian family. Under their joint influence King Ethelbert was baptised and gave his support to the mission of St Augustine, who became the first Archbishop of Canterbury. Thus two hundred years after the last Roman legion had left Britain, Rome once more had a footing on the island.

The illustration shows the ruins of the Church of SS Peter and Paul, of which St Augustine laid the foundation stone, before its restoration in the nineteenth century. King Ethelbert and his queen are buried here.

The Synod of Whitby

was a decisive test of strength between the Roman Catholic and Irish-Celtic Churches in Europe. It was a meeting of the Northumbrian clergy held in A.D. 664 before King Oswy of the Anglo-Saxon Kingdom of Northumbria to decide whether the Celtic or the Roman rule was to be followed there. Its decision in favour of the Roman rule had repercussions all over the British Isles and also on the Continent, where the Irish Church was to remain influential for some time yet to come. This outcome of the synod, so important for the history of Europe, was a logical consequence of the success of St Augustine's mission in Kent, and again owed something to the influence of a Catholic queen, Eanfled of Northumbria. It owed a great deal also to the energy and eloquence of St Wilfrid, the leader of the Catholic party.

It was reserved for this same King Oswy to inflict a decisive defeat on the pagan King Penda of Mercia, who had been responsible for the death of two of his predecessors. The weather-beaten inscription, above, recalls a vow Oswy made just before the battle. He vowed that if he was victorious he would dedicate his daughter Aelfled, then still a child, to religious life. The gravestone, which comes from the ruins of Whitby Abbey, is that of this princess, who was abbess there for thirty-three years, dying in 714.

An important section of the Northumbrian Church felt unable to submit to the Whitby decisions, and Colman, Abbot of Lindisfarne, who had led the Irish party at the Synod, withdrew from Northumbria and returned with several of his fellow missionaries to Iona, which until its destruction by the Vikings in A.D. 804 remained a stronghold of the Irish-Celtic Church. Before he left, Colman persuaded King Oswy to appoint in his place as abbot Eata of Melrose, who had been a pupil of Aidan at Lindisfarne and a strong supporter of the Irish-Celtic rule, but had now decided in the interest of Christian unity to submit to Rome.

The new abbot's right-hand man, whom he appointed as prior, was Cuthbert. Of Anglo-Saxon origin, St Cuthbert was one of the last great saints in the Irish-Celtic tradition and one of the first of the unified English church. He had entered Melrose Abbey at the age of seventeen. When his abbot Eata was invited by a son of the Northumbrian king to found a new monastery at Ripon, in what is now Yorkshire, he took Cuthbert with him. Not long after its foundation Ripon Abbey became involved in the conflict between the Irish-Celtic and Roman Catholic Churches. The king's son, whose mother, as we have seen, was Catholic, came down on the side of Wilfrid, the Roman enthusiast, who was installed as Abbot of Ripon in place of Eata. Eata returned to Melrose with Cuthbert and other monks who would not accept the Roman rule. At Whitby Cuthbert, now Prior of Melrose, was again on the losing side.

After twelve years as Prior of Lindisfarne, St Cuthbert, who had by now attained great celebrity for his holiness, was permitted by his abbot to withdraw to a solitary hermitage on Farne Island, about seven miles out to sea. Here he lived for nine years. Three years before his death he yielded to the entreaties of the King and his nobles to return to the mainland and accept consecration as Bishop of Lindisfarne. He died in 687.

The mortal remains of St Cuthbert had an adventurous history. When in 875 the Vikings had destroyed Lindisfarne, the monks who had survived the catastrophe, led by Bishop Eardwulf and Abbot Eadred, forsook their island and wandered for seven years from place to place. They bore with them a coffin containing the bones of St Cuthbert and the skull of St Oswald, the first Christian king of Northumbria. Their wanderings ended finally in Chester-le-Street, County Durham, and here the cross illustrated below was found in the saint's clothing as his bones were being moved to a new resting place.

In 1104 the bones of St Cuthbert were moved once more, in solemn procession to Durham, and there laid to rest, with great pomp, in the Cathedral. The mounted fragments of a wooden coffin, also from Durham Cathedral, illustrated below, are adorned with carvings representing Christ, the symbols of the four Evangelists, Mary with the Child, and the Twelve Apostles. The style is Northumbrian, seventh century. There can hardly be any doubt that this was the coffin in which St Cuthbert's body continued its earthly journey for so long after his death.

Fifty years after the death of Constantine the Great

Rome had abandoned Britain. Probably another half century under the *Imperium Romanum* would have sufficed to make Roman Britain a completely Christian country even before the sixth century. Under Theodore of Tarsus, who became seventh Archbishop of Canterbury in A.D. 668, the goal for which so many brave men had been striving for six centuries was finally attained.

Theodore organised the English Christians on the system which had so well proved itself throughout the Roman Empire both during the persecutions and after. It was to prove itself in England, too, in the confusion of the Danish invasions.

Among the collaborators whom Theodore brought to England with him was Benedict Biscop, a Northumbrian of good family and great learning. He had been trained in the Monastery of Lérins on the coast of Provence, which so many important men of those times had visited. In England Biscop founded the two neighbouring monasteries of Jarrow and Monk-wearmouth.

The stone slab, above, with the dedicatory inscription of Jarrow Church, is the oldest written evidence we have of the foundation of a church in England. The inscription says that 'on April 23, in the fifteenth year of King Ecgfrith, in the fourth year of Abbot Ceolfrith, by the will of God, this church was dedicated to St Paul.' The fifteenth year of King Ecgfrith was 685.

Besides being a man of learning and of good works, Benedict Biscop was also a patron of the arts, and brought to England stonemasons and glass-workers from Gaul. Until that time in England wood had been almost the only building material. Under the guidance of these foreign and widely travelled masters the English craftsmen took the first steps on the road that was to lead to the masterpieces of English cathedral architecture in later centuries. It was here in Jarrow Abbey that the Venerable Bede wrote the history of Christianity in Britain from its beginnings up to A.D. 731. He is considered a thoroughly reliable historian, and published many other learned works – commentaries, translations, and works of exposition – in which he made the thought of the Greek and Latin Church fathers available to English readers. Thus he performed the same inestimable service for England as Cassiodorus for Italy, Gregory of Tours for France, and Isidore for Spain.

The Sutton Hoo Ship Burial

was found in southern England in 1939. The ship was about eighty feet long, much larger than any known Viking ship of a later period. The excavation presented a number of puzzles. The ship contained weapons evidently of pagan origin, but besides these there were some Christian objects, among them a hanging bowl of bronze (below) with three drop-

handles and a fish on a small pedestal attaching it to the floor of the vessel. Further, there were two silver spoons, one inscribed with the word 'Saulos' in Greek letters, the other with the word 'Paulos'. This suggests a baptismal present to a convert who at baptism changed his name, just as the Apostle had changed his, from Saul to Paul. The burial must have taken place between A.D. 654 and 664, and from the treasure's magnificence it is inferred that it must have been that of a king. But no trace of a body has been discovered. It is supposed, therefore, that it must have been the death ship of a Christian king which was buried in accordance with the old pagan ceremonies while the king himself was given a Christian burial elsewhere.

In 1958 another valuable treasure was found, this time in the far north on the islet named after St Ninian in the Shetlands. It contains twenty-five pieces which when found, were completely coated in verdigris, so that they were at first thought to be made of bronze. They

are, however, all silver, and the oxidised coating was due to an unusual amount of copper impurity in the original metal. On the clasp here illus-trated the engraved inscription is partly in Latin, partly in Pictish. On one side it reads 'IN NOMINE D(EI) S(UMMI)' – 'In the name of God the All-Highest'. This treasure, which must undoubtedly have belonged to Christians, had been buried at the end of the eighth century under a stone slab on which a small cross had been scratched.

The money-box and the Ruthwell stone cross are interesting examples of the mixture of styles that characterised the great period of Northumbrian art, in the eighth century. In the Mediterranean, the money-box, as we know from many examples, would have been a casket of ivory. The northern equivalent is made of whale-bone. Scenes of Roman and Christian myth and scenes from northern legend are depicted side by side. On this same casket we find Romulus and Remus, the con-quest of Jerusalem by Titus, an adoration of the Magi, with the word inscribed in runes, and the vengeance of Wieland the Smith on King Nidhard. In the last-named scene Wieland is shown first killing the two sons of the king and then holding the skull of one of them in blacksmith's tongs so as to make a drinking cup out of it in accordance with the grue-

some Viking custom. A long runic inscription reads: 'This is whalebone. The ocean cast the fish upon the rocky coast. The sea was stirred up as it grounded on the beach.'

The stone cross, left, is covered with reliefs in which Celtic ornamental designs are very happily combined with representations of Christian scenes showing Gallic influence. Engraved in the stone are passages from the 'Dream of the Cross', an old English mystical poem of great beauty in which the Cross itself tells the story of the Crucifixion. The upper part of the stone cross has been restored.

This Anglo-Saxon Christianity, which both in its practice and ways of thought and in its works of art drew so fruitfully on a mixed Irish and Mediterranean ancestry, was not destined to last long. The Anglo-Saxon Church flourished but there was no corresponding development of political institutions. Out of the warring Anglo-Saxon kingdoms no State emerged strong enough to defend the island against sea attack. Towards the end of the eighth century the Danish invasions began. In England the south put up more resistance to the raids and the Church there remained strong. Very soon there were Christian converts among the Scandinavians, and it was not long before Oda, a Dane, became Archbishop of Canterbury. The Danish raids in England went on for some two hundred years. During this period an important group of Vikings had settled in France, about the lower Seine, and there become Christian and created the Duchy of Normandy. These were the Normans who in the eleventh century crossed-over and conquered England. Since the Norman conquest no other invader has succeeded in occupying England.

304

EVEN BEFORE the collapse of the Western Roman Empire there was a brief moment in the history of Europe during which the south of Britain, the whole of Gaul, and part of Germany were all Christian. Germany west of the Rhine, that is, and south of the *limes*, the frontier line drawn across central Europe by the Roman emperors, was Christian. Germany east of the Rhine and north of the *limes* never belonged to the Roman Empire. It had to wait for centuries more before it was reached by the light of the Gospel. The battle in the Teutoburg Forest saved the Germans from coming under Roman rule. This was by no means an unmixed blessing. Had they lost this battle, Christianity would have come to them five hundred years sooner – years that would have been passed in the school of Mediterranean civilisation. And however highly we esteem the later services of the Germans to Christianity, there have been occasions in their history when this schooling has been greatly missed.

In this story the decisive turning point was the baptism of Clovis, King of the Franks, at Reims in 496. This event had two important consequences. After Clovis had succeeded, in a relatively short time, in bringing the greater part of the old Roman Gaul under his rule and then restoring it to the Roman Church, the other Germanic tribes between the Rhine and the Pyrenees, who were mostly followers of the Arian heresy, gradually gave up their resistance to Rome and went over to Catholicism. Thus the whole of Gaul was recovered for the Roman Church. The second consequence of Clovis' baptism was possibly even more important. The Frankish kings, rather as Constantine the Great had done, skilfully used the organisation of the Church to strengthen their own young State. In return, Rome itself received from the Frankish kings and their Mayors of the Palace a protection against the many dangers that threatened it. This protection, which Byzantium was hardly in a position to provide, became increasingly important as time went on, and the whole development culminated in the coronation of Charlemagne as Roman Emperor at the hands of Pope Leo III at St Peter's in Rome. The same Germans who had destroyed the Roman Empire gave new life to the idea of the *Imperium Romanum*. The same Germans who had endangered the very existence of Christianity were to be among the strongest guarantors of its future.

From this Frankish and Christian Gaul of the Merovingian period Irish and English monks set out to preach the Gospel to the heathen. They went into Alsace, to the Upper Rhine, down to Lake Constance, to Bavaria and

Austria, and finally up to the Main. Gradually the whole region, which had once belonged to the Western Roman Empire, was reclaimed for Christianity. The north of Europe, however, was still closed to it, and at the heart of this pagan stronghold was the land of the Saxons.

The northern neighbours of the Saxons, with whom they managed to keep on terms of close friendship, were the Frisians. To the south of them were the Hessians and Thuringians. The assault on the pagan stronghold began in Frisia. Under Dagobert I, King of the Franks, in 630, the Bishop of Cologne had founded a church in Utrecht. Bishop Wilfrid, the powerful Abbot of Ripon, who at the Synod of Whitby had brought about the decision in favour of Catholicism, in the course of one of his journeys to Rome in 678, landed on the Frisian coast. As luck would have it, there was in this year a particularly abundant herring season, and the pagans attributed it to the holy man's arrival amongst them. He was given a friendly reception and baptised a few nobles and a number of commoners. His work was continued, from about 690 onwards, by a pupil of his, Willibrord, a Northumbrian educated in Ripon. The headquarters from which St Willibrord made his missionary journeys into pagan Frisia was Utrecht. Though he had some success among the Frisians he did not succeed in converting the whole people.

The effective ruler of the kingdom of the Franks at this time was Pepin of Heristal, who since 687 had been Mayor of the Palace, the office that had by now usurped the power of the Merovingian kingship. Pepin extended his temporal authority over the South Frisians whom Willibrord had been converting. Near the end of the century he sent Willibrord to Rome with a letter to the Pope requesting his consecration as archbishop. Pope Sergius, a Syrian, performed the consecration of the Anglo-Saxon archbishop in 695. At a time when the Churches in his native Syria and in Palestine and Egypt were being cut off from Rome by the Arab conquests, there knelt before Sergius the representative of a people that only very recently had been pagan. It was not quite a hundred years since his predecessor Pope Gregory the Great had sent the monk Augustine as his legate to England. And now the converts of this monk were themselves adding new dioceses to the Roman Church in lands where the Roman imperial power and civilisation had never penetrated.

St Willibrord laboured in Frisia for almost half a century. He died in 738 and was buried at the Monastery of Echternach, which he himself had founded.

Among those who had served under him was one who was to become one of the greatest missionaries of Christendom, the Anglo-Saxon Winfrid. His dream it had been from boyhood to convert the Frisians and the Saxons, 'the land of our fathers, inhabited by men of our own blood'. As the Apostle of the Germans Winfrid is better known to history by the name which he was given later: Boniface. The dream of his boyhood, however, was not destined to be fulfilled, and the work of St Boniface in Frisia was crowned by martyrdom. The conversion of the Saxons was reserved for the sword of Charlemagne.

The Tassilo Chalice, the work of a Bavarian master, dates from the end of the eighth century. It was presented to the Monastery of Kremsmünster, in Upper Austria, by Duke Tassilo of Bavaria, whose name is engraved round the margin of the base. This fine piece is still in the keeping of the monastery to which it was given over a thousand years ago.

309

Only two weeks

were needed by a Roman force stationed in Lyon to reach the Porta Nigra at Trèves, after receiving the alarm at a performance in the Amphitheatre and hurrying by forced marches all the way. The fourth century was the last period in which the Roman Empire still had the strength to resist the pressure of the barbarians from the East. Minor invasions could not be prevented, but the Emperor Constantine did succeed in securing for a further century the peace that Augustus had created. Lyon, whose amphitheatre is here illustrated, was an important centre of commerce. The smaller sea-going ships at that time sailed up the Rhone as far as Lyon From there the merchandise was transported overland to the Rhine and

then again by ship downstream. Lyon was the first city in Gaul to have a bishop. Trèves was the Roman centre of the north-west, and was elevated by Constantine the Great to the status of an Imperial Residence, of which there were only four in the Roman Empire.

From the Rhine to the Pyrenees, from the English Channel to the Alps, Europe was at this period a region of highly civilised cultural uniformity, in which the Celts of Gaul and the Germans on the Rhine shared equally in the classical heritage of Greece and Rome. They eagerly absorbed what was given and built abundantly on the foundations thus laid. Despite all the confusions of the migration of peoples, the northern regions never entirely lost what they had learned from the classical tradition.

The illustration, above, of a Roman Christian glass bowl from Cologne shows one of the sons of Constantine. The other bowl, left, was found at Homblières on the Aisne in a fourth-century grave. The easily identifiable Bible scenes show aniel in the lion's den and Adam and Eve with the serpent in Paradise. The Christogram in the centre is surrounded by stars, symbolising heaven.

From the very beginning

Christianity was characterised by its world-wide outlook. Nations and territorial frontiers never had much importance for the preachers of the Gospel, which was destined for all men. It was Christianity, indeed, that gave a new meaning to the concept of 'mankind'. So the first missionaries to Gaul came not from Rome but from Asia Minor. In A.D. 177 or 178 there were severe persecutions of Christians in Lyon and Vienna, and while in prison the martyrs wrote to the brethren in Phrygia and in the Province of Asia. In this letter it is expressly said of some of the martyrs that they come from Asia Minor. The ninety-year-old Bishop of Lyon, who also suffered martyrdom in these persecutions, had the Greek name of Po hinus. Both he and his successor, Bishop Irenaeus of Lyon, were pupils of the venerable Bishop Polycarp of Smyrna, who had been a pupil of the Apostle John.

Gaul was converted by Asia Minor, Russia by Byzantium, England by Ireland, Germany by Ireland and England, and Scandinavia by England and Germany. However acute the differences that today divide the nations of Europe from one another, what groups them together as Europeans is their common Christian past.

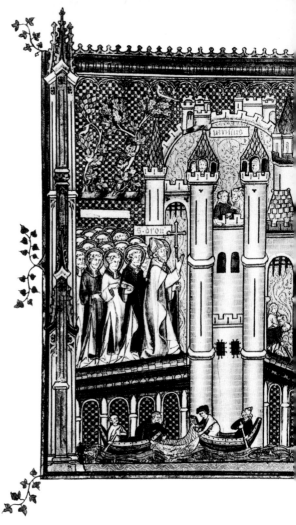

In Toulouse there is preserved a magnificent fourth-century sarcophagus on which Christ is depicted with eight Apostles. The left-hand side of the sarcophagus is of particular interest. The small building there shown in relief, and illustrated above, is an *aedicula* – a shrine. In appearance it is remarkably similar to the reconstruction of the *aedicula* recently discovered beneath St Peter's in Rome, and illustrated on p. 120. It can hardly be doubted that the *aedicula* on the Toulouse sarcophagus represents the Shrine of St Peter. The dead man had presumably been on pilgrimage to Rome and wanted a permanent record of this, the most important event of his Christian life, carved on his sarcophagus. A second sarcophagus with an exactly similar *aedicula* is to be found in Rodez, in south-western France. St Denis, whose name in Latin was Dionysius, was the first Bishop of

Paris. He suffered martyrdom in the middle of the third century. Very little is known about him otherwise. There was a legend that after his head had been struck off on the 'martyr's hill', or Montmartre as it has been called ever since, his body rose up and, conducted by an angel, carried the severed head to the spot where the saint's church now stands. King Dagobert I at the beginning of the seventh century erected the celebrated Abbey of St Denis where nearly all the French kings are buried. The miniature, left, shows the saint's processional entry into Paris. St Denis is one of the fourteen 'helpers in need', the guardian saint of Paris, and the patron saint of France.

Lists of bishops and sarcophagi

are the most important evidences of Christianity in third- and fourth-century Gaul. About the middle of the third century there is mention of a Bishop of Reims. It was in Reims Cathedral in later ages that the French kings were crowned. In Autun, too, there were Christians at this period.

In 314 a Church Council, convened by the Emperor Constantine, was held at Arles. From the list of those who attended it we learn that there were at that time seven bishops in Aquitania, or south-western Gaul, and twelve in the Lyon region. At the time when Constantine ascended the throne Roman Gaul had at least thirty bishoprics.

A number of sarcophagi have been preserved in Arles, and one of them today serves as an altar in the Church of St Trophimus. With a technique which is still quite Roman a number of scenes from the Bible are reproduced in relief. The female figure in the attitude of prayer in the centre is probably intended to portray the lady who was buried in this costly sarcophagus.

in Gaul after Bishop Irenaeus of Lyon was St Martin of Tours. He was born in Hungary in 315, of pagan parents. At the age of fifteen he was already an officer in the Imperial horse guards. While on garrison duty at Amiens, he was riding out of the town one day when he saw at the gate a half-naked beggar. Martin drew his sword and, cutting his cloak in two pieces, gave one to the beggar. That night Martin had a dream in which Christ appeared to him wearing the half of his cloak which he had given the beggar.

For a while Martin stayed with his regiment, but then one day he refused to go on duty, saying that he would no longer fight for the Emperor but only for Christ. He was baptised, and when reproached with cowardice declared himself ready to go into battle unarmed in the front line. The conscientious objector was put in prison but released again as the result of a chance amnesty. He thereupon went to St Hilary, Bishop of Poitiers, one of the leading champions of Nicene orthodoxy against the Arian heresy, and was enrolled among his pupils.

St Martin journeyed through Illyria and Italy, preaching fiery sermons against the Arians. For a time he lived as a hermit on the isle of Gallinaria in the Gulf of Genoa. Returning to Poitiers, he founded at Ligugé in 361, only a few decades after the foundation of the first monasteries in Egypt, the first important monastery in Europe. In 371 he became Bishop of Tours. He died in 397. The shrine containing his bones was destroyed in 1562 by the Huguenots.

Although his work of conversion must have been shared with other bishops, such as his friend and contemporary Victricius, Bishop of Rouen, the personality of St Martin seems to have overshadowed them all. He was credited with many miracles, and his reputation, which went on growing after his death, was that of an outstandingly active and courageous Christian rather than a man of learning. Among those who visited him at Tours, towards the end of his life, to receive instruction in preaching to the heathen, tradition includes St Ninian, the wandering bishop who converted the south of Scotland. It was the work of St Martin and his fellow bishops in taking Christianity not only to the towns but into all the country districts that enabled it to survive the destruction of Roman power in the following century. Unlike Britain, Gaul had become so thoroughly Christianised by the time of the German invasions that a good deal of Christian life was able to maintain itself both then and through the Hun invasions that followed later in the century.

Innumerable churches throughout Europe have been dedicated to St Martin of Tours. In France alone there are four thousand, and five hundred French villages bear his name. On the capital of the Eglise de La Madeleine in Vézelay there is sculptured in relief a representation of one of the many miracles performed by St Martin.

315

The columns of Greek temples have never entirely disappeared from European architecture. The Baptistery of Fréjus in Provence dates from the fifth century. The architects found it natural to lighten the somewhat austere structure with columns of a light-hearted pagan elegance, and felt no sense of incongruity in doing so.

The Christianisation of Gaul went on making further progress despite the great political changes that occurred there during these centuries. The gradual transition from the late Roman to the Merovingian, and then to the Carolingian, style can be followed with particular clearness in Christian art.

The clasp from the girdle of St Caesarius of Arles, sixth century, contains elements that are still classical. It shows the sleeping guards at the tomb of Jesus. Caesarius, a Benedictine, was Archbishop of Arles, and in the course of his long life presided over many Church congresses. At the Synod of Orange in 529 he obtained recognition of twenty-five articles summarising the doctrine of original sin and divine grace, somewhat modifying the views of St Augustine. The synod was called to combat the false doctrine of the British-born heretic Pelagius, which was widespread in Gaul and Spain, and which denied the existence of original sin and the necessity for grace. The relief (opposite) of the two martyrs bound to the cross, separated by a column still of classical proportions, also comes from the Poitiers neighbourhood. It has been assigned to the end of the seventh century. Art here reflects the spiritual life of man. The relief shows artistic development tending, through a period of primitive vigour, towards the Romanesque, which was to be the characteristic form of expression of the northern peoples converted to Christianity.

Beside the door to the Church of Saint Germain-des-Prés

in Paris, which was founded at the beginning of the sixth century by Childebert, one of the four sons of Clovis, there are sculptured in stone these portraits of King Clovis, St Remigius, Queen Clotilda, and King Chlodomer, who was also a son of Clovis.

The baptism of this warrior king was the turning point in a period of great weakness and confusion for western Christianity. In the middle of the fifth century the Western Roman Empire collapsed. The Germans flooded across Gaul. South of the Loire the Visigoths had taken possession of Aquitania. The valley of the Rhône and Saône was occupied by the Burgundians, the lands between the Rhine and the English Channel by the Franks. These Franks were still pagans. The Visigoths and Burgundians were Christians but mostly of the Arian persuasion. Clovis, the son of Childeric, was one of the three regional kings of the Salic Franks, who were established in the neighbourhood of Tournay. To the Germans breaking out of their

eastern forests Christianity had a different aspect from that which it had for the Romans of the first few centuries. It had been now for many generations the religion of the Roman Empire. So to these intelligent barbarians Christianity was the religion of an admired civilisation. At that time belief was the gateway to the promised land of knowledge and education. Today knowledge and education are often enough the gateway to the desert of unbelief.

In 493 Clovis married a Burgundian princess, Clotilda, niece of the King of the Burgundians, who was not an Arian but a Catholic. When in the battle of Zülpich Clovis' warriors began to waver before the Alemanni, the Frankish king swore to have himself baptised if the 'God of Clotilda' would grant him the victory. He won the battle and kept his word. On Christmas Day, 496, he went through the ceremony of baptism, together with three thousand of his warriors before Bishop Remigius in Reims.

Remigius, himself a man of good family, a son of the Count of Laon, half Gaulish, half Roman, was old enough to have had the education of a young patrician. So it was that the barbarian king, who was to be one of the founders of a new world order, received baptism at the hands of one of the last representatives of the old. And the form of words he used was in the best Ciceronian tradition. While the holy water poured over the neophyte, the bishop said to the king:

> 'Proud Sugambrian, bow thy head. Pray to that which thou
> hast burned. Burn that which thou hast prayed to.'

With these words the history of France begins. A few years later Clovis defeated the Burgundians at Dijon and the Visigoths at Poitiers. The defeat of the Burgundians and Visigoths meant the defeat of Arianism in Gaul. The dominions of Clovis now extended from the Rhine to the Pyrenees, and his kingdom of the Franks, notwithstanding the confusion that set in after his death among his successors, was destined to be the strongest prop of Christianity in Europe.

Through all the turmoil

which followed Clovis' death the spread of Christianity in Gaul progressed steadily. The Gallo-Roman aristocrats who apparently continued to fill the higher Church offices under the Merovingian kings, gave way gradually to Franks, with whom their families were in any case intermarrying. The continuity of the Church's authority formed a link between the old times and the new, and even provided an element of security and refuge through the collapse of the social order. The high standard achieved by the works of art of the sixth and seventh centuries in Gaul is some evidence of this.

Among the most famous of these were the works of St Eligius (Eloi), the goldsmith-bishop who was appointed by King Clothaire II Keeper of the Mint at Limoges, an office that included the functions of State treasurer. The chalice, above, from the Monastery of Chelles, founded in A.D. 622 by Queen Bathildis, was his work. It is no longer extant. The drawing dates from the seventeenth century, and was undoubtedly made from an older drawing. It does show, however, the elegance and fine detail of the original chalice.

A remarkable piece of an unusual kind is the Diptych of Ariobindus, who was Consul of Constantinople in A.D. 506. On the front it shows the Consul, full face, holding in his left hand a staff on which is engraved the name of the Emperor Anastasius, in whose reign

he took up office. On the back is an ivory carving which was added in the ninth century in Tours. It has an elaborate arrangement of scenes representing the earthly Paradise. The representation of the Garden of Eden begins at the top with Adam and Eve. Then there come a series of fantastic, half human, half animal creatures. Below them come the symbolic animals – lion, griffin, unicorn – then horned, then unhorned beasts, and finally exotic animals. This 'evolutionary ladder', which might almost have been the work of an early medieval Darwinist, is in fact derived from St Augustine.

By what route the Diptych came from Constantinople to Tours is not known. But whereas Byzantium for us is a pale, far distant memory, for the Christians of early Europe the great Roman Empire of the East was a source of comfort and hope. The links were closer than we imagine. At this period, moreover, the Christians of the West began to make pilgrimages to the Holy Sepulchre in Jerusalem. When the Emperor Heraclius in 629 defeated the Persians and recaptured from them the True Cross of Christ which they had carried off, it was a day of rejoicing for the whole of Christendom. It is still celebrated to this day as a holiday in the Roman Catholic and Greek Orthodox Churches.

A glimpse across the centuries

is given in this photograph of the recent excavations in Cologne Cathedral.

The masonry above on the left is the base of a Gothic pillar of the fifteenth century. The wall in the centre and to the right supports the threshold of the porch of the earlier ninth-century cathedral. The stone-work at the bottom of the trench is the base of a pillar that belonged to a Roman street colonnade of the third or fourth century. The trench in the foreground is an early Roman street gutter from the first century A.D. Through the Roman colon-nade the contemporaries of the Emperor Constantine used to wander. Over the threshold of the

porch the archbishops of Charle-magne's time used to pass into the old cathedral. The Gothic pillar was built at the time when Colum-bus was discovering America. All this history is contained in one corner of a building.

The detail from the mosaic of the Mysteries found in the Cornmarket at Trèves, where Constantine lived for a time, shows the birth of Helen, Castor and Pollux from the egg, which is lying on an altar. In style this piece has many similarities with the early Christian mosaics of the same period, when pagan and converted lived side by side.

The filigree glass from the wine-growing village of Niederemmel on the Moselle is a drinking vessel from the time of Constantine. The glass is wrought from a single piece and unusually well preserved. These filigree glasses are of extraordinary rarity, not more than seven or eight examples being known. They are among the most celebrated examples of the ancient glassworker's art. The great Roman officials evidently had a feeling for the style of glass out of which the wines of the Moselle should be drunk.

The photograph, below, shows a double grave of two martyrs, found in Xanten Cathedral. They must have been buried between A.D. 358 and A.D. 363, during the reign of the Emperor Julian the Apostate. From documents, traditions, and archaeological finds the experts infer that they were the two martyrs Victor and Mallosus, who, to judge from their names, must have been Africans, probably soldiers of a Roman legion.

These finds have been amplified by others from Christian graves, a number of which have been investigated. There must have been a flourishing Christian life towards the end of the fourth century in the Roman frontier provinces of Germania Inferior, with its capital at Mainz. It was these regions which suffered most severely from the collapse of the Roman military defences and the irruption of the new peoples from the east. While the Church in Gaul remained in being, Christian life was extinguished on the Rhine in much the same way as in Britain. And as in Britain so on the Rhine it was Irish monks who planted new Christian life among the ruins.

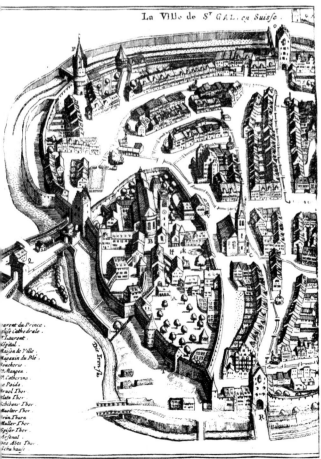

La Ville de S^T GAL en Suisse.

The wandering monks of Ireland were for several centuries a characteristic sign of the times in Western Europe and their activities were of critical importance for the progress of Christianity.

The portrait, left, represents St Columbanus, before a background filled with scenes from monkish life. Thirty years after St Columba had set out for Scotland to found the Monastery of Iona, Columbanus, at the age of fifty, left Ireland. He was accompanied, like Columba, by the evangelical complement of twelve monks, and landed in 590 in Brittany. There he was invited by the King of Burgundy to found a number of monasteries in his kingdom. The saint himself laboured for twenty years in Burgundy and about the Upper Rhine. Then he went to Lake Constance and from there at the invitation of Agilulf, King of the Lombards, to Upper Italy where he built the Monastery of Bobbio. There, in 615, he died. St Columbanus had left Gallus, his friend and companion for many years, behind at Lake Constance, where he lived for a time, on the Swiss side, as a hermit. Soon, however, other monks gathered round him and the hermitage of Gallus became the nucleus of the monastic community of St Gall.

These early medieval monasteries had a beneficial effect on their surroundings, both in their own works and by the force of their example. The monks cleared woodlands and made them arable, drained marshes and cultivated the fields. They raised cattle and introduced fruit and vine growing. They built churches and schools, and taught men to pray. They cared for the sick and performed the last offices for the dying. The monasteries of the East were places of meditation and prayer, while those of the West were more actively engaged in good works.

The strict monastic discipline of St Columbanus was for long enforced in the monasteries of Gaul and the Rhineland, until the arrival of St Benedict of Nursia from across the Alps. The Benedictines were as pious as the Irish and as active in good works, but they were rather milder in the demands which they made on themselves and on others.

Charles Martel, the famous Mayor, and his son Pepin the Short, the first Carolingian king, richly endowed St Gall. Othmar, who is said to have been its first abbot, introduced the Benedictine monastic rule and founded the School of St Gallen, which continues to be a stronghold of learning in Europe. North of the Alps St Gall became the principal monastery of the Benedictines of Monte Cassino.

St Gall is close to Lake Constance in which lies the island of Reichenau. On this island St Pirman founded a monastery, which had a famous scriptorium in Ottonian times. The church at the eastern end of the island is reputed to be the earliest in Germany.

To meet violence with bravery

was often enough the test of Christian faith in these centuries, as it had been under the early Roman Emperors. This picture shows the scene of carnage as St Kilian and his two companions, the priest Colman and the deacon Totnan, were beheaded.

St Kilian was the missionary of the country today called Franconia. He too came from Ireland. In 686 he went to Rome and was consecrated bishop by Pope Conon and put in charge of the mission to the eastern territories of the Frankish kingdom. The conversion of Germany to Christianity was not left to the enthusiasm of individual missionaries but was systematically directed from Rome.

With his two companions, the priest Colman and the deacon Totnan, St Kilian went up and down the Frankish territories of the Main. Thousands were baptised, and eventually Duke Gosbert, a local ruler, decided to follow their lead. Duke Gosbert had his seat on the 'Virteburch', where Würzburg is situated today. He was married, however, to his brother's widow, Gailana, which is forbidden by ecclesiastical law. So the Duke resolved to be separated from his wife. In his absence the Duchess plotted revenge. She persuaded the castle chamberlain and the cook to murder the vexatious priest and his companions. The picture on the previous page shows, in the background, how the murderers were afterwards so filled with terror at the prospect of the returning Duke's anger that they took their own lives, while the Duchess Gailana was carried off by the Devil.

The rays crowning the head

of the spear-carrier on the Frankish figured stone from Niederdollendorf, near Königswinter, have posed a number of problems for the archaeologists. The stone is seventh-century work. The sides are ornamented with Germanic animal designs. On the obverse of the stone, not shown here, there is an armed warrior.

The figure of the spear-carrier has been identified with Wotan. But the halo, the crown of rays, is unknown in Germanic art. This symbol of holiness comes from the Orient, and found its way into northern art only with Christianity.

The workmanship suggests a natural artistic talent but is primitive in its execution. Perhaps the most likely explanation for this puzzling combination of *motifs* is the suggestion that it was the work of a newly baptised convert from paganism who was still very little acquainted with Christian teaching, and could imagine Christ only as the sort of warrior-god he had worshipped up till then.

The stone cross of Moselkern is also attributable to the seventh century. The harmonious relations and simple strength of the whole, and the well con-

ceived loosening of the heavy block of stone by means of the apertures, all point to a master of his craft. Here too it is uncertain whether this monument can be identified as a Christian work. The cross is frequently used in Germanic art of the pre-Christian period. The figure in the upper half is embracing the cross with both arms, a mode of representation not found anywhere else. The figured stone and the stone cross both seemingly belong to a transitional period in which Christianity and paganism were not yet separated from one another.

St Boniface, the Apostle of the Germans,
came from Wessex in England, where he was born between 672 and 675. His real name was Winfrid. After his first missionary journey, which had taken him to Frisia, he went in 718 to Rome. There his energy, intelligence, and enthusiasm won the confidence of Pope Gregory II, who conferred on him the name of Boniface ('man of good fortune') and sent him to Thuringia. In 722, after his missionary labours, Boniface returned to Rome, and the Pope consecrated him as bishop. At this cere-

mony Boniface swore the oath of loyalty to the Pope in the form in which the bishops of the Roman Church Province swore it, only in Boniface's case the undertaking of loyalty to the Emperor in Constantinople was omitted. Boniface then returned northward with a letter to Charles Martel from the Pope.

St Boniface's oath of loyalty and Gregory II's letter to Charles Martel, as the course of history was to show, were of the greatest importance for Western Christendom.

For a quarter of a century St Boniface 'laboured mightily' among the heathen in Hesse and Thuringia. His methods recall the courageous determination with which St Patrick had set about converting the Irish. They are symbolised by the famous story of the thousand-year-old oak of Thor at Geismar, near Fritzlar in Hesse, to which St Boniface laid his axe in defiance of a threatening crowd of armed heathen. After one blow, instead of lightning from Thor to blast the saint, there came a gust of wind and the tree crashed to the ground. This miracle was followed by numerous conversions and the wood of the ancient oak was used to build a monastery.

Boniface preached and baptised, and built other churches and other monasteries. His earliest foundations, apart from Fritzlar, were Amöneburg and Ohrdruf. The

S. BONIFACIVS *Arch*
Ultraiectinus II. *natione*
norumq; Apostolus, in Docku
est an. 755. *conditusq; Fulden*
Ioan Galle excudit

...piscopus Moguntinus I. et
...Anglo-Saxo, Frisiorum Germa...
...apud Frisios martyrio coronatus
...in monasterio, a se constructo.

last of his foundations was the one he loved the best: Fulda, which he had modelled on Monte Cassino. He collected a staff of able assistants, including a number of women. Among these was St Walburga, who came from England, and founded many churches, schools, and convents, the most famous being Heidenheim, of which she herself was abbess.

One result of St Boniface's labours was that the whole of central Germany became Christian. But he achieved more than this, for he was not only a great missionary, but also a great diplomatist and politician. His policy was based on his realisation that the only way to secure Christianity's hold on the new territories was by means of a firm organisation, and moreover that Rome alone could not supply this. Without the support of the temporal power in these newly converted lands, he was doubtful if Christianity could maintain itself.

The letter to Charles Martel, which Boniface brought back from Gregory II, gave substance to a papal policy that had been initiated by Gregory the Great more than a century earlier. It envisaged the reorientation of the Roman Church, away from the ancient centre of power in Byzantium to the new centre in the Frankish kingdom to the north.

In 732 Pope Gregory III raised Boniface to the rank of missionary arch-bishop and on his third visit to Rome in 737–738 appointed him Papal Legate.

Boniface, under the protection of the Frankish rulers, especially the two sons of Charles Martel, then took in hand the reorganisation of the Church in the Kingdom of the Franks. Under the later Merovingians it was becom-ing increasingly decadent. A number of synods were held for the pur-poses of Church reform, and in 747 a great all-Frankish synod was held at Mainz, where Boniface was now resident archbishop, and every bishop present swore an oath of loyalty to St Peter and his successor at the Holy See. Of Charles Martel's two sons, Carloman, who ruled the eastern king-dom, retired to a monastery in this same year, and in 751 his brother Pepin the Short deposed the last Merovingian King, Childeric II, and had himself crowned King of All the Franks in his place, thus founding the Carolingian dynasty. After he had been raised on the shield in the old Frankish manner, it is recorded that it was Boniface who anointed him king. In 754 Pope Stephen II made his fateful journey to Paris to petition King Pepin's help against Aistulf, King of the Lombards. He was received with with all reverence and, after an assurance of Frankish support, re-anointed Pepin *Rex Dei Gratia* – King by the Grace of God.

In the same year, when he was nearly eighty, and regardless of the long life's work already behind him, Boniface set out from Mainz in pursuit of his boyhood dream of converting the Frisians and Saxons. At Dokkum in Frisia a band of heathen robbers made a surprise attack on his camp, and he and his companions were massacred. His body was brought back to Fulda and given solemn burial.

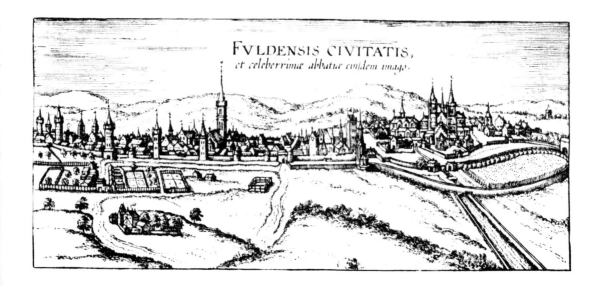

FVLDENSIS CIVITATIS,
et celeberrima abbatiæ eiusdem imago.

The most important Abbot of Fulda,

the monastery that St Boniface had founded, was Hrabanus Maurus, who laboured there in the first half of the ninth century. He was a pupil of Alcuin, the Anglo-Saxon divine from York who had been the teacher, advisor, and friend of Charlemagne. Hrabanus Maurus, called 'Preceptor of Germany', made his monastery into a centre of German learning. We are indebted to the Fulda Library, in which Hrabanus Maurus collected manuscripts of the classics, for the preservation of the works of Tacitus, the only source other than Julius Caesar of information about the ancient Germans. It was Alcuin and Hrabanus Maurus who made the decisive contribution to the spread of classical education in Germany. Among the many writings of Hrabanus Maurus was his *De Universo*, an encyclopaedia of the knowledge of his time in twenty-two volumes. He was probably also the author of the hymn 'Veni Creator Spiritus'.

The final victory of Christianity in the heart of Europe

is linked with the name and deeds of Charlemagne – Charles the Great. When he entered on his inheritance as King of the Franks, he found it threatened on every side by incalculable dangers. It took him thirty-five campaigns to overcome them all. After the death of his father Pepin the Short in 768, Charles shared the kingdom with his brother Carloman,

becoming sole ruler when Carloman died in 771. At his own
death in 814 (his tomb is in the
cathedral, left, at Aix-la-Chapelle)
Charlemagne had been for fourteen years Emperor of the West,
the first to bear that title since the
deposition of the boy-emperor Romulus Augustulus by the Roman
Army of the West in 476.

The hazards through which he
fought his way to this position may
be illustrated by a single famous
instance. He was in Pamplona, in
northern Spain, which he had just
conquered, when he received the alarming news that the Saxon hordes were
marching with fire and sword on Cologne. He had to drop all his successes
in Spain and hurry by forced marches to the Rhine. During his return
through the Pyrenees his rearguard, led by Hruotland, or Roland, Mar-
grave of Brittany, was waylaid by the Basques in the Valley of Roncesvalles.
La Chanson de Roland, the French heroic ballad, tells the story of the last
fight of Roland, who covered his king's retreat.

Charlemagne fought against Avars in the east and Moors in the south. He
subdued the Bavarians and the Saxons. On the Mediterranean coasts he
made war against the Saracens, on those of the North Sea against the Danes
and Norwegians. The empire that he ultimately ruled extended from
the Elbe, the Drava, and the Sava to the Atlantic Ocean and the Pyrenees,
and included almost the whole of Italy. Where Theodoric the Great, King
of the Ostrogoths, had failed three hundred years earlier, Charlemagne
succeeded in founding a German empire that could maintain itself in
company with the world powers of Byzantium and Islam and at the same
time had the strength to keep out the ceaseless pressure of peoples from the
steppes and forests of the East. In 802 Charlemagne sent an embassy of
peace and friendship to his 'sister empress', Irene in Byzantium, and is
recorded by some authorities as having asked for her hand in marriage.
Such a union, if it was ever meditated, might have restored a semblance
of the original Roman Empire, but the same year Irene, who had procured
the deposition and blinding of her own son, was deposed in her turn. In
800 the Patriarch of Jerusalem sent Charlemagne the keys of the city and

seven years later the Caliph Harun-al-Rashid confirmed his claim to imperial privileges in the Holy City, gestures symbolic of the greatest power attained by a Western ruler for four centuries.

The sword of Charlemagne achieved in many campaigns what had remained a distant dream for St Boniface. Apart from the Scandinavians, the last great Germanic tribe on the Continent to hold out against Christianity were the Saxons, and it was Charlemagne who carried through their conversion by force. The motive for his campaigns against the Saxons, however, was not simply evangelical. The experience of the Roman Empire had shown the danger constituted by the warlike and predatory Germanic tribes on the other side of the Rhine for the flourishing civilisation on its own side. Charlemagne wanted to secure his dominions against the invasions that had destroyed the Western Roman Empire. There is no doubt his campaigns against the Saxons were cruel and ruthless, but the Saxons were cruel and ruthless too. It may be doubted that he ever had 4,500 Saxons beheaded in a single day. Possibly this tradition may be based on a chronicler's slip – a confusion between '*decollare*' ('behead') and '*delocare*' ('deport'). But massacres and mass deportations there certainly were before the Saxons were finally converted and subdued.

Whatever Charlemagne's methods, their outcome was received without qualms as good news. When the news reached Rome of the conversion of the Saxon Duke Widukind and his people, the Pope proclaimed a general holiday for the whole of Christendom.

The bronze statuette, right, was made about a generation after the death of Charlemagne.

It is not to be regarded as a true likeness. Such a thing did not exist at that time. None the less, the artist has succeeded, in the portrait of this stern man with the Frankish cavalry moustache, the straight thin nose, and the soldierly bearing, in conveying something of the impression of majesty he made when alive.

Rather like Augustus before him, but in a very different cultural situation, Charlemagne is remembered in history not only for the feats of arms that enabled him to build an empire, but also for the vision and dedication with which he set about bringing order and improvement into every aspect of its life and government. His zeal for Christianity did not stop at conversion of the heathen. He exercised strict supervision of the Church, gave orders to its bishops, and concerned himself with a hundred details of Church life. He was generous, also, with gifts and endowments to monasteries and places of worship. His own imperial palace at Aix-la-Chapelle, with its chapel, was the work of the architect Odo von Metz. It was destroyed by bombing in the Second World War, but has been completely rebuilt since.

Among the peoples subdued by Charlemagne were the Lombards, against whom he marched, as his father had done, on behalf of the Pope. The crown (facing page) with which he crowned himself their king is today preserved in the Monza Cathedral treasure. The iron hoop visible inside the crown was forged, according to tradition, from a nail from the cross of Christ.

Among the personal possessions of Charlemagne which have been preserved is a sapphire pendant. It has had an interesting history. The grave of Charlemagne was opened once in 1000 by Otto III and once in 1165 by the Emperor Frederick Barbarossa. On both these occasions a number of valuables which had been put into the grave with Charlemagne's body were transferred to the Aix-la-Chapelle Cathedral treasure, where most of them are still kept. In 1804, when Napoleon came to Aix-la-Chapelle, some of these objects were presented to the Empress Josephine, the pendant among them. From her it passed by inheritance into the possession of the Empress Eugénie, wife of Napoleon III, and she on her deathbed entrusted it to the Abbot of Farnborough, Dom Fernand Cabrol, with the request

that he would take it to Cardinal Lucon, Archbishop of Reims. Thus this precious relic of Charlemagne came to Reims Cathedral, where almost all the great emperor's successors on the French throne have been crowned.

The illustration (facing page) shows the front of this pendant, which is set with a large oval sapphire, bright blue, and of the first water. Through the sapphire can be discerned a splinter of wood, which according to tradition comes from the cross of Christ. There is no longer any trace of a hair of the Virgin Mary, which is also supposed to be contained in it. The design of the pendant and the technique of the goldsmith's work point to a date near 800. The reliquary was worn by Charlemagne in life and death.

The imperial crown that was set on Charlemagne's head by Pope Leo III on Christmas Day, 800, has not been preserved. His chronicler, Einhard, relates that this coronation took Charlemagne by surprise. But he accepted both the crown and the title of Roman Emperor. Europe, through all the centuries when it had been laid waste in countless wars, plundered by innumerable conquerors, torn apart by dynastic struggles, impoverished, harassed, and plunged back into savagery, had never forgotten the old idea of the Roman Empire.

Charlemagne's empire did not long survive his death. It was revived by Otto the Great nearly a hundred and fifty years later. In 1157 Frederick Barbarossa added the word 'Sacrum' – 'Holy' – to its style. The crown

which was made for Otto the Great's coronation in 962, became the crown of the 'Holy Roman Empire of German Nation'. The workshop that produced this famous masterpiece of the medieval goldsmith's art was prob- ably that of Reichenau Monastery, where the imperial chancellery was lodged at that time. The crown was later altered in certain details. On the hoop the following inscription is set in pearls:

CHVONRADVS DEI GRATIA ROMANORV(M)
IMPERATOR AVG(VSTVS)

('Conrad by the Grace of God Emperor of the Romans Augustus')
The ruler referred to was Conrad II, who reigned from 1024 to 1039, and in whose reign the State was first referred to in documents as 'Romanum Imperium'. Among the oldest parts of the crown are the enamel plates, on one of which is a representation of King Solomon as the symbol of wisdom, on another of King David as the symbol of justice. Every part of the crown has a definite symbolic meaning connected with the liturgy of the imperial coronation. But its ultimate and deepest meaning was given to this crown of the Emperors, the temporal rulers of the West, by the highest symbol of Christendom – The Cross.

St Nicholas, born in Parrara in Lycia, became Bishop of Myra in Asia Minor in the fourth century. He is a popular figure, particularly with sailors and with children whose patron saint and benefactor he is. He was much revered in Christian Russia. In this stained glass pane we see him drawing a ship to land, while the False Pilgrim falls overboard.

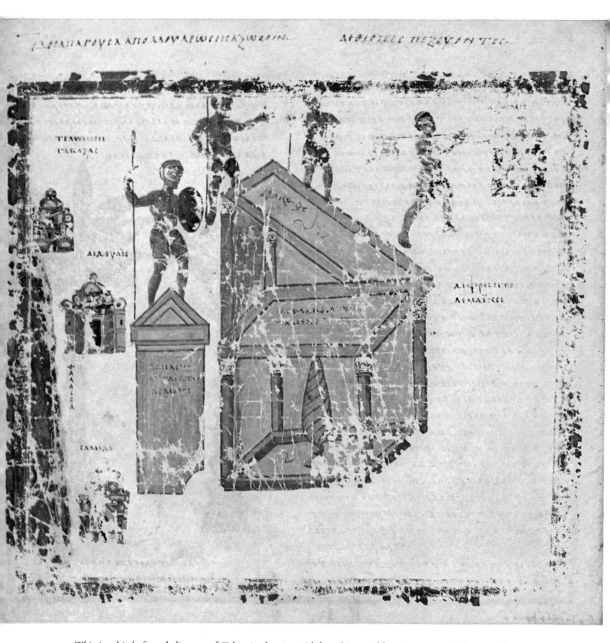

This is a kind of symbolic map of Ethiopia showing Aduli and its neighbouring towns, Gabazas and
Samidi, all three represented by stylized buildings. The place-names are given in Greek. To the right
of Aduli is a stele or column inscribed PTOLEMY THE EMPEROR (literally 'great king'),
and in the centre a cathedra in the form of a solium. Above the throne, Ethiopian foot soldiers march
from Aduli to Axum.

Aduli, which Cosmas Indicopleustes in his Topographia Christiana describes as a Christian
town, has long since disappeared.

Postscript

This colourful fish was found in the interior of a Saxon hanging-bowl from the Sutton Hoo ship burial (see page 301), which dates from the seventh century. It is of bronze and was originally spotted with enamel studs. The fish was, of course, the cryptic symbol of the Early Christian Church; but by the seventh century it is scarcely used any more in Christian art, outside the Coptic Church. It is surprising, therefore, that it should still occur in the North in recently converted Anglo-Saxon Britain.

The story of Jonah and the whale belongs to the Old Testament, but was repeated in the Koran. A representation of this legend finds a place also in a manuscript of the Universal History (Jama at Tawarikh) by Rashid ad-Din, and is reproduced opposite. This is a Persian painting of the Mongol period in tempera on paper, dating from the end of the fourteenth century. It is an example of the work of the Tabriz school. Rashid ad-Din, besides being a historian, was a capable physician, a sponsor of the arts and sciences and a powerful minister at the Persian court.

The early Christians imbued the story with symbolic meaning, and used it allegorically in one of their favourite prayers: 'O Lord, liberate my soul as you have liberated Jonah from the whale!'

THE STORY OF the spread of Christianity is our own story. A society is characterised not only by its relations with other societies but also by its past. We are accustomed to think of ourselves in the West today as belonging to one great society. The fact that a number of States scattered over a globe choose to be known as 'the West' can be explained only by reference to past history, going back to the Roman Empire of the West, from which we feel ourselves to be descended.

There are States described as 'Western' today on both sides of the Meridian of Greenwich and both sides of the equator, indeed on either side of any great circle that can be drawn around the globe. What they have in common is a certain historical descent. For when we look back into what we have been taught to think of as our own past, we see a succession of societies that seem in some way to have grown out of one another. We see first, nearest to us in time, the growth of a civilisation which is today spread all over the globe, and which began as the civilisation of Christian Europe. Behind that, and separated from it by a period of confusion and anarchy, we see the Roman Empire, embracing first the Mediterranean region and then expanding into western and central Europe; behind that again, the Hellenistic world that resulted from the conquests of Alexander the Great.

At this point the succession divides. For Alexander was undoubtedly a product of classical Greece, and had no less a tutor than Aristotle. Educated Europeans have at most periods been glad to acknowledge themselves the heirs of Greece. But there were times, too, when their cultural past, as it reached out behind the Hellenistic age, was apt to identify itself not with the history of the Greek city States but with that of the Jews as recorded in

This is the opening page of the Gospel of St Luke, and shows the Evangelist surmounted by his Symbol the winged bull; on either side are three pairs of scenes from the life of Christ, each annotated with a quotation in Latin from St Luke's Gospel. The delicate colouring is still in a particularly good state of preservation, though the text on the reverse side can be seen through the parchment at the top of the picture.

This fine illumination is to be found in the sixth-century 'Gospels of St Augustine', now in Corpus Christi College, Cambridge. The manuscript was probably written and illuminated in Italy, but had found its way to England by the seventh or eighth century. The corrections on it show that by the eleventh century it was at St Augustine's Abbey, Canterbury. No doubt it was amongst those books which Bede mentions as having been sent to St Augustine by Pope Gregory the Great shortly after the former's arrival in England in 596.

the Old Testament. At such times the Hebrew patriarchs and prophets were more intimately a part of the European heritage than the Greek heroes and demigods. The 'rediscovery' of the classics, indeed, is enshrined in our tradition as a revolutionary development and, under the name of the Renaissance, as a recognised watershed of European history.

Behind the Greeks and the Jews the lines of European ascent reach far back into prehistory. But even about this prehistory we have an intimate feeling of its being our past. Its importance to us can be measured by the amount of archaeological effort expended by Europeans on the Near and Middle East as compared with any other part of the world.

As we have seen in the previous pages there is an ambiguity about our Western descent. So far as it is Christian it ought to include Byzantium among its ancestors, yet the 'Western' point of view is that the Byzantine Empire is part of a different line, ending in Russia. Moreover, there is yet another, and wholly different, world community to which the Byzantine Empire stands in much the same ancestral relation as the Western Roman Empire to Western Europe. That is the world of Islam and the Arabs. The Muslims share both the Greek heritage and the Jewish tradition with the Christians but have made something entirely different out of them.

The notion that the past consists of civilisations and cultures, not simply of States and empires, has been given currency by modern sociology and anthropology, but it also reflects feelings about the modern world that do not find adequate expression in terms of political units. Civilisations are conceived as arising out of one another in a manner that disregards or transcends race and nation. They have ancestries or family trees and are often talked about in biological terms of birth, growth, aging, and death. The definition of a civilisation almost always involves reference to a religion, typically a higher religion with a comprehensive State cult. In recent times this notion has given rise to a kind of apocalyptic literature with its own vocabulary, culminating in the work of Arnold Toynbee.

The power groupings which confront one another in the modern world are separated by differences that can claim to be religious, and adherence to one group or other is determined as much by present beliefs and past history as by force or economic subjection. And this way of thinking about the past has been found peculiarly satisfying in such a world, which seems to be longing for political unification but fearing the price that may have to be paid for it. For those who feel themselves confronted by an impasse, it is comforting to think of great historical processes and patterns of organisation in which such impasses are circumvented or swallowed up.

This world in which we live has resulted from the spread of Christianity, and there are today more nominal Christians living in the world, forming a higher proportion of the world's population, than at any previous period in history. But it is not a Christian world. There are two explanations for this, one concerned with the failure of Christianity to make headway in other cultures, and the other concerned with its loss of command in the Christian communities themselves.

Taking the first one first, we have seen how in the early centuries of one era the Christian faith spread far outside the frontiers of Roman rule and scored spectacular successes in Asia but how it failed to maintain itself there and was either obliterated or reduced to a few scattered communities. We have seen also how in the latter half of the first millennium Christianity suffered its first great setback in the conquests of the Arabs and the rise of Islam. In Western Europe the Muslim invasion was stopped and driven back but it was not until the fifteenth century that the Moorish holdings in Spain were finally liquidated. At the other end of the Mediterranean during this same span of time the Muslims – Arabs, Persians, Turks – succeeded ultimately in overwhelming the Roman Empire of the East and occupying south-east Europe.

After the fifteenth century Western Christianity suffered no further territorial losses. In fact, it was already launched on its period of greatest expansion. In the far west, a great new continent, the existence of which had been unknown to the Romans, was discovered and incorporated in the Christian world. Bit by bit the coasts of Africa and Asia, the islands of the Pacific, were opened to European colonisation and trade. European rule was established in India, on the borders of China, and other ancient countries of Asia. In the far south another new continent was discovered and peopled by Europeans. While the interior of Africa was explored and the whole continent parcelled up among the western European nations, the Islamic world of the Middle East and North Africa was gradually brought under European control.

Not every country conquered by the Europeans was thereby converted to Christianity. India remained true to its older religions and the conversion of the Indian people did not form part of British policy there. But in other parts of the world societies more or less Christian usually resulted from the European conquest, particularly of course in those countries where the Europeans themselves settled in large numbers. In North America, above all, there grew up a new English-speaking nation which by the mid-twentieth century had become the dominant power in the Western world.

The rise of American power coincided with other developments which made it look as if European expansion had passed its peak. Europe was weakened and European self-confidence undermined by the effects of internal wars which eventually spread over the whole globe – the two World Wars. Free play was thereby given to certain tendencies which were implicit in European expansion. Europe consisted of nations, and nationalism was among Europe's principal exports. The sense of mission which, following on the pursuit of wealth, took Europeans into all parts of the world contained, besides a certain racial arrogance, assumptions about the welfare of the inhabitants of European colonies. After European rule had been imposed on the archaic civilisations, primitive cultures, and regions of anarchy which the Europeans overran, their non-European subjects began to give an obvious interpretation of their own to what the conquerors had taught them. As Europe weakened or lost confidence, they began to resist or throw off European rule.

Christianity was of course often implicated in these struggles but not in any direct or simple way. Despite the part played in the European expansion by the slave trade, by piracy and other forms of rapine and plunder, there was at most stages a definite accompaniment of missionary work, and the idea, not merely hypocritical, of bringing the Gospel to the heathen. This idea, it is true, was sometimes allowed to give respectability to proceedings that bore more resemblance to the early Viking raids than to the journeys of the Irish missionaries. The ruthlessness and arrogance towards other races so often shown by the conquering European has sometimes been laid to Christianity's charge. Christianity is no doubt an intolerant religion and the duty to proselytise is laid on every Christian, but it would be difficult to show that the aggressions and brutalities committed by Christian Europeans were different in kind from those committed by pagan peoples

Desiderius was a great benefactor of the monastery of Monte Cassino, of which he was abbot in the eleventh century. It was on his instructions that a life of the monastery's founder St Benedict was written and richly illuminated. This picture, taken from this book, shows a seated St Benedict holding a book in his left hand and blessing Desiderius with his right. The buildings behind the two figures probably represent the monastery. At Desiderius's feet lie other books, while the smaller buildings, the mountain and the trees below are the abbot's estates which, according to the inscription, he is also donating.

St Benedict, who was born in 480, founded Monte Cassino in 529, thereby creating monasticism for the West. In due course his Order grew to become one of the most important in Europe.

Cum dominus multos pluseis peract accipe libros.

Ruffer lectus presto. Celi michi prestator esto.

The temptation of St Anthony in the desert is the most frequently represented scene from the life of the Saint. Usually his tempters are depicted as hideous devils, but in this picture he is shown confronted outside his cell by a seductive young maiden with scarcely visible demon's wings. Nevertheless, St Anthony appears to have little difficulty in rebuffing the advances with a deprecatory gesture of his left land. The picture is by the Sienese painter Sassetta, who has brought a very personal touch to the temptation scene. It was painted c. 1436 and constitutes one of the surviving panels from the Asciano polytych.

The martyrdom of St Denis, the first bishop of Paris and patron saint of Paris, is here depicted in two parts separated by the Holy Trinity. Above the crucified Christ appears God the Father, surrounded by the angelic host. On the left the bishop is seen in prison being given the Eucharist by Christ Himself; the scene on the right shows him being beheaded. Of the Saint's two companions Rusticus and Clenthorius, one is already beheaded and the other is waiting with bowed head for the executioner's axe. The picture was painted by Henri Bellechose, who belonged to the Flemish School; he worked for the Dukes of Burgundy 1415–1440.

in similar circumstances and at similar stages of cultural development. It could with more force be argued that it was Christianity which first furnished a criterion, and which was responsible for improvements in European behaviour here and there, for the eventual abolition of the slave trade, the growth of self-criticism inside European society about its attitudes to subject races, and the developing sense of a common humanity.

Whatever the practice of individual Christians, the moral commandments preached by Christianity in its simplest form were unequivocal and provided an unchanging standard by which the actions of Christians were to be judged. There were always, even at the worst times, saintly characters to set an example. Christian morals have maintained, and in some cases increased, their hold on a society in which, for a century or more, institutional Christianity has itself been losing ground.

This brings us to the second explanation of why the world we live in is not a Christian one. Inside the Christian communities there is widespread loss of faith, and in many Christian countries the believing and practising members of the Christian Churches are now in a minority. The attitudes of the rest of the population towards institutional Christianity vary from outright hostility to the commonest case, a simple abstention from church-going; and their attitudes to religion vary from militant atheism through various forms of agnosticism to a mere lack of interest.

The situation is in fact strikingly reminiscent of that situation in the early Roman Empire in which Christianity itself arose. There is even a modern parallel to emperor-worship. In our time one entire province of Christendom has been detached from it by the victory of a political creed. Communism, a form of atheism that propagates the ideology of anti-faith, was established in Russia by the Russian revolution. The honours exacted by the new Soviet State and its ruler soon began to resemble those of a secular cult. Not only were its total demands on the individual such as to leave no place for any religion, but Christianity for many years was actively persecuted. It was this revolutionary creed which later took possession of China and enabled it to drive out the Europeans established in its treaty ports. It there displaced

The episode of doubting Thomas, who later became the Apostle of India, fills one of the quatrefoils of the Syon Cope, on which scenes from the life of Christ and that of the Virgin Mary are represented. The Cope with its interlaced quatrefoils is worked in silks on a linen foundation with silver-gilt thread added. Made in England in the first quarter of the fourteenth century, it is one of the best-preserved and most beautiful textiles of medieval times.

SCS ✠ IOHA

not only Taoism and Buddhism but above all Christianity, which had been – ironically enough in view of China's past experience of that religion – the inspiration of the first Chinese revolution earlier in the century.

Communism originated in the same development of ideas that led to the loss of Christian faith. Both were connected with the growth of modern science. Science has not only transformed the world materially, it has presented the greatest challenge to Christianity since its inception. What modern science offers is nothing less than an alternative account of the world and its origins, and the scientific challenge in its crudest form is a claim to supersede religion entirely. The extreme formulation of this claim is the assertion that religion was a mere phase in human development which we have now outgrown. Since science itself is a product of the European Christian and classical tradition, its argument with modern Christianity has the same intimate character as that of early Christianity with Greek philosophy. Today Christians find themselves in the same need of coming to terms with a secular system of thought as in those first centuries. The argument is already one and a half centuries old, and despite the dwindling of Christian congregations in many countries there are churchmen who think that Christianity may in the long run have gained by it, and under-gone much-needed renovation. It has been realised that the world for which science can account so fully has been put there by science. There are other worlds for which science cannot account. The intrusions of scientific method into Bible studies, Church history, and Christian archaeology are welcomed insofar as they clear the way to a truer understanding of Christian belief. The unexpected corroboration of Bible stories that has often been given by these methods has likewise been welcomed, but has not been allowed to affect the new appreciation by Christians of the function of myth in formulating truths about the world. It is no longer possible, as it was in the time of Sir James Frazer, to discredit the Gospel story by showing how many mythological elements it had in common with other cults among which it arose. Rather, a study of these similarities and echoes, which were freely and vigorously discussed at the time by the early Christian fathers but

The Godesalc Gospels were written and illuminated between 781 and 785 by the scribe Godesalc for Charlemagne. The manuscript was probably produced in Trèves, and the saints who are given most prominence are Maximinus of Trèves, Nazarius of Lorsch and Boniface of Fulda. Trèves had at that time a Syrian colony and the illuminations have certain Syrian characteristics; but the general influence of late antiquity is also very noticeable in such details as the chair on which the Evangelist sits.

345

later forgotten with paganism itself, is once again encouraged, for it is believed that they serve to root the faith more firmly in the human past.

Checked in its expansion and forced to retreat from older civilisations into which it had once gained entry, the Christian West today is no longer so certain of its mission or its future. It fears annihilation by the hydrogen bomb. It is menaced externally, and to a lesser extent internally, by a political creed, militant and revolutionary, which has gained control of a third of the world's population. It no longer has the faith it once had in science as holding the key to the future, but it has not yet regained its faith in Christianity. It has found itself giving sympathetic attention to other world religions, more ancient than Christianity, which have made prominent Western converts. The debate, however, between science and Christianity continues, and Christian doctrine has been strengthened by it. There can never have been in the whole history of Christianity a time when it was more profitable to study its origins than today.

ACKNOWLEDGEMENTS

The Author and Publishers would like to thank the following for their valuable help in providing illustrations and information: Donald Bullough, Edinburgh; Erica Cruikshank, Hamilton; C. R. Dodwell, Cambridge; Michael Edwardes, London; Henry Ellison, London; Dr Emslie, London; Michael Gough, Edinburgh; Baroness Elisabeth von Herwarth, London; Professor Max Hirmer, Munich; Professor Karnapp, Essen; Stephen Longstreet, Beverly Hills, California; Georgina Masson, Rome; F. L. Van Nice, Washington; Liam de Paor, Dublin; Thomas Pakenham, London; John Ward Perkins, Rome; C. A. Ralegh Radford, Uffculme, Devon; W. Staude, Paris; Dr Schaezler, Munich; Professor D. Talbot Rice, Edinburgh; Charles Thomas, Edinburgh; A. Trampitch, Paris; Professor E. K. Waterhouse, Birmingham; Professor G. Zarnecki, London.

They are indebted also to the following Museums, Libraries and other Institutions for their willing cooperation in placing documents at their disposal and in providing photographs together with permission to reproduce:

Accademia, Venice; American School of Classical Studies, Athens; Archaeological Museum, Istanbul; Archives Photographiques, Paris; Bayerische Staatsbibliothek, Munich; Bibliothèque Communale, Amiens; Biblioteca Laurenziana, Florence; Bibliothèque Nationale, Paris; Bibliothèque de Tours; Bildarchiv, Marburg University; Bodleian Library, Oxford; Bord Fáilte Éireann, Dublin; The British Academy, London; The British Museum, London; Byzantine Institute, Dumbarton Oaks, Washington, D. C.; Musée Cherbourg; China Society, London; Corinium Museum, Cirencester; Master and Fellows, Corpus Christi College, Cambridge; Courtauld Institute of Art, London; Cyprus Museum, Nicosia; Dean and Chapter of Durham Cathedral; Domgrabung, Cologne; Direzione Generale dei Musei e Gallerie Pontifici, Rome; École des Hautes Études, Sorbonne; Ehemals Staatliche Museen, Berlin-Dahlem; Gabinetto Fotografico Nazionale, Rome; H. M. Ministry of Works, London; H. M. Stationery Office, London; India Office Library, London; India House Library, London; John Rylands Library, Manchester; Kunsthistorisches Museum, Vienna; Kupferstichkabinett, Berlin; Lateran Museum, Rome; London Museum, London; Louvre, Paris; Magyar Nemzeti Muzeum, Budapest; Manx Museum, Isle of Man; Metropolitan Museum of Art, New York; Musée d'Art et d'Histoire, Ghent; Museo, Barcelona; Museo Arqueologico Nacional, Madrid; Museo Provincial,

Burgos; Museum of Art, Rhode Island School of Design, Providence, R. I.; Museum of Eastern Art, Oxford; National Buildings Record, London; National Central Museum, Taiwan (Formosa); National Gallery, London; National Museum of Antiquities of Scotland, Edinburgh; National Museum of Ireland, Dublin; National Museum of Wales, Cardiff; Pontificio Commissione di Archeologia Cristiana, Rome; Reverenda Fabbrica della Basilica di San Pietro in Vaticano, Rome; Rheinisches Landesmuseum, Bonn; Rheinisches Landesmuseum, Trier; Rheinisches Museum, Cologne; Römisch-Germanisches Museum, Cologne; Royal Institute of British Architects, London; Royal Irish Academy, Dublin; Russell Trust, University of Edinburgh; San Donato Museum, Zadar, Yugoslavia; Staatliche Museen, Berlin; Städtisches Museum, Cologne; Stiftsbibliothek St Gall, Switzerland; Trinity College, Dublin; Tunisian Embassy, London; Turkish Embassy, London; Uffizi, Florence; Dept. of Archaeology, University College of South Wales and Monmouthshire, Cardiff; University Museum, University of Pennsylvania, Philadelphia; Vatican Library, Rome; Vatican Museum, Rome; Victoria and Albert Museum, London; Warburg Institute, London; Dean and Chapter of Westminster Abbey, London; Yale University, USA.

They are particularly indebted to the following for providing photographs: Geoffrey Ashburner, ARPS, London; Roloff Beny, Rome; M. B. Cookson, London; John R. Freeman, London; Professor Max Hirmer, Munich; Ida Kar, London; Vincent Megaw, London; Rosemarie Pierer, Hamburg; Josephine Powell, Rome; Sansaini, Rome; Edwin Smith, London; Eileen Tweedy, London; Alinari, Florence; Anderson, Rome; Böhm, Venice; Bulloz, Paris; Gibson and Son, Penzance; Giraudon, Paris; Gudiol, Barcelona; The Impartial Reporter, Enniskillen; Izis, Israel; Mansell Collection, London; Mas, Barcelona; Paul Popper, London.

NOTES TO THE COLOUR PLATES

8 The Discovery of the True Cross is one of the frescoes with which Piero della Francesca began to fill the walls of the Church of San Francesco at Arezzo, a small town south of Florence, very soon after 1452. The subject of the frescoes, with which Piero was occupied for twelve years, is the Story of the True Cross, largely based on the *Golden Legend* of Jacopo Voragine. The plate shows a detail from the upper fresco on the east wall of the church, in which the Empress Helen watches as Judas raises one of the three crosses from the ground.
Photo Josephine Powell.

9 The four Evengelists in this Persian Manuscript, a 15th-century copy of a 13th-century diatessaron, are represented by their symbols: Mark by the lion; Luke by the bull; Matthew by the angel; and John by the eagle. They ar also each linked, as we are told by the Arabic inscription, with one of the four rivers of Paradise, and also with a foodstuff: the Solium and milk are associated with Matthew; the Tigris and wine with Luke; the Fison and honey with Mark; and the Euphrates and butter with John. The picture on the reverse of the leaf, Christ entering Jerusalem on an ass, shows through upside-down.
Cod. Medceo Persiano XVII, now 81.f.28 1 r.
By courtesy of the Direzione della Biblioteca Laurenziana, Florence.
Photo Alinari.

10 The Stoning of St Stephen. The saint is shown in the *orans* position and with his right knee bent, He is in the centre of an amphitheatre, in the podium of which are three arched doors and four windows. Behind it, in a semi-circle, are eight young men in the act of casting stones at the saint. The Greek inscription below St Stephen's feet reads: 'Stephen, the first Martyr, being stoned by the Jews', and above his head is the prayer 'Lord Jesus, receive my spirit'. The scene is an illumination in a 9th-century copy of the 6th-century *Topographia Christiana* of Cosmas Indicopleustes, which describes events and places of the Christian world.
Cod. Vat. Grec. 699. f.82. v.
By courtesy of the Direzione della Biblioteca Vaticana, Rome.

11 St Jerome in the Wilderness. In this picture the saint kneels before a rude cross, at the base of which crawls a serpent. He is more usually represented praying to a crucifix. The landscape in the background is so like the Jordan valley that it seems probable that the artist, Giovanni Battista Cima da Conegliano (1459/60–1517/18), had actually been there. St Jerome was born in Dalmatia in 840, and a great part of his life was spent in Bethlehem, where he died at the age of eighty-one; the cell in which he lived with the lion is still to be seen at the Church of the Nativity. One of the great fathers of the Latin Church, St Jerome is particularly important for Christianity as the translator of the Vulgate from Greek into Latin.
By courtesy of the Trustees of the National Gallery, London.
Photo Zoltan Wegner.

14 The Oppenheim Reliquary. According to tradition the reliquary originally came to Pope Innocent IV (1245–1254) from a member of his family who had taken part in the sack of Constantinople in 1204. The Pope presented the relic of the True Cross which it contained to the Church of Lavagna, but the enamelled box became an heirloom of the Fiesco family. It received its present name when it passed into the collection of Baron Albert von Oppenheim of Cologne.
Depicted in enamel over gold plates on the top and sides are a number of saints and apostles; and beneath the lid appear Biblical scenes: the Annunciation, Nativity, Crucifixion and Ascension; the reliquary is shallow, and has a sliding lid. The relic was contained in a cavity in the shape of a patriarchal cross.
By courtesy of the Metropolitan Museum, New York.

15 Mosaics from the Monastery Church of the Nea Moni on Chios. The magnificent mosaics of this 11th-century church follow a scheme common to all Byzantine churches of the period: they depict scenes from the New Testament in chronological order, from the Annunciation and the Nativity (destroyed) to the Descent of the Holy Ghost and the Ascent into Heaven. The mosaic in this plate shows Christ stretching out his hand to awaken Adam to eternal life. The picture of King David and King Solomon on page 182 is a detail from the left half of the same mosaic.
Photographed by Rosemarie Pierer at the suggestion of the author.

16 The Prophet Elijah. An icon representing Elijah and his raven painted on wood, and dating from the 11th–12th century. This unusual and colourful piece is in a private collection in the USA.
By courtesy of Stephen Longstreet, Beverly Hills, California, USA.

17 Isaiah at Prayer. The 9th-century psalter from which this illumination is taken contains fourteen similar scenes on different parchments. The miniatures must all have been painted in the court workshops at Constantinople, but the psalter was probably compiled over a period of time, and their dating has been the subject of much controversy.
From the Psalter, B. N. Grec. 139.
By courtesy of the Bibliothèque Nationale, Paris.
Photo Eileen Tweedy.

336 St Nicholas and the False Pilgrim. The legend goes that St Nicholas sometimes appeared to sailors of the Lycian coast in order to bring their ships safely to harbour. When he himself travelled by sea he calmed storms, and once he healed a sailor who had fallen from the mast. This scene is one of seven stained glass panes in the north window of the Jerusalem Chapel in Westminster Abbey. The glass is 13th-century.
By courtesy of the Dean and Chapter of Westminster Abbey, London.
Photo Eileen Tweedy.

337 Map showing the Christian town of Aduli and its neighbours, from a late 9th-century copy of the 6th-century *Topographia Christiana* by Cosmas Indicopleustes.

Notes to the colour plates

Cod. Vat. Grec. 699 f.15 v.
By courtesy of the Direzione della Biblioteca Vaticana, Rome.

338   Above: The fish from a 7th-century Saxon hanging-bowl, found in the ship burial at Sutton Hoo, Suffolk. The use of the fish as a Christian symbol stems from the Greek for a fish, **ΙΧΘΥΣ**, each letter forming the initial of the words in the formula 'Jesus Christ, Son of God, Saviour'. The theory that these hanging bowls, probably produced in Celtic Northumbria, were used either as liturgical lamps or as stoups is supported by the way the fish stands on its pedestal and is thus visible swimming in the liquid with which the bowl would have been filled.
By courtesy of the Trustees of the British Museum.
Photo Geoffrey Ashburner, ARPS.

Below: Jonah and the Whale. 14th-century Persian painting; tempera on paper.
33.113 Pulitzer Bequest Fund.
By courtesy of the Metropolitan Museum, New York.

339   Opening page of the Gospel of St Luke from the 6th-century 'Gospels of St Augustine'. Flanking the Evangelist seated beneath his symbol, the three pairs of scenes from the life of Christ, with their Latin references, are as follows:

Left, top   1 Zacharias and the Angel (Luke I, 12)
            2 Christ among the doctors (Luke II, 48)
middle   1 Christ teaching from the boat (Luke V, 3)
            2 St Peter falls at Christ's feet (Luke V, 8)
bottom   1 Raising of the son of the widow of Nain (Luke VII, 12)
            2 The call of Levi (Luke V, 27)
Right, top   1 Christ and the lawyer (Luke X, 25)
            2 Christ hailed by a woman (Luke XI, 27)
middle   1 Foxes have holes (Luke IX, 58)
            2 The parable of the fig-tree (Luke XIII, 6)
bottom   1 Miracle of the dropsical man (Luke XIV, 2)
            2 Christ and Zachaeus (Luke XIX, 4)
CCCC. MS. 286 f.129.
By courtesy of the Master and Fellows of Corpus Christi College, Cambridge.
Photo Eileen Tweedy.

342   Abbot Desiderius hands over books and other possessions to St Benedict, the founder of the Monastery of Monte Cassino. St Benedict had been so greatly shocked by the wickedness of Rome that he went to the mountain hermitage of Subiaco, where he passed three years of rich spiritual development. The fame of his holiness spread. Numerous disciples from far and near gathered round him. They were so many that he founded twelve small monasteries, over which he ruled for twenty years. He then left Subiaco to found the great Monastery on the site of the famous Temple of Apollo on Monte Cassino.
Vat. Inst. 1202 f.2 r.
By courtesy of the Direzione della Biblioteca Vaticana, Rome.

343   Above: The Temptation of St Anthony in the desert. The panel belongs to the Jarvis Bequest, Yale University Art Gallery.
By courtesy of Yale University Art Gallery, USA.
Photo Anna Wachsmann.

Below: The Martyrdom of St Denis. The artist, Henri Bellechose, who belonged to the Flemish School, died before 1444. He probably painted this picture in 1415.
By courtesy of the Louvre, Paris.
Photo Eileen Tweedy.

344   The Syon Cope is one of the treasures of the Victoria and Albert Museum. It belonged formerly to the Nunnery of Sion in Middlesex and is one of a large group of English medieval embroideries called Opus Anglicanum. The fame of these embroideries spread to the Continent, and such large quantities were exported that more pieces survive in Europe than in England. One closely related cope is now in the Museo Christiano in the Vatican.
Photo Victoria and Albert Museum.
Crown copyright reserved.

345   The Godescalc Gospels, from which this illumination is taken, belong to a series of manuscripts together known as the Ada Group, so called after Ada, the patroness of one of these splendid old codices. A later tradition has it that Ada was the sister of Charlemagne.
B.N. Lat. 1203 f.3 r.
By courtesy of the Bibliothèque Nationale, Paris.
Photo Eileen Tweedy.

NOTES ON THE ILLUSTRATIONS

I How it began

17 Monogram of Christ between St Peter and St Paul on a gilt glass medallion dating from the 4th–5th century.
Photo Metropolitan Museum of Art, New York.

23 Jerusalem, the Divided City; a photograph showing the no-man's-land between the Jordanian and Israeli part of the city.
Photo Izis.

24 Pentecost; a wall painting of c. 1350–55 by Andrea da Firenze in the vault of the Spanish Chapel in Sta Maria Novella, Florence. The Holy Ghost, symbolised by a dove, is seen descending upon the Virgin and the Apostles surrounding her. In front of the house citizens stand listening.
Photo Alinari.

25 The Twelve Apostles; an illumination in the margin of a Greek Psalter of 1066. Three of the Apostles are replaced by Paul, Mark and Luke; each is talking to a group representing different peoples.
British Museum Add. MS. 19.352. ff. 19v. and 20r.
By courtesy of the Trustees of the British Museum.

26 St Peter holding his emblem, the keys of heaven; a 12th-century stone sculpture from the Abbey of Cluny.
By courtesy of the Museum of Art, Rhode Island School of Design, Providence, R. I.

27 A stone slab of Theodotus with a Greek inscription, found in the Ophel Synagogue, Jerusalem. From E. K. Sukenik, *Ancient Synagogues in Palestine and Greece*, Schweich Lectures of the British Academy, 1930.
By courtesy of the British Academy.

28 The Stoning of St Stephen; a detail from one of the tapestries designed by Raphael for the Sistine Chapel, c. 1519, showing the Saint having a vision of Paradise, and some of his tormentors. In the foreground the clothing is guarded by the young Saul.
Galleria degli Arazzi, Vatican Museum, Rome.
Photo Alinari.

29 The Conversion of St Paul; a 16th-century engraving by Marten van Heemskerk, from his series *The Acts of the Apostles.*
By courtesy of the Trustees of the British Museum.
Photo Thames and Hudson archive.

30 The Roman Gate at Damascus; a lithograph from L. de Laborde, *Voyage en Orient*, II, 1838.
By courtesy of the Trustees of the British Museum.
Photo Thames and Hudson archive.

31 Bird's-eye view of Damascus; a Dutch engraving of 1668 showing many ancient buildings of Damascus in imaginative reconstructions.
Department of Prints and Drawings, British Museum.
By courtesy of the Trustees of the British Museum.
Photo Thames and Hudson archive.

32 View into the courtyard of the Omayyad Mosque in Damascus, with the Jesus minaret of Madinet Isa.
Photo Roloff Beny.

The Straight Street in Damascus still follows the line of the Roman street. Parts of the colonnade with which it was flanked survive.
Photo Courtauld Institute of Art, London.

33 St Paul being lowered by night from the walls of Damascus, a relief cast in bronze from the Triumphal Column of Bernward in Hildesheim Cathedral, c. 1030.
Bildarchiv-Foto-Marburg.

35 Ruins of Caesarea.
Photo Izis.

36 The Roman road leading through the desert from Damascus to Antioch.
Photo Dr M. Emslie.

37 Personification of Antioch; a late 4th-century silver statue from the Esquiline Treasure symbolising the town and the river Orontes.
By courtesy of the Trustees of the British Museum.

38 The modern Turkish village, Antakya, which is built upon the ruins of Antioch.
Photographed by Rosemarie Pierer at the suggestion of the author.

39 The Chalice of Antioch, a 4th–5th century silver goblet, decorated with vine leaves and symbolical scenes.
In the Metropolitan Museum of Art, New York.
Photo Giraudon.

40 The church of Panaya Chrysopolitissa in Paphos, Cyprus, with ancient columns from the Palace of the Roman Governor in the foreground.
Photo Cyprus Museum, Nicosia.

41 View of Tarsus in Asia Minor, with the Taurus mountains in the background; a 19th-century lithograph published by the Working Men's Educational Union.
Department of Maps, British Museum.
By courtesy of the Trustees of the British Museum.
Photo Thames and Hudson archive.

42 Paul and Barnabas at Lystra; a detail from the cartoon by Raphael for one of the tapestries for the Sistine Chapel, c. 1516.
Photo Victoria and Albert Museum, London.
Crown copyright reserved.

43 A view from the sea of Kavalla and the Roman aqueduct; a lithograph from M. A. Walker, *Through Macedonia*, London, 1864.
Photo Thames and Hudson archive.

Old Roman Road on the coast near Kavalla; a lithograph from M. A. Walker, *Through Macedonia*, London, 1864.
Photo Thames and Hudson archive.

44 Ruins of an ancient arch of Philippi; a steel engraving from L. Heusey and H. Daumet, *Mission Archéologique de Macédoine*, 1876.
Photo Thames and Hudson archive.

45 St Paul and Silas as prisoners in Philippi during the earthquake, which is symbolised by a human figure. A tapestry made for the Sistine Chapel from a design by Raphael, c. 1519.
Galleria degli Arazzi, Vatican Museum, Rome.
Photo Alinari.

46 View of the port and town of Thessalonike from the sea; an engraving from *Die Hoche Stein-Klippen und Geburge Cyaneae, Olympus und Athos ... Dem Curiosen Leser zur Nachricht und Belustigung, Historisch und in Kupffern vorgestellt, 1689.*
Photo Thames and Hudson archive.

Notes on the illustrations

page

47 St Paul preaching at Athens; detail from the cartoon for a tapestry for the Sistine Chapel by Raphael, c. 1516.
Photo Victoria and Albert Museum, London.
Crown copyright reserved.

The Stoa of Attalos in the Agora of Athens; reconstructed with the help of old plans and descriptions by the American School of Classical Studies, Athens, upon its original foundation, and exactly as it appeared when it was first built in the 3rd century B. C. It was finished in 1958.
Photo American School of Classical Studies, Athens.

48 The Mocking of St Paul; an illumination in Codex 64 of the St Gall library, dating from the first half of the 10th century.
By courtesy of the Stiftsbibliothek St Gallen, Switzerland.

49 Bird's-eye view of Ephesus with the estuary of the Kaystros. 18th-century travellers' archaeological accounts of this cannot be corroborated to any great extent by subsequent excavations. This map is nevertheless important as it shows how far sand had choked up the bay 250 years ago.
Pitton de Tournefort, *Relation d'un voyage du Levant*, II, 1717.
Photo Thames and Hudson archive.

50 The Temple of Diana at Ephesus; an engraving showing a fairly accurate reconstruction of the ancient temple, 300 years before it was excavated. In A. Tempesta, *The Seven Wonders of the World*, 1609.
Photo Thames and Hudson archive.

51 Diana at Ephesus; a statue with the head of bronze. A Roman copy of 3rd century A. D.
Museo Nazionale, Naples.
Photo Alinari.

52 Ruins of the Theatre, Ephesus.
Photographed by Rosemarie Pierer at the suggestion of the author.

53 St Paul on Malta; an ivory, the so-called Carrand Diptych, produced in 380–400.
Now in the Museo Nazionale, Florence.
Photo Alinari.

54 Onesimus sent back to his master Philemon by Paul; a woodcut from the *Malermi Bible*, Venice, 1490.
By courtesy of the Trustees of the British Museum.
Photo Thames and Hudson archive.

II The Silent Centuries

55 Vision of Christ and The Seven Lamps as described in the Apocalypse; an early 13th-century illumination.
British Museum Cotton MS. Nero D. I. f.156.
By courtesy of the Trustees of the British Museum.

61 The symbols of the Four Evangelists from the so-called Pax Gospel-cover, dating from the 12th century; repoussé and filigree inlaid with precious stones and enamel plaques.
San Lorenzo, Chiavenna.
Photo Alinari.

63 A fragment of St John's Gospel, dating from the first half of the 2nd century. The famous *Rylands Greek Papyrus 457.*
By courtesy of the John Rylands Library, Manchester.

page

64 A fragment from an unknown Gospel, dating from the first half of the 2nd century.
British Museum Egerton Papyrus 2.
By courtesy of the Trustees of the British Museum.

65 The Evangelist Mark; a 6th-century mosaic from the Church of San Vitale, Ravenna.
Photo Anderson.

66 View of Smyrna; a lithograph from L. de Laborde, *Voyage en Orient*, I, 1838.
By courtesy of the Trustees of the British Museum.
Photo Thames and Hudson archive.

67 Chapel erected in Smyrna in memory of St Polycarp; an engraving from *Die Hoche Stein-Klippen und Geburge Cyaneae, Olympus und Athos ... Dem Curiosen Leser zur Nachricht und Belustigung, Historisch und in Kupffern vorgestellt, 1689.*
Photo Thames and Hudson archive.

The martyrdom of St Polycarp; a coloured woodcut from the *Legenda Aurea*, Augsburg, 1494.
By courtesy of the Trustees of the British Museum.
Photo Thames and Hudson archive.

68 Fragment of Tatian's *Diatesseron*, from a papyrus found in Dura Europus.
Photo Dura Europos Publications, Yale University, USA.

Head of Christ; a gilded glass medallion of the 3rd–5th century.
By courtesy of the Trustees of the British Museum.

69 Pliny the Younger; a seated figure on the west facade of Como Cathedral, 16th century, by A. de Lurago.
Photo Alinari.

71 The Emperor Trajan, engraved after a Roman coin; in J. de Strada, *Epitome Thesauri Antiquitatem*, 1553.
Photo Thames and Hudson archive.

72 An olive tree more than two thousand years old, in the vicinity of Bethlehem.
Photo E. Cruikshank.

73 Solomon's Cedars of Lebanon; a lithograph in L. de Laborde, *Voyage en Orient*, II, 1838.
By courtesy of the Trustees of the British Museum.
Photo Thames and Hudson archive.

74 Reconstruction of North Wall of the Christian Baptistery of Dura Europus.
In Yale University Art Gallery.
Photo Dura Europos Publications, Yale University.

75 The Good Shepherd; a wall painting from Dura Europus. The probable original state of this picture is shown on the left in the reconstruction.
In Yale University Art Gallery.
Photo Dura Europos Publications, Yale University.

76 Moses and the Burning Bush, from the Synagogue in Dura Europus.
Now in the New Museum of Damascus.
Photo Dura Europos Publications, Yale University.

78 Ruins of Palmyra in the Syrian desert.
Photo Roloff Beny.

78–79 Rusafa; the view from the north-east corner of the ruined town wall towards the former town centre, taken during the excavations conducted by Professor Karnapp.
Photo Professor Karnapp, Essen.

79 Rusafa; a reconstruction of the North Gate by Professor Karnapp.

81 View of Edessa.
Photo Turkish Embassy, London.

352

page

82 St Simon Stylites; from a 6th-century silver plaque. *Now in the Louvre, Paris.*

83 The Monastery of St Simon Stylites, Kalat Siman; from De Vogué, *La Syrie Centrale*, 1865. *Photo Thames and Hudson archive.*

Fragment of the column of St Simon Stylites in Kalat Siman. *Photo E. Cruikshank.*

84 Bird's-eye view of Patmos, the island of St John's Vision of the Apocalypse; an engraving from Pitton de Tournefort, *Relation d'un voyage du Levant*, I, 1717. *Photo Thames and Hudson archive.*

85 The Cave of St John on Patmos; an engraving from T. Milner, *The Seven Churches of Asia*, 1832. *Photo Thames and Hudson archive.*

St John on Patmos; a detail from the wall painting by Giotto of c. 1320 in the Peruzzi Chapel, Sta Croce, Florence. *Photo Anderson.*

87 View from the theatre of Pergamon looking towards the Turkish city of Bergama. *Photographed by Rosemarie Pierer at the suggestion of the author.*

88 Asia Minor; a composite view from the title page of L. de Laborde's *Voyage en Orient*, I, 1838. *Photo Thames and Hudson archive.*

89 The Ruins of Laodicea; an early 19th-century engraving from R. Walsh and T. Allom, *Constantinople and the Seven Churches of Asia Minor*, n. d. *Photo Thames and Hudson archive.*

90 St Thekla; an illumination in a Greek Menologium of the 12th century. *British Museum Add. MS. 11870 f.174v.* *By courtesy of the Trustees of the British Museum.*

91 The walls of Konia (Iconium) the capital of the empire of the Seljuks; a lithograph from L. de Laborde, *Voyage en Orient*, I, 1839. *By courtesy of the Trustees of the British Museum.* *Photo Thames and Hudson archive.*

92 Silver reliquary from Cirga, Turkey, c. A. D. 500. *Now in the Museum, Adana.* *Photo Michael Gough.*

Minoan Goddess between beasts, from a seal of c. 2000 B.C. found at Mycenae; in Sir Arthur Evans, *The Mycenean Tree and Pillar Cult*, 1901. *By courtesy of Macmillan and Co. Ltd.*

III Roma Aeterna

93 The Good Shepherd was a favourite symbol of early Christianity. This stone sculpture, reminiscent of the Greek Orpheus, dates from the late 3rd century. *Now in the Louvre, Paris.* *Photo Archives Photographiques.*

101 The Dream of the Emperor Constantine; a wall painting by Piero della Francesca of c. 1460 in San Francesco, Arezzo. This depicts Constantine asleep in his tent before the fateful battle of Ponte Milvio, dreaming that victory will come to him at the sign of the Cross, which an angel holds in the upper left corner of the picture. *Photo Alinari.*

page

102 The Catacombs of Praetextatus as they looked to the 19th-century draughtsman of the *Bulletin d'archéologie chrétienne*, 1872. *Photo Thames and Hudson archive.*

103 Sermon on the Mount; a relief from a 4th-century sarcophagus found in a catacomb. *Now in the Terme Museum, Rome.* *Photo Bulloz.*

104 Oil lamps from a catacomb; a 17th-century engraving by A. Bosio in his *Roma Sotterranea*, 1632. *Photo Thames and Hudson archive.*

105 The Vatican Obelisk and Sta Maria delle Febbre; a drawing made in the 16th century by Marten van Heemskerk, showing the Obelisk's original place at the side of St Peter's. *By courtesy of the Kupferstichkabinett, Berlin.*

106 An ancient circus scene, engraved after a reputedly 5th-century rock-crystal, formerly in the collection of the King of Naples. From James Jassie and R. E. Raspi, *A Descriptive Catalogue of a General Collection of Ancient and Modern Gems*, 1741. *By courtesy of the Trustees of the British Museum.* *Photo Thames and Hudson archive.*

107 The Colosseum with the Cross in the centre, erected in memory of the Christians martyred there. This 19th-century lithograph by Wightwick and Baynes shows how it appeared before excavations took place. *Photo Thames and Hudson archive.*

108 The Colosseum. Today the Cross has been moved to one side following the excavation of the centre. *Photo Georgina Masson.*

109 'Domine, quo vadis?' Painting by Annibale Caracci. *By courtesy of the Trustees of the National Gallery.*

110–111 The capture and decapitation of St Paul; 16th-century reliefs by Matteo Pollaiuolo on the ciborium of Pope Sixtus IV. *Grotte Vaticane, Rome. Photo Alinari.*

111 The translation of the bodies of SS Peter and Paul; a 17th-century engraving after a lost relief, formerly in the Old Basilica of St Peter. The soldiers are symbolic of the threat to Christians. From A. Bosio, *Roma Sotterranea*, 1632. *Photo Thames and Hudson archive.*

112 Pilgrims' graffiti invoking St Peter and St Paul, in the Catacombs of S. Sebastiano, Rome. *Photo Richter.*

113 The seven-branched candlestick; a detail of a relief on the Arch of Titus, Rome, representing the military campaigns of the victorious general. *Photo Anderson.*

114 This Roman floor mosaic was discovered during recent excavations under the Church of St John of the Lateran, Rome. *Photo Pontificio Commissione di Archeologia Sacra.*

115 View of the Church, Baptistery and Palace of the Lateran, from J. Ciampini, *De Sacris Aedificiis a Constantino Magno Constructis*, 1693. *Photo Thames and Hudson archive.*

116 Interior view of the Constantinian Basilica of St Peter, Rome, from J. Ciampini, *De Sacris Aedificiis a Constantino Magno Constructis*, 1693. *Photo Thames and Hudson archive.*

Notes on the illustrations

page

149 Seal of the Patriarch of Constantinople; an engraving from G. Schlumberger, *Sigillographie de l'Empire Byzantin*, 1884.
Photo Thames and Hudson archive.

Onyx bust of Constantine, once part of a sceptre; an 18th-century engraving, formerly in the Sainte Chapelle.
In the Cabinet des Medailles, Bibliothèque Nationale, Paris.
Photo Thames and Hudson archive.

150 Eagle with serpent; a 5th-century floor mosaic from the Great Palace of Constantinople.
Photo Professor Max Hirmer.

151 5th-century mosaic with portrait of a barbarian prince from the Great Palace of Constantinople.
Photo Professor Max Hirmer.

152 The translation of the relics of St John Chrysostom to the Church of the Apostles in Constantinople, showing the church which was later destroyed by the Turks. Illumination from *MS. Vat. Grec. 1613 f.353.*
By courtesy of the Direzione della Biblioteca Vaticana.

153 The Church of St Irene photographed from Hagia Sophia, Constantinople.
Photo F. L. van Nice, Dumbarton Oaks, Washington, D. C.

154 Fragment of a pediment from the first Hagia Sophia in Constantinople.
Photo Professor E. K. Waterhouse.

Cornice with lambs, from the first Hagia Sophia.
Photo Professor E. K. Waterhouse.

155 Marble bust of the Empress Helena; 4th century, probably made during the Empress's lifetime.
Sambon Collection, Paris. Photo Giraudon.

156 St Helena; detail of relief from the Kelloe Cross showing the Invention of the Holy Cross.
Photo Otto Fein, Warburg Institute, London.

157 Constantine and Helena with the Cross; a fresco at Goreme, Ürgüb.
Photographed by Rosemarie Pierer at the suggestion of the author.

158-9 Reconstruction of Jerusalem in Biblical times; a 17th-century engraving by Daniel Hertz.
By courtesy of the Trustees of the British Museum.
Photo Thames and Hudson archive.

160-1 A True Picture of Ancient Jerusalem; a representation of the Jerusalem of the Old Testament with the Temple of Solomon in an engraving by Henry Overton after a drawing by Wenzel Hollar, London, 1715.
By courtesy of the Trustees of the British Museum.
Photo Thames and Hudson archive.

161 The Omar Mosque in Jerusalem, also known as the Dome of the Rock, with the Haram esh-sherif, the sacred precinct upon which the Temple of Solomon once stood.
Photo Paul Popper.

162 Holy Sepulchre and its Church; a 14th-century drawing. *MS. Cod. Urb. Vat.* 1362.
By courtesy of the Direzione della Biblioteca Vaticana.

Church of the Holy Sepulchre, Jerusalem, as it appears today.
Photo E. Cruikshank.

page

163 Christ enthroned before the hill of Golgotha, with the holy buildings of Jerusalem in the background. A mosaic of c. 400 in the apse of Santa Pudenziana in Rome.
Photo Alinari.

Church of the Holy Sepulchre; an engraving by G. Sandys in *Relation of a Journey*, 1615.
Photo Thames and Hudson archive.

164 Cross-section of the Church of the Nativity; an engraving by B. Amico da Gallipoli, in *Trattato delle piante et imagine dei sacri edificii di Terra Santa*, Rome, 1609.
Photo Thames and Hudson archive.

165 Church of the Nativity, Bethlehem. Since the wall dividing nave and choir has been removed it is again possible to have an unobstructed view of the apse.
Photo Roloff Beny.

166 The Councils of the Church, mosaics from the Church of the Nativity, Bethlehem; an engraving from J. Ciampini, *De Sacris Aedificiis a Constantino Magno Constructis*, 1693.
Photo Thames and Hudson archive.

167 Nicaea. A 15th-century woodcut from H. Schedel, *Liber Chronicarum*, Nuremberg, 1493.
By courtesy of the Trustees of the British Museum.
Photo Thames and Hudson archive.

168 A gate in the town wall of Nicaea. An early 19th-century lithograph from C. Texier, *Description de l'Asie Mineure*, I, Paris, 1839.
By courtesy of the Trustees of the British Museum.
Photo Thames and Hudson archive.

169 The first Council of Nicaea, as shown by Michael Damaskinos, a 16th-century Cretan painter in a picture in the Church of St Menas, Heraklion, Crete.
Photographed by Rosemarie Pierer at the suggestion of the author.

170 Illumination from a Greek manuscript of 1066. On the left, discussion of the problem of iconolatry is taking place; on the right iconoclasts are whitewashing an icon.
British Museum, Add. MS. 19352. f.90 v.
By courtesy of the Trustees of the British Museum.

171 A 6th-century silver gilt liturgical fan, with a representation of an archangel.
Archaeological Museum, Istanbul.
Photo Professor Max Hirmer.

172 A medaillon showing the crucifixion, found in Kertsch in the Crimea.
In the Louvre, Paris.
Photo Fonds Louvre Antiquités Chrétiennes.

Rock crystal fish of the 6th century with engraved decoration. Probably Egyptian work.
Collection of A. Trampitch, Paris.

173 View of Hagia Sophia from the south after it had become a mosque. In G. J. Grelot, *Relation d'un Voyage de Constantinople*, 1680.
Photo Thames and Hudson archive.

174 Interior of Hagia Sophia, seen from one of the galleries.
Photo F. L. van Nice, Dumbarton Oaks, Washington, D. C.

175 Head of an angel; a fragment of a 9th-century mosaic recently discovered in Hagia Sophia.
By courtesy of the Byzantine Institute, Dumbarton Oaks, Washington, D. C.

Notes on the illustrations

page

176 Coronation of Romanos and Eudoxia; ivory, c. 950.
Cabinet des Medailles, Bibliothèque Nationale, Paris.
Photo Professor Max Hirmer.

The Veroli Casket, ivory, 10th century, is characteristic of the classical revival of that period.
Photo Victoria and Albert Museum. Crown copyright reserved.

177 The crown of the Emperor Constantine Monomachos, dated between 1042 and 1055, is decorated with enamel plaques bearing figures.
By courtesy of the Magyar Nemzeta Museum, Budapest.

178 Interior of the Cathedral of St Sophia in Kiev, showing the arrangement of the frescoes. C. V. Bezsonov, *Istoriya Ruskoĭ Arkhitektury,* 1956.

179 St Sophia, Kiev. The 10th-century church was later enlarged and its interior elaborately decorated. C. K. Loukomski, *L'architecture religieuse russe du 12ième au 17ième siècle,* 1926.

Tomb of Yaroslav the Wise, in St Sophia, Kiev. C. V. Bezsonov, *Istoriya Ruskoĭ Arkhitektury,* 1956.

180 This interior view of the Cathedral of St Sophia, Novgorod, clearly shows its affinity to the Byzantine churches. G. K. Loukomski, *L'architecture religieuse russe du 12ième au 17ième siècle,* 1926.

181 The cloister and church of Nea Moni lie in a remote part of the Greek island of Chios.
Photographed by Rosemarie Pierer at the suggestion of the author.

182 The kings David and Solomon; an 11th-century mosaic in the Church of Nea Moni, Chios.
Photographed by Rosemarie Pierer at the suggestion of the author.

183 This group of nuns was painted c. 1400 and belongs to the Typicon, formerly at Lincoln College, Oxford, and now in the Bodleian Library, Oxford. 'Typicon' is the name given in the Eastern Church to a liturgical handbook which gives the divine services for the ecclesiastical year.
Bodleian Library. MS. Grec. 35.
Photo Professor Max Hirmer.

185 The ruined walls of Constantinople, which for so long protected the West from the East.
Photographed by Rosemarie Pierer at the suggestion of the author.

186 Portrait of Sultan Mohammed II by the Venetian painter Gentile Bellini, dated 1480.
By courtesy of the Trustees of the National Gallery.

V   On the Margin of the Antique World

187 Christ crowned with thorns; a detail from an 18th-century Abyssinian manuscript.
Bibliothèque Nationale. Fonds Ethiopiens 60–62.
By courtesy of the Bibliothèque Nationale, Paris.

193 A page of the 4th-century Codex Sinaiticus, with part of the Epistle to the Galatians.
By courtesy of the Trustees of the British Museum.

194 A bird's-eye view of Etchmiadzin in Armenia, with its three churches. An engraving from G. Chardin, *Journal du Voyage en Perse,* 1686.
Photo Thames and Hudson archive.

page

195 One of the three churches in Etchmiadzin, Armenia. It is a characteristic example of Armenian architecture, which is notable for its affinity to the Romanesque churches of Western Europe.
Photo Ida Kar.

196 Erivan with Mount Ararat and Noah's Ark on its peak; an engraving from G. Chardin, *Journal du Voyage en Perse,* 1686.
Photo Thames and Hudson archive.

197 St Gregory the Illuminator, the national saint of Armenia; an illumination from the Chikbak Gospel. *Armenian MS. 10 f.257, John Rylands Library.*
By courtesy of the John Rylands Library, Manchester.

198 Martyrdom of Gregory the Illuminator; an illumination from a 12th-century Greek manuscript. *British Museum Add. MS. 11870 f.242 v.*
By courtesy of the Trustees of the British Museum.

199 The Church of Achtamar in Armenia, famous for its rich sculptured decoration, built in the 10th century by King Gagik.
Photo J. Powell.

200 A Seraph; a relief from the Church of Achtamar.
Photo J. Powell.

Winged genius on a door jamb from the Persian royal palace at Pasargadae, 6th century B.C. Between this relief and the one in the preceding figure there is an interval of 1500 years. Engraving from C. Texier, *Description de l'Arménie,* II, 1852.
Photo Thames and Hudson archive.

201 The Forty Martyrs of Sebaste; a Byzantine ivory of the 10th or 11th century.
Berlin-Dahlem, former State Museum.

202 Recovery of the relics of the Forty Martyrs of Sebaste from the sea; an illumination from a Greek Psalter of 1066.
Add. MS. 19 352 f.82 v.
By courtesy of the Trustees of the British Museum.

203 The Robe of Christ forms part of the arms of Georgia. A woodcut from a Georgian Bible, printed in Moscow in 1740.
By courtesy of the Trustees of the British Museum.
Photo Thames and Hudson archive.

King Mirian, the first Christian King of Georgia. A woodcut from M. Tamarati, *L'Eglise Georgienne,* 1910.
Photo Thames and Hudson archive.

204 According to tradition the church at Pitzounda, Armenia, was founded by the Apostle Andrew. It was restored during the reign of the Emperor Justinian. A lithograph from F. Dubois de Montpereux, *Voyage en Caucase,* 1843.
Photo Thames and Hudson archive.

205 Gold reliquary with enamel plaques showing St George and St Demetrius. It has a Georgian as well as a Greek inscription. Byzantine, 12th century.
By courtesy of the Trustees of the British Museum.

206 Interior of the same reliquary with a fragment of wood from the True Cross.
By courtesy of the Trustees of the British Museum.

207 Fire Altars of the followers of Zoroaster; a lithograph from F. Flandin and P. X. Coste, *La Perse Ancienne,* IV, 1851.
Photo Thames and Hudson archive.

208 Two Persian kings, Shapur II and Shapur III; an engraving after a Persian rock relief. From M. Dieulafoy, *L'Art antique de la Perse,* II, 1884–89.
Photo Thames and Hudson archive.

page

208 Battle between a Roman and a Persian on horse-back. Sardonyx.
Cabinet des Médailles, Bibliothèque Nationale.
Camée 360.
By courtesy of the Bibliothèque Nationale, Paris.

209 The Immaculate Conception is foretold to the three holy kings; an illumination from an Arabic manu-script.
Biblioteca Laurenziana Med. Pal. 387, Florence.
Photo Collection chrétienne et byzantine, Ecole des Hautes Etudes, Sorbonne, Paris.

210 View of the Monastery of St Catherine at the foot of Jebel Musa on Mt Sinai; a lithograph after a drawing by D. Roberts in G. Croly, *Syria, Arabia, Egypt,* 1843.
Photo Thames and Hudson archive.

211 Ground plan of the Monastery Church of St Cathe-rine on Mt Sinai; an engraving from R. Pocock, *Description of the East,* I, 1743.
Photo Thames and Hudson archive.

212 Interior of the Monastery of St Catherine, Mt Sinai, in the early 19th century. The interior of the monastery has changed little in the last 150 years. Lithograph after a drawing by D. Roberts in G. Croly, *Syria, Arabia, Egypt,* 1843.
Photo Thames and Hudson archive.

213 Ancient Arabic inscriptions on a rock from Sammat al-Nadhun, Yemen.
Photo Paul Popper.

215 Portrait of Julius Varus Philippus, known as Philip the Arab; an engraving of a bronze coin from J. de Strada, *Epitome Thesauri Antiquitatem,* 1553.
Photo Thames and Hudson archive.

House and street in Saana, a small village in the Yemen, which already had a Christian community in the 6th century; an engraving from R. Manzoni, *Il Yemen,* 1884.
Photo Thames and Hudson archive.

216 Church at Axum, Ethiopia; an engraving from G. A. Annesley, *Voyages and Travels to India, Ceylon, the Red Sea, Abyssinia and Egypt,* IV, 1809.
Photo Thames and Hudson archive.

217 Obelisk at Axum, erected shortly before the intro-duction of Christianity into Ethiopia; a lithograph from H. Salt, *Twenty Four Views of St Helena,* 1809.
Photo Thames and Hudson archive.

219 The Church of Ganetta Mariam, one of the rock churches of Ethiopia, is here photographed from above so that the crosses on its flat roof can be clearly seen.
Photo Thomas Pakenham (Paul Popper).

220 View of the cruciform roof of the Church of St George in Lallibela, Ethiopia, also cut out of the rock.
Photo Thomas Pakenham (Paul Popper).

221 Roof decorated with panelling, from the Church of Imraha Christos, Ethiopia; 12th century.
I. Bidder, *Lalibela – the Monolithic Churches of Ethiopia,* 1958.
View of the roof of the nave of the Church of Bethlehem, Ethiopia, which was built in the 13th century, and only recently discovered and photo-graphed for the first time.
Photo Thomas Pakenham.
The miraculous deliverance of an Abyssinian monk is shown in a fresco in a church built in the 'Cave of Birds' in the heart of the mountains.
Photo Thomas Pakenham.

page

222 Story of an Abyssinian monastery transferred to a new site by boat is the subject of an illumination in an Abyssinian manuscript of the 17th–18th century, in which the miracles of the Virgin are described. The manuscript is in Gondar, Ethiopia.
Photo Thomas Pakenham.

Alexander the Great, who is a saint of the Abyssi-nian Church, is carried up to heaven by griffins. From the same Abyssinian manuscript in Gondar.
Photo Thomas Pakenham.

223 St Thomas the Apostle; a stone bas-relief from the Apostle's tomb near Mylapore.
F. Plattner and B. Moosburger, *Christian India,* 1955.
Ancient Cross with Sassanid Pehlevi inscription, on St Thomas' Mount in Madras, India.
H. Yule, *The Book of Ser Marco Polo,* 1901.

224 View of Suratte on the west coast of India; an engraving from Philippus Baldaeus, *Naauwkeurige Beschryvinge van Malabar en Choromandel,* 1672.
Photo Thames and Hudson archive.

225 St Thomas preaching to the Hindus; a scene described by Hayton and depicted in the *Livre des Merveilles,* a 15th-century manuscript.
Bibliothèque Nationale MS. 2810 f.228 r.
By courtesy of the Bibliothèque Nationale, Paris.

226 Bridge near Little St Thomas Mount, which can be seen in the background; an aquatint from Thomas and William Daniell, *Oriental Scenery, Twenty-four Views in Hindustan,* Series II, 1807.
Photo Thames and Hudson archive.

227 Tomb of St Thomas at Mylapore, described by Jean de Mandeville and depicted in an illumination from the *Livre des Merveilles.*
Bibliothèque Nationale MS. 2810 f.186 v.
By courtesy of the Bibliothèque Nationale, Paris.

Alfred the Great; a medieval representation in an illuminated manuscript of Matthew Paris, *Chronica Majora I. CCCC. 26 f.129.*
By courtesy of the Master and Fellows of Corpus Christi College, Cambridge.

228 Relief representing one of the chargers of the Emperor T'ai-tsung, from his tomb, erected in 637.
By courtesy of the University Museum, University of Pennsylvania, Philadelphia.

229 The 8th-century Nestorian stele at Hsi-an, report-ing the spread of Christianity in China, was rediscovered in 1623. From a cast in the Museo Cristiano Lateranense.
By courtesy of the Direzione Generale dei Musei e Gallerie Pontifici.
Photo Sansaini.

230 Crosses on Chinese monuments found between 1619 and 1638 near Ch'uan Chou; from A.C. Moule, *Nestorians in China,* 1940.
By courtesy of the China Society, London.
Photo Thames and Hudson archive.

231 Confucian Literati engaged in painting, music and games; from a Chinese Famille Verte porcelain of the K'ang-hsi period, 1662–1722.
By courtesy of the Museum of Eastern Art, Oxford.

232 A portrait of Jenghiz Khan.
National Central Museum, Taiwan, Formosa.

Kublai Khan receives the brothers Nicolo and Matteo Polo; an illumination from the 15th-century *Livre des Merveilles.*
Bibliothèque Nationale, MS. 2810 f.2 v.
By courtesy of the Bibliothèque Nationale, Paris.

Notes on the illustrations

VI   Between East and West

VII Saints and Conquerors

Notes on the illustrations

282 An aerial view of part of the Hill of Tara, Co. Meath. A portion of the Rath of the Synods, where in ancient times Irish tribal gatherings were held, is to be seen in the top left-hand corner. Centre, between two ring-forts, the Forradh and 'Cormac's House', is a 19th-century statue of St Patrick.
Photo Bord Fáilte Éireann.

283 A ground plan of the great Banquet Hall of the High Kings of Ireland at Tara, from the 12th-century *Book of Leinster*. This hall follows the plan of Laoghaire's great hall where Patrick gained his victory against paganism.
Trinity College Dublin MS. H. 2. 18 f.15 r.
By courtesy of the Board of Trinity College, Dublin.
Photo Thames and Hudson archive.

284 The crook of the Crosier of Maelfinnia, a covering for a staff of yew, from the Columban monastery at Kells. The silver crook-casing is 10th-century workmanship, while the collar-knop of silver with niello inlay is in the Scandinavian 'Ringerike' style of the 11th century.
By courtesy of the Trustees of the British Museum.

The bronze bell of Cumascach, son of Ailill, and steward in the monastery of Armagh, who died in A.D. 908. This is the only dated example of these early bells, which occur not only in Ireland but also in Wales and Scotland.
Photo National Museum of Ireland, Dublin.

285 A standing stone, depicting a priest with bell and crosier, still in place, on White Island, Lough Erne, Co. Fermagh.
Photo Impartial Reporter, Enniskillen.

286 The 'Mên Scryfys', from Madron, Cornwall, dated to the 5th–7th century. It records in a Latin formula the Celtic name of 'Realobranus son of Cunovalus'.
Photo Gibson and Son, Penzance.

Aerial view of Tintagel, North Cornwall, showing the Celtic settlement and medieval castle.
Photo H. M. Ministry of Works.
Crown copyright reserved.

287 A reconstruction of the 7th-century chapel and habitation site on Church Island, Valencia, Co. Kerry. After M. J. O'Kelly in *Proceedings of the Royal Irish Academy*, 59, C2, 1958.
By courtesy of the Royal Irish Academy, Dublin.
Specially drawn.

288 St Brendan celebrating Easter Mass on the whale's back; taken from an engraving of the 16th century from Robert-Yves Creston, *Journal de Bord de Saint-Brendan*, 1957.
Photo Thames and Hudson archive.

289 St Ninian's Cave, Glasserton; a photograph taken in the late 19th century before the removal of the cross-slabs.
By courtesy of the Controller of H. M. Stationery Office. Crown copyright reserved.

290 A detail of an initial from the 6th-century *Cathach of St Columba*.
By courtesy of the Royal Irish Academy, Dublin.

291 St Columba; a pen drawing from a 9th-century manuscript, Adamnan's *Vita Sancti Columbae*, written and preserved in the Irish foundation of St Gall, Switzerland.
MS. 555 f.166.
By courtesy of the Stiftsbibliothek St Gallen, Switzerland.

291 Iona. A view from the north showing the Benedictine abbey standing within the ditch and bank of the Columban settlement. To the right of the abbey precincts can be seen the little chapel, Releig Odhrain, where Blathmac was slain by the Norsemen for refusing to reveal the whereabouts of the shrine containing the relics of St Columba. The adjoining graveyard was in later times the burial place of the kings of Scotland, and here are supposed to lie Duncan and Macbeth.
Photo J. V. S. Megaw.
By courtesy of the Russell Trust, University of Edinburgh.

292 The Devil tempting Christ to cast himself down from the Temple; an illumination to St Luke's Gospel in the Book of Kells. The Temple is represented in the form of an early Irish church.
Trinity College Dublin MS. Kells f.202 v.
By courtesy of the Board of Trinity College, Dublin.
Photo Thames and Hudson archive.

293 An 8th-century reliquary in the shape of an early Irish church, from Monymusk, Scotland.
Photo National Museum of Antiquities of Scotland, Edinburgh.

St Rule's shrine, from St Andrews, Fife. St Rule is associated with Raghail of Mucinis, a companion of St Columba. The style belongs to the 9th century, and the carving of the cornice slabs shows a connection with Irish work.
From Stewart Cruden, *The Early Christian and Pictish Monuments of Scotland*, 1957.
By courtesy of the Controller of H. M. Stationery Office.

294 The first verse of St Matthew's Gospel from the 7th–8th century Lindisfarne Gospels, the greatest manuscript of the Northumbrian 'Golden Age'.
British Museum Cotton MS. Nero, C. IV f.27.
Courtesy of the Trustees of the British Museum.

295 Lindisfarne Priory, Holy Island, Northumberland, showing the ruins of the Benedictine abbey on the site of Aidan's Celtic foundation. In the distance can be seen the Castle of Beblowe, partially built from the abbey masonry.
Photo Edwin Smith.

296 St Augustine's Abbey, Canterbury. In the centre are the ruins of the Church of St Peter and St Paul, founded by St Augustine in 597.
Engraving by S. and N. Buck, 1755.
Photo Thames and Hudson archive.

297 A memorial stone from Whitby Abbey, Northumberland, records that Aelfled, daughter of Oswy of Northumbria, died abbess of Whitby in 713.
By courtesy of the Trustees of the British Museum.

298 A 12th-century wall-painting in Durham Cathedral depicting St Cuthbert in bishop's robes.
From (Ed.) C. F. Battiscombe, *Relics of St Cuthbert*, 1956.
By courtesy of the Dean and Chapter, Durham Cathedral. Photo Thames and Hudson archive.

299 The 6th–7th century Cross of St Cuthbert, found in 1827 'deeply buried amongst the remains of the robes which were nearest to the breast of the Saint'; it is of gold inlayed with shell and garnets. The shell was an importation from the East, and indicates the widespread trading contacts of the time. The cross was beyond doubt amongst the relics of the saint deposited with his body in 687.
From (Ed.) C. F. Battiscombe, *Relics of St Cuthbert*, 1956.
By courtesy of the Dean and Chapter, Durham Cathedral. Photo Thames and Hudson archive.

VIII In the Heart of Europe

Notes on the illustrations

Postscript

NOTES TO THE MAPS

These maps are based on the originals drawn by Ruth Daniel for the German edition

INDEX

A page number with an asterisk indicates a colour plate opposite that page

Index

Index